Shamanism for Everyone

Shamanism for Everyone

Gini Graham Scott

International Standard Book Number: 0-914918-86-9
Library of Congress Catalog Card Number: 88-63396
Cover design by Ultimo, Inc.

Published by Whitford Press
A division of Schiffer Publishing, Ltd.
1469 Morstein Road
West Chester, Pennsylvania 19380

Manufactured in the United States of America

This book may be purchased from the publisher.
Please include $2.00 postage
Try your bookstore first.

Contents

Introduction

Magic, shamanism, channeling, ESP—the whole world of otherworldly phenomena have suddenly captivated the public. The signs of this are everywhere. New popular books on this subject by Castaneda, Andrews, MacLaine, Knight and others. Hit films on reincarnation and time travel. Celebrities on the lecture and TV-talk show circuit demonstrating their ability to channel or use ESP. The booming market in crystals. And more.

All these signs show a deep hunger to understand this ordinarily unseen world, even in these highly rational high-tech times. People seek the wisdom, guidance and support available by tapping into other realms, and they recognize the potential source of power that comes with this higher knowledge and help.

Many teachers and leaders have appeared to help them on the way. Their names are widely known, and they have gained a wide following as wise psychics, channelers, gurus, shamans and healers who have special knowledge.

Yet this knowledge is available to others too, directly, because the ability to contact and work with this other world and its powers is in us all. SHAMANISM FOR EVERYONE is designed to show you how you can access this realm of wisdom and power by developing your own abilities to see into, contact and work with the forces and energies of this world which are normally unseen. You can then mobilize these powers, much as the psychics, channelers, gurus and shamans do, for your own benefit and the benefit of others.

SHAMANISM FOR EVERYONE provides one route to getting and working with this power. It is based on the teachings which I learned when I studied for over a year with a master shaman, Michael Fairwell, who has been teaching these principles for most of his life. Now, four years later, I am still studying with Michael, learning advanced techniques.

Michael's teachings represent a kind of modern-day blend of the traditional shamanic practices employed since the dawn of time, the wisdom of the Eastern shamans, the teachings of the American Indians and the shamanic traditions described in the writings of Carlos Castaneda and most recently Lynn Andrews. Michael has experimented with these various methods in the field and has synthesized them into a series of step-by-step teachings the average person can learn to gain access to this often mysterious world of unseen energies and forces. His emphasis has always been on direct hands-on experiences and the application of these principles to everyday life, rather than a more theoretical understanding of how and why these principles work.

I first wrote about my experiences in meeting Michael and learning about these teachings in my book SHAMAN WARRIOR, published by Falcon Press. However, this was a more personal journey in which I described what happened as I went through Michael's introductory six-month training program along with several other initiates. I talked about Michael's teachings in each class I attended, but mostly I reported on my own and other's experiences in working with these techniques. A reader might read between the lines and begin to put these teachings into practice himself, but it could be difficult.

Now, however, Michael feels it is time to let others know of these teachings more widely, and he has chosen me to spread these teachings. The first step is this book, which is designed to show each person in a step-by-step fashion how he or she can gain the skills of the shaman to contact and work with the other world, and thereby gain personal power. Then, other teachers will be selected to pass on the teachings described in this book.

A central tenet of the book and Michael's teachings is that each person has the ability to gain this connection with the other realm by getting in touch with his generally unconscious inner or higher self. One way to do this is by developing one's power of "seeing," which permits one to see into oneself, into others and into other levels of reality. The process is hard to explain, but basically through seeing and the power of awareness and knowing that comes with this, one can tune into that higher inner world and into the powerful energies and forces of nature which exist both within and outside the self.

As Michael explains in his teachings, these forces of nature assume four basic forms which have been recognized in traditional systems of learning. They are manifested in the powers of earth, air, fire and water which have both the physical form we are all familiar with and a more symbolic or metaphorical form, so that we can work with these elements as energies which exist both outside and within the self. The shamanic techniques which Michael teaches are designed to tap into these powers. By learning them you can use these techniques to contact and direct these universal energies to develop personally and gain personal power. Then, you can apply it to attain your own objectives in your personal life.

However, as Michael cautions, it is important to direct this power to benevolent or beneficial ends. The power itself is purely neutral, and it can be used with any intent. However, if used destructively, that power can easily turn on you and harm you, and it exposes you to having that power used on you destructively by others. But when this power is put to good uses, it opens up tremendous potentials for the good of each person, for the people he or she connects with directly, and for society as a whole.

In short, these techniques have tremendous power, and now, according to Michael, it is time to make them available to the general public, so that all can now learn the secrets of the shamans in working with power. The one caution is to direct these powers to the good and use them in an ethical way.

This book is designed to present a training program for this purpose lasting from between three to six months, depending on how quickly you want to work with the material presented in each chapter. If you spend about a week working with each chapter, the program will take three months; if you spend about two weeks with each chapter, the program will take about six months to complete. Of course, you can always simply read the book in a few hours or over a few days period. But the way to use this book most productively to develop the powers described is to actually do the exercises and practice with them. This way you can make these techniques an integrated part of your life and apply them on a regular basis.

To this end, the book is divided into the following chapters. Chapter 1 begins with the basic procedure necessary to all else in mastering the shaman's path—learning to "see." You need this ability to see into and contact your higher self and the forces or energies of nature. Then, Chapter 2 deals with some practical ways of using seeing to pick up insights about yourself and others.

Chapters 3 and 4 show you how to use this seeing process to get in touch with your dreams. It explains how you can not only get information from your dreams, but you can learn to control and direct them. And by programming your dreams you can get insights on certain topics. You can also have precognitive dreams to make predictions and you can manipulate your dreams in various ways. You can even have shared dreams with others.

Chapter 5 to 8 deal with techniques for projecting your vision so you can see into other places and into the future. In turn, this information can help you better understand people and make decisions.

Chapters 9 and 10 will help you get in touch with your inner voice so you can better know what you know and apply this in everyday life.

Chapter 11 is designed to help you become more receptive to the forces of nature outside and within yourself by taking what is called a "solo." This is a time to go off by yourself for about thirty minutes to an hour and put yourself in a very quiet, receptive space. Then, like a radio or television receiver, you can pick up these forces and energies and gain a much deeper understanding into yourself.

Chapter 12 discusses how to develop the balance and personal control you need to work most successfully with these forces. This ability becomes especially important as you become more receptive and sensitive to these energies. Specifically, the chapter explains how to balance the masculine and feminine polarities and the energies of earth, air, fire and water which exist within yourself.

Finally, Chapter 13 will help you overcome any blocks or barriers to your personal power so you can move full steam ahead in charting your own course.

These chapters provide a basic introduction to the techniques needed to develop the abilities of a shaman yourself, so you can similarly work with the normally unseen powers and forces of nature. As you work with these techniques you will find you are becoming more aware of and sensitive to these forces and more able to exercise your own personal control and power to gain your own ends.

Then you can work on refining and perfecting these techniques and exploring still other realms of personal power to be described in subsequent books in this series. I am learning these techniques from Michael now.

Chapter One

Learning To See
Into Other Dimensions

The Use of "Seeing"

Seeing is basic to the shaman's path to knowledge, because you need this to see into the other reality or dimension of being. You need to be able to see the energies that exist out there and see into yourself.

The ability to see is crucial because the energies you see out there are really aspects of yourself and through seeing you can project these parts of yourself out into the universe and at the same time get in touch with them. In this way, you can both become aware of and communicate with these universal energies which are in yourself and in nature. The result is you are both working in cooperation with nature and learning more about yourself in the process. Through this knowledge, you can gain more control over both the nature that is out there and over yourself, for you and nature are one.

This process is quite different from that used by many others who try to use magical powers to command the forces of nature around them. You are not trying to order the elements outside or within yourself to act in a certain way. Rather, you are using your ability to see and understand to flow with nature and get in tune with the natural processes, so you gain support for what you want to do. The result is you do achieve your ends, but you do so in a more gentle harmonious way.

So seeing is the key to opening the door into this other world. It's like the telescope you use to peer into this altered space, see what's happening, and step into that world yourself.

What You Can See

When you start seeing, one of the first things you will observe is auras. You'll see the auras around people and, as you start learning how to really look at objects, you'll see auras around them too. For example, if you go out in an open area at night and look around you at the bushes and trees, you'll start seeing shapes emerge around them. Or maybe you'll see reflections or after-images. Whatever you want to call them, you'll start seeing these fragmentary shapes and forms which represent the energies or forces of the natural world or projections of the energies within yourself.

Seeing is also a way to get new insights into others. For example, you can pick up feelings about people's energies through the aura and use this feedback to figure out where people are coming from. Then you can readily apply this information in everyday life.

For example, let's say you are going to a job interview. You can use your seeing to get a sense of who that person is and what he or she wants to hear about. These insights can be extremely useful because people have different personal styles. For instance, some people want lots of details; other people want you to be very direct and get right to the point, still others like people who are warm and affable. By picking up this kind of information about these people, you have a better sense of how to relate to that person and what to do.

How Seeing Works

In seeing, you don't look at something directly; you want to look into the spaces between things. It's like seeing into the air. If you've ever had the experience of looking at things when they are very far away and just letting your eyes go out of focus, that's a little like what the seeing process involves.

Another way to describe the process is that your eyes are focused, yet unfocused, because you're looking into the spaces between, in front of, or behind things, rather than directly at the object. Thus, when you look at an object or another person in this way, you want to gaze or stare at this object or person. Don't try to do anything as you look; let your eyes stare, then let go of them and let them do what they want. You'll find yourself in a very intense state where you are in fact concentrating. Yet you're not forcing yourself to concentrate. You're just doing it because you're totally involved in the process.

It's a hard process to explain, but you know when you are really seeing in this altered intense state because you'll feel totally involved and connected with whatever you are doing or looking at. For example, if you've ever been involved in doing a project and you become so caught up in it that you lose all track of time, that's the quality of concentration you'll start feeling as you start looking at something in this intense seeing way.

Learning How to See Yourself— Exercise #1

The following exercise is designed to help you learn how to see yourself. Find a quiet place where you can get very comfortable and relaxed. It helps to have low lighting also.

Take a moment to get into a relaxed, calm state. Perhaps close your eyes or concentrate on your breathing for a minute or two to help you calm down.

Now pick an object in the room and get ready to look at it for about five minutes. Set an alarm if you have one handy. Be aware that you may blink from time to time as you do this. If you are very relaxed, you will not have to blink very much, and you should try not to if you can avoid this easily.

Once you start looking, don't try to direct what will happen. Just look in this focused, yet unfocused way just described. And don't try to see anything in particular; just be receptive to whatever you see.

However, there are certain things you may be likely to see, and if so, pay attention to them. For instance, as you look you may notice the aura or energy field around the object emerge. As you look at this energy field, you may start seeing the movements or changes in the luminescences around things. So things may suddenly start to get darker or lighter, or you may see the energy form into shapes or move around.

Don't try to analyze any of these images or sensations if you perceive them, since that will only interrupt your perceptions. Just be open and receptive and notice whatever comes. Later you can think about what these images mean or suggest if you want. Now you simply want to focus on learning to see.

So when you're ready settle back and do this. Give yourself about five minutes . . . choose an object and gaze at it . . . and now let go!

Assessing Your Experience

After the time is up for doing this exercise, take a little time to review what you observed. As you do this a number of times, you can also pay attention to whether there are any patterns in the images, colors or perceptions of movement you experience. These observations can be ways to get insights, as you become more experienced in seeing into the object or into yourself. The more you work with these techniques, the better you will become at discerning the source of the information you are picking up.

For now, though, just review and perhaps write down what you have seen. Or if you are doing this exercise with others, share what you have experienced in a group. For example, some of the perceptions you may have which you should note include:

-size and shape of the aura or surrounding energy field
-texture or color of the aura; any multiple colors
-any changes or movements in the aura

-any images
-any feelings or sensations
-any sounds
-any changes in the lighting or visibility of the object (sometimes, an object may seem to grow brighter or disappear)
-any changes in the background of the object, such as the wall or surrounding room (sometimes the wall or surrounding room may go black)
-any changes in your perspective or position in looking at the object
-any sense of the object taking on a new or different reality, such as the object seeming to come alive or look at you.

Such a review can be especially useful for learning more about your own perceptual abilities, so that later on you can work on distinguishing between what is coming from you and what is coming from the object itself. Later on, these distinctions can be helpful when you work on contacting and working with the forces of nature or picking up information about other people.

One common experience for some people is to see everything they look at as having the same color in the aura. If this happens to you, what this commonly means is you are picking up your own resonant color, which is the color that represents you. If you are picking up your own color and are aware of this, you can look beyond this color to notice the other colors that are also in the aura, for these are the colors associated with the object, whereas your resonant color is being projected on it by you.

The Importance of Practicing

When you first start working with seeing, it's important to practice these new skills in the beginning. It's like learning any other skill. You need to do it again and again in the beginning, until these skills become a regular part of your life.

You should spend about a week or two practicing this and the other seeing techniques described in this chapter. Plan to spend about ten to fifteen minutes a day working with them. When you first start doing this, you may find you don't see much of anything, particularly if this type of work with altered states of consciousness is new to you. But as you work with these techniques more and more on a regular basis, you'll find your ability becoming better and better. And soon you'll be able to see much more, as well as better discern the meaning of what you see.

Seeing with a Partner: Exercise #2

Working with a partner can help you expand your ability to see even more, because now you can work on gaining insight into others and also get feedback on the relationship between what you are seeing and what the other person is thinking or feeling. This next exercise is designed to help you begin this process. You can do this with a friend, or if you are doing these exercise in a group setting, it's better to experiment with someone you don't know or know very little. This way you are less influenced in what you see by what you already know about the person.

Begin by sitting across from each other. You should both get in a relaxed position. Then, get ready to start looking at each other. When you do this, you should look at a spot in the center of the other person's forehead or at the tip of his nose. You shouldn't look directly at each other's eyes because this is too intense.

Then, when you are ready, you will begin looking at each other in the same way that you looked at an object. Focus your attention, yet gaze in a relaxed, unfocused way. Try not to blink, but blink if you feel like doing so. And don't try to direct what happens. Just let the experience you have occur as it will. But if your attention or gaze should wander from the other person's face, gently bring it back and resume looking.

Again, don't try to see anything in particular, although there are certain things you may see. If so, don't be surprised and just acknowledge them.

Once again, you are likely to see an aura or energy field emerge around the person. You may also see people's faces disappear, or you may see through them. You may pick up insights into who they are or what they are thinking or feeling.

Again, don't try to analyze or explain these perceptions when they occur. Simply acknowledge them and put them on the shelf so you can think about them later.

When you're ready, allow yourself about five minutes. Use an alarm if you have one. Then start gazing at each other and experience whatever happens now.

Assessing Your Experience

After the time limit is up, share with your partner what you both experienced. Take turns doing this.

Whoever is describing their experience should be as detailed as possible. You should report images, auditory sensations, feelings, whatever you observed. Also, in describing images, note any colors, abstract shapes or realistic pictures or scenes that come to mind.

The reason for all this detail is that after one person describes what he has experienced, the other person should note if he feels any connections or associations with what he has said. Often there will be such hits, and this is a way of demonstrating to you that your seeing is picking up information about the other person. Then, as you work with these techniques more, you can start to tell whether the information you are picking up is coming from the other person or is something you are projecting out of yourself. It is all part of the process of learning discernment, and as you learn this, you will gradually come to feel an automatic sense of knowing or certainty about what you are picking up from where.

This initial exercise with a partner is designed to give you some beginning intimations of how this process works. For example, when I did this exercise with a group, one man reported seeing a white aura that was suffused with green around another man, who then announced that he normally saw the color green himself whenever he looked at things and commented "I have a thing for green." In another case, a woman reported seeing the woman's face in front of her turn into that of a very old woman, and then she saw the face of an Indian woman followed by the image of a strong powerful male. When her partner responded, she confirmed that almost everything had something to do with herself. As she stated: "I have always wanted to be older, and I have a lot of fantasies about being different. I sometimes think about wanting to paint my body and dance around like an Indian. Also, I feel a lot of strong male energy about myself. I've always been a kind of tomboy all my life."

As these reports and responses suggest, you may be able to pick up some insights into other people's backgrounds and feelings with very little training in this area. This is the case because when you let yourself see and open yourself up to the experience, you tap into this higher mind of yours which has great wisdom and insight. So even though you have little formalized knowledge about something, your inner wisdom may give you these insights which you aren't aware you have. As you learn to work with this vision more closely, you can better understand what your insights are telling you and direct your vision so you pick up the information you want.

More specifically, some of the information you may get and should look for when you think about your experience in seeing with another person is the following:

- the size and shape of the person's aura
- the color of the person's aura
- any changes in the appearance of the aura as you look
- the placement of the aura and its colors around the person's body
- any movements in the person's aura
- the clarity or fogginess of the image
- any images of other faces (if so, are they of specific people you know, archetypal images, old or young faces, faces from another country or historical period, etc.)
- any sense of the person's face being like a mask or unreal
- any special lights, reflections, areas of darkness
- any abstract or geometrical images
- any flashes of scenes
- any images of objects
- any special sounds, sensations, feelings
- any changes in the appearance or lightness or darkness of the room
- any sense of time change
- the disappearance of the person in front of you
- any changes in your own bodily responses

The Power of Seeing Into the Other Person

The technique of just looking at another person can be a very powerful technique because it can give you great insights into the other person, as well as produce changes in and around you. In fact, as you become more experienced in seeing, you do not even have to have the actual person in front of you, you can put up an image of that person and work with that. Also, you can use other images which you create yourself to help you gain information as you look at this person in reality or in your mind.

One way to use another image to gain more information is to put up the image of a rose against the seven chakras or energy systems in each person. These energy systems begin at the base of the spine and go up to the top of the person's head. They are like seven centers of energy and each one is associated with different qualities. For example, the lowest center at the base of the spine is survival. The next, located at the pelvis, is associated with sexuality. The one at the abdomen is associated with will and power, the one at the heart with emotion and feeling, the one at the throat with communication, the one at the center of the forehead with vision, and the one at the top of the head with spirituality.

The way to use these centers and your power of imaging in conjunction with seeing into the person is to imagine the rose in front of each energy center in turn. Then, watch what happens to the rose. If you see the rose blossom when in front of the survival center, this means one thing such as a strong, vibrant person. But if the rose blooms at the communication center, this means something else such as an openness to others, and if this same process occurs at the heart center, the flowering means something else again—such as a great deal of love. If the rose withers or does anything else in front of a particular energy center, that suggests still other interpretations.

Beginning with the process of just looking, you can pick up tremendous information about someone you have met. Your basic seeing technique helps to open up this window and give you some insights. Then the additional imagery helps you to look at the person even more closely so you pick up additional information about the person on different levels. The process is a little like putting on someone's head and experiencing what he is thinking and feeling at each energy level of being.

Sometimes when you tune into someone through seeing you may end up feeling so connected that you literally start thinking and feeling in tandem. For example, sometimes you may find that when you see some image as you look at the person, the other person is seeing or thinking that image too. Or maybe you are having simultaneous feelings. You'll discover these parallels in the course of sharing about the experience. The reason this happens is that you are seeing into the other person's mind or the other person is projecting his thoughts or feelings into you. So again, it's like you have stepped into someone else's head so that you are both having the same vision or experience.

Noticing Other Transformations That Occur Through Seeing

This seeing process also can open up channels of perception for you in addition to picking up information about the other person. That is why it is the key to moving into other levels of reality which we will be talking about more in later chapters of the book.

For example, as you look at a person or an object, you may feel special energies in the room, or you may have the experience of the room changing. What this suggests is that you are becoming more receptive to usually unseen energies of the universe or that you are becoming aware of an opening into this other realm.

You may also get a sense of time changing. Frequently, this is a sense of time moving very slowly, almost standing still, as a myriad of sensations and experiences crowd into a small instant of time. Or alternatively, it may seem like you have been doing something for just minutes, when in fact hours have passed. Again this is a sign you have moved out of ordinary reality and are operating mentally and perceptually on another level.

Another thing that sometimes happens is that the person or object you are looking at may seem to disappear, so that you are suddenly looking through that person or object—another sign of this movement of your consciousness to another level. For instance, you may be looking at a person when you suddenly see the label on the back of his clothing. If this happens, see if you can read it and then check out what you saw later for accuracy. In some cases people have reported being able to read such things, although they had no knowledge of what they were reading in advance, and later found that they were accurate.

You may also find that there are changes in the speed of your own bodily responses. Probably the most common response here is for you to feel that things are really slowing down for you such as your heart and your pulse. And when you move, your reactions may be much slower too. The slowness of your body occurs because your mind and other senses are picking up so much more. With your body quieted, you are able to expand your powers of perception. Your brain and other body control systems have less to pay attention to. Thus, that energy is released so you can do more in exploring with your vision and your mind.

Gaining the Ability to Discern What You Are Seeing and Experiencing

Initially, when you experiment with seeing you are likely to pick up a jumble of information, some of it coming from you, some from the other person you are looking at, and you may also pick up information from other people or objects in the room. This occurs because as you open up, all sorts of energies can come in from outside of you, and all sorts of images and sensations can well up from your own unconsciousness also.

The first step of the process is to let yourself be as open and receptive as possible, so you do pick up this information from your inner self and from the ordinarily unseen energies all around you and from others. Then gradually you will learn to become more discerning about the sources and meanings of what you are picking up, and you should seek to develop this discernment.

For example, you want to be able to distinguish between whether some image you are seeing is your own projection onto someone else, which gives you information about yourself, or whether you are really picking up information about the other person. The way to do this is by getting feedback about the images and sensations you experience whenever you work with someone else. Then you can learn if the images or sensations are something the other person connects with and therefore are a source of information about that person or if the images or sensations are really coming from you. By practicing with this mutual seeing technique and getting feedback, you can gradually start sorting out what information is coming from where, and soon you'll get a sense of knowing what the source of your information really is.

Developing Your Ability to See—Exercise #3

One way to develop your ability to see, discern what you are seeing, and check the accuracy of your perceptions is to work with someone else who is consciously concentrating on different images or feelings. Then you try to pick them up.

When I first worked with these techniques, my partner thought about her energy going one way and then the other and then concentrated on expanding and contracting it. I didn't know what she was doing, and simply tried to pick up what I experienced was happening with her aura. Then, after we shared, and I explained how I had seen her aura moving and changing, she described what she had done, and there seemed to be an almost perfect match in the sequence of what she did and what I saw. Essentially what she did is that she used certain power images to help make her aura expand, such as thinking about a lion, and then she used other images, such as thinking about herself growing very small to make her aura contract. She had also thought about throwing her energy like a ball to the right and the left.

The idea of the following exercise is to take turns consciously projecting and changing your energy and picking up what the other person is projecting. The way to do this is as follows.

Sit across from each other as in the mutual seeing exercise. Then, one person will be the sender the other the receiver. The receiver should look at the other person with his eyes open and should concentrate on really seeing just as before.

Meanwhile, the sender will try to do things with his energy, and will pay attention to what he is doing so he can report on the sequence of these activities. The sender can keep his eyes open or closed, whatever feels comfortable to him.

As the sender, you might imagine your aura or energy expanding, getting larger, or more powerful, and perhaps you might use power images like lions, tigers or whatever means power to you, to help you do this. Or you might think of your energy or aura getting smaller and contracting with images like mice, small objects, fish or whatever feels small to you. Or maybe think of your energy going to your right or left or swirling around or doing anything else you want. Or even think of random images.

In other words, the person who is being looked at, the sender, should concentrate on doing things with his mental imagery and aura so it changes in some way. Meanwhile, the other person should concentrate on picking up whatever he can of their aura, their imagery or the energy around them.

As sender you can think of as many images or make as many projections as you want. And you can seek to consciously direct the sequence or actively project them at the other person. Or you can simply let your mind be more receptive, and pay careful attention to the images and perceptions that flow through your mind. You can choose what you want to experience or do with your energy. The important thing is that you don't tell the other person what you are doing and that you remember what you did.

After the exercise, you can both compare. First, the receiver should describe what he experienced in as much detail as possible. He should also try to report his experiences in sequence. Then, the sender should describe what he did following the same guidelines. Afterwards look for correlations between what the receiver picked up and what the sender did. Often there may be at least a few parallels, and as you practice with this technique more, the number of correspondences should increase because you'll become increasingly sensitive to what the other person is putting out.

An alternate way to keep track is for the sender to write down his images or projections as they occur. When the receiver reports what he experienced, you can check these directly against what was written down. Or perhaps both the sender and receiver can record their experiences, and then you can compare what you have both written to look for parallels.

When you are ready, start the process. Decide who will be the sender and receiver first, and then concentrate on doing this for about three to five minutes. Then share for a few minutes, and afterwards, switch, concentrate, and share again.

If you wish, do this two or three times, and notice if your accuracy goes up. Generally it will. Or do this exercise once or twice regularly over a period of days, and again notice your accuracy. Over time you should become more sensitive to picking up these images and energies, so your accuracy should increase.

Types of Images and Energies to Work With

Normally, a sender should feel free to work with whatever images and sensations come to mind. However, sometimes a person who is new to working with the imaging process may have difficulties coming up with images. If so, the following is a list of common images and energy projections you can use:

-seeing your energy expand and contract
-sending your energy to your right or left
-projecting your energy towards or away from the receiver
-visualizations of strong power images associated with the expansion of energy, such as lions, tigers, authority figures, military symbols, etc.
-visualizations of weak, gentle images associated with the contraction of energy such as rabbits, mice, small fish, babies, etc.
-images of birds flying (some common images are of hawks and eagles)
-classic images of women such as a maiden in white, the mother, the elderly crone
-abstract geometrical shapes such as squares, circles and triangles
-changes in the atmosphere, like a shift from a sunny day to clouds to rain to fog
-changes in the color of an aura or energy field
-changes in sensations of temperature
-perceptions of vertical or horizontal movement
-images of water
-perceptions of light and shadow
-images of ancient Indians or other peoples
-images of strong natural features such as a large rock or cliff, a waterfall, a meadow, an unusual tree, etc.
-images of common animals such as cats, dogs, horses
-images of faces or masks of known or unknown people
-perceptions of changing colors or patterns of colors such as a rainbow, fireworks or an explosion of colors

Picking Up Images and Energies from Other Sources

Even though you may be focusing on picking up images from one person who is concentrating on thinking of these images or sending them to you, you may still pick up interfering images and energies from other sources. This can be especially true if you are doing this exercise in a group setting.

This might be especially likely to occur if somebody else is visualizing something which is a very powerful image for them. The intensity they are experiencing could create a strong energy signal, much like a television transmission, so that even if you aren't focusing on them you could still pick up what they are imagining.

This is where your power of discernment comes in, so that you can sense when you are picking up information from an extraneous source. When you learn some of the protections, like putting up energy shields against energy you don't want, you may be able to tune out the energy coming to you from certain directions. That way you can better zero in on the exact source you want to tap for picking up energy, and avoid getting it in from somewhere else. The process is a little like tuning a television channel and getting rid of the static and noise coming in from other channels.

The Importance of Practice and Keeping Records

After you try out these first three seeing exercises, it is important to keep working with them for a while until you feel comfortable using your power of seeing. In fact, your goal should be to make this process second nature so you can use your seeing in the course of everyday activities when you want to pick up information about something or someone.

You should plan to practice with these exercises for perhaps a week or two. Spend about ten to twenty minutes a day in regular practice, and then consciously try to use these techniques from time to time during the day.

As you can, get feedback on what you are doing. If you are working with a partner, you can always ask and compare experiences as previously discussed. Also, you can use the automatic writing technique as you experience things previously described so you can create an ongoing record of experiences which you can subsequently check out.

But even when you are trying out your seeing when practicing alone or in the course of everyday activities, you can seek some feedback. For example, if you meet someone at a cocktail party, try to sense where that person is coming from before that person even says anything. Notice the person's aura and any images that appear, and quickly interpret what they mean to you. Then, as you talk to that person, you can notice if you were correct, or observe what information you got was valid and what was not. Also, you can compare where you were correct and where you were not with the feelings you got as you worked on seeing, and later you can work on recreating that feeling you got when you were correct in the past. In other words, as you practice with the seeing process, you can work on refining your accuracy so you will increasingly get correct and valuable information when you attempt to see.

Chapter Two

Using Your Seeing To Pick Up Insights About Yourself And Others

Once you have developed your basic ability to see, you can use this ability to pick up insights about yourself and others. Also, you can use power tools or objects as a way to intensify and direct this seeing ability. In this chapter, we will start by considering how to expand your vision into other levels of reality through power objects, and then we will consider how to apply these seeing techniques to gain information and otherwise improve your everyday life.

Using Power Objects to Improve Your Ability to See

One of the best tools for intensifying and directing your seeing ability is the staff. You can use any kind that feels comfortable for you. If you prefer, you can create your own staff from the branch of a tree, or you can pick one up in a store.

This staff is especially good for doing magical rituals, since you can use it to call up and focus your own power, draw in power from the area around you and create a protective encapsulated environment where you can feel safe and totally involved in what you are doing. You can then direct that power toward your ritual goal. For example, you can use the staff to create a magical circle around you by drawing a circle symbolically on the ground around you. Likewise, you can use the staff to draw a series of protective pentagrams or five-sided stars in the air, which are a symbolic way of setting up a protective capsule around yourself.

If you get a staff which is already made, a walking stick is ideal. Also, it is recommended that you obtain a staff which is black or a dark color. This is because you can best work on seeing into the other psychic world when it is dark so you aren't distracted by the light which helps to pull you back into everyday reality. In turn, a dark staff will better blend into this darkness, so you can better see the energy you put out.

Even though a staff can be an excellent tool for working with energy, since it is long and thereby acts as a kind of extension of your arm to concentrate and direct power, you can do the same procedures with virtually anything. You do not have to use a staff. For instance, you can use a ritual knife to create a magical circle or draw other magical images.

The key is to use whatever tools work for you, because essentially what you are doing is using the tool as an extension or projection of your own energy. So you do not need any equipment to do anything. You can go out and work with energy directly with your hands.

However, these tools are valuable to help you get into a ritual space, since they serve as a physical signal that now you are going to do something to work with energy or magic. They help you accomplish that ritual successfully by extending and intensifying your energy as you project it into and through that object. These tools work much like a laser beam to focus your energy. And when you work with this focused energy, it is much more powerful, and you can better direct and control it to achieve your particular ends.

Using Power Objects in the Field and in Everyday Life

An ideal way to work with your tools is to use them to intensify your ability to project and direct energy in an outdoors field setting where you can work directly with the elements of nature. Then take that ability you have gained to generate and direct power and apply that to whatever you are doing in everyday life. You can both experience your own powers and the energies of nature in the field, and then use the knowledge you have gained about power and energy to achieve your everyday goals.

For example, if you go out in the field and imagine projecting your energy through the tool you are using, say a staff, you will soon start seeing an aura around this, as well as around the objects in the field you are looking at. Also, you will see your own energy projecting out of the tip of the tool so you can direct this around like a flashlight beam. Knowing you can do this, you can take this experience of working with energy in the field and use it to direct that same energy in daily life. Suppose you are doing a project. You can imagine focusing your energy, as you have done in the field, to get it done. Or if you find the project is encountering some difficulties, you can imagine creating the same kind of protective magical circles you have made for yourself in the field. With that protective image, you can shut out distractions and interferences standing in the way of the project and get it done.

Alternatively, you can use a tool as a powerful receptor, both in the field and in everyday life to pick up useful information. For instance, say you are out in a park or wilderness area experimenting with these techniques. You can use your staff like a radio receiver to experience if there are other people around you, maybe over a hill. The way you do this is by moving your staff around, and then you may experience a feeling of intensity, a kind of energy surge in those areas where there are extra people. Or you may perhaps see a brief interruption or indentation in the beam of energy projecting out of your staff, suggesting that it has encountered the energy of another person. You might not have the sensitivity to pick up this change in the energy on your own, but perhaps you can by using your tool like a radio receiver.

In an everyday situation, you might be able to use this increased sensitivity to tell when others are nearby and this could be an extremely valuable skill to have in a situation of possible danger. Suppose you are walking into a lonely garage to pick up your car or passing through a quiet street in a tough neighborhood. If you have developed this increased sensitivity, you might pick up that someone is lurking ahead in the garage or on the street and change your path to avert the danger.

Working With Your Own Power Object—Exercise #4

To experience how you can project and see energy using a power object, obtain something you can use as a tool. Find something which is long and thin such as a staff, stick, sword or knife. Ideally, you should acquire a power object you can devote specifically to this purpose. Then you can charge it with your own energy and keep recharging it when you use it for generating and projecting energy. If you do not have anything special, you can work with any kind of long and thin object you happen to have around the house.

Now pick up this object and hold it in front of you. Imagine that you are projecting your energy into it and through it. As you do this, notice that an aura seems to form around this object, and notice that a beam of light seems to project beyond it. Commonly you will see the color of this surrounding aura or beam of light as white, amber or blue.

Notice how far out this beam extends. See if you can get this beam to go out even further by focusing the energy you are projecting out and sending more of your energy into that beam. Next, see if you can direct that beam. Move your power object to the right or left. Notice how the beam continues to project out as you change directions. Then, move the object up and down, and perhaps move it around in a spiral. As you do, see the energy beam ahead of it moving in the same direction. It is like moving a flashlight around and watching its beam.

If you are with another person, you can take turns watching each other do this. Or a group leader can do a demonstration in front of a group. The person who is working with the object should move it around, while projecting energy through it. Meanwhile, the person who is watching should pay attention to the size and movement of the aura and notice the power and direction of the beam.

Using Energy Projections to Achieve Your Goals

The value of projecting your energy in this way is you can use that projection to gain help and support for whatever you are doing and thereby achieve your goal. In a field setting you can send out this energy as a way of attracting or calling up the spirits or energies of nature to respond to you and help you. The way this process works is you project out a beam of your own energy and you focus on the various aspects or elements of nature, earth, air, fire and water, which are also aspects of yourself. Then, see them responding to you. To do this, concentrate on calling them forward as if your energy beam is an invitation to them to come out and respond, and when you see or feel these forces respond, you can find ways to have them interact with you. Using your projected energy beam, you can have them move forward and back, circle around in different directions or actually come to your assistance in accomplishing some goal or project you want to do.

The process works because you are really projecting out your own energy, and by visualizing or feeling it, and using a tool to intensify and direct it, you have gained both more power and more control over it. Also, by calling on particular aspects of that energy—earth, air, fire or water, you are drawing on the qualities you especially need for a particular purpose, so the energy you are working with is even more focused, directed and powerful.

The process of working with these different energies in the field helps you to get that experience of what the qualities of these different energies is like. For instance, the energy of the earth is stronger and more solid, that of air lighter and more uplifting, while fire is intense yet changeable, and water is smooth and flowing. Then you can take your experience of those energies and apply them to everyday projects.

I had this experience when I first started writing. To get in a creative mood I would use a visualization in which I imagined the earth energy coming up from the earth and into my feet. I would experience this energy swirling around and going up into my body. At the same time, I imagined the energy of the air coming down into my head and swirling around in the other direction. I saw the two energies, the solid energy of the earth and the uplifting energy of the air, whirling around in me to form this big white ball of energy. And then I would see this energy pouring out through my hands, and I went to the typewriter with this image and began to write. For me, this imagery opened up any blocks I had to writing, and I found I just needed to go to the typewriter feeling this outpouring of energy, and I could easily write.

You do not need any equipment to do these kinds of visualizations and energy projections. But the equipment can help you both send out the energy from yourself and pull in the energy from elsewhere. Also, it is a way to help you get into an altered state, so you can draw on these energies. But there is nothing mystical about using the equipment. You can use it or not, and you can choose different types of equipment, whatever feels right for you. As mentioned, the staff is ideal because it is long and thin, and therefore good for concentrating and intensifying your energy. But if you prefer working with a knife, stick or anything else, that is perfectly fine.

Choosing Your Equipment

One important consideration in choosing equipment for many people is whether to use traditional materials or objects or opt for something made by modern methods of production with modern materials. For traditionalists, the traditional materials and methods of creating magical tools are preferred because they are time-tested with roots in the past. For example, as these traditionalists point out, at one time people used to get their magical gear by going out in the wilderness. Then, they would get branches to make into staffs, and they would even talk to the spirits of the trees in the process so they could become more in tune with the trees. This way they could feel they had more understanding and control of the energy in the object they were using to project their own energy and call on the powers of nature.

Not all traditionalists feel it is necessary to go through the process of getting living branches in this way. But many still like using wood or other natural materials, because over the centuries these materials have acquired a certain power, resulting from their traditional use in magic.

However, it is not really necessary to use traditional materials. You can use any materials you feel comfortable using. In fact, now that ours has become a very technological society there is no reason why we cannot use technological objects and materials to work with energy. People have used the traditional materials because that was what was available to them at the time. But now we have new materials such as plastics, acrylics and fiberglass.

Choose whatever feels right for you. If you feel more comfortable using a natural living staff and taking a branch from a tree, use that. Or if you prefer, use plastic or anything else that feels comfortable for you.

Preparing Your Equipment by Charging It—Exercise #5

When you first start experimenting with power tools, you are just learning to see and project the energy, so there is no need to do anything special to make that a regular working or ritual object. However, as you work with a tool more and more on a regular basis, it will gradually become charged with your energy since you are constantly projecting your energy through it. If you get a new object that you want to specifically devote to working with power, you can consciously charge it with your energy in advance which helps to give that object even more power, because you are consciously directing your own energy into it to make it your own.

You can also choose whether to let others handle your power tools when you do this charging. Some feel concerned about others using their tools because they are afraid that other people may mix their energy with their own, so that their tool will become less powerful for them. But you can readily charge your tool in such a way that others can use it too. When you focus on directing your own energy into your tool to charge it, you can also imagine a protective shield of energy forming around your own energy or the tool itself to keep others' energy out. If you have not previously charged your own tool, you can always clear out the energy of others before you use it. You simply focus on any alien energy dissipating out of your tool, and after cleansing it of this other energy, you project in your own energy to give it your own charge. So again, choose the approach that works for you.

The following exercise is designed to help you charge your staff or any other tool you decide to use.

You should begin by obtaining the tool you want to charge. Then, find a quiet place and lay it down in front of you. This could be on an ordinary table. Or if you have a special place, such as an altar, which you have set aside for working with magic or energy and power, then use that.

Get yourself relaxed and in an altered state of consciousness. You want to be in the same kind of altered space you use in seeing.

When you feel ready, pick up the tool you are charging. Hold it out in front of you, and as you do, imagine your own energy projecting out into this tool. See your energy flowing from your hands and coursing into the tool. As this happens, notice the aura growing around it and look for the beam projecting out of its tip.

Continue to focus on sending your energy and seeing the energy field around the object expand. Focus on the beam getting brighter and longer.

Keep sending bursts of energy and seeing this energy around and projecting from this object for several minutes. As you do, feel your energy in the object grow stronger and stronger.

Finally, if you wish, visualize an energy shield around your own energy to keep the energy of others out.

When you feel complete about changing your object, let the visualization go and return to an ordinary state of consciousness. Your power object is now charged with your energy, and that charge will stay there and add to the power of this object when you work with it.

Thereafter, when you work with this object, you will continue to charge it each time, so you will probably not need to recharge it again. However, if you do not use the object for some time, your energy may gradually diffuse out of it. So when you pick it up again after a period of not using it, it is a good idea to charge it again if you feel the original charge is weakened or gone.

Cleaning Up Your Energy

After you have done some work with projecting energy, it is important to disperse that energy or draw your leftover energy back into yourself. That way you do not leave any remnants of this energy hanging around where it can potentially interfere with what other people are doing or be turned back against you to harm you.

When you first start working with these techniques you may not be aware of these leftover energies. But as people become more experienced they can see not only the energy forms they create or draw to them, but those left over from other people. When I first started going out in the field with Michael, I was not able to see such things. However, from time to time he would notice some leftover energy forms hanging around, such as the remnants of a magical circle or pentagram created by someone else. He would either direct us to stay away from the area to avoid those energies, or he would do his own working to send those energies away.

The reason it is important to get rid of these energy forms you create is because sometimes if you do not they linger and can disrupt other people. Or alternatively, if you come back to the area, they can harm you in some way on a psychic or spiritual level. This can happen because you have left some energy of your own out there, and it could potentially turn against you if you do not pull it back in again after you are done working with energy.

Another way to think of this is that you do not litter in the public parks with your leftovers when you leave. By the same token, you should not litter with your psychic energy. Many people may not be aware of this litter. But as people become sensitive they can see these things, and you will too.

Applying the Perception of Energy to Your Own Experience

As you get better at perceiving these energy forms and forces in the field, you will find you can perceive them in everyday life also. Michael found these kinds of perceptions critical for him when he was working in an ambulance on emergency duty in Los Angeles. The ambulance traveled in some very rough parts of town, and sometimes he would get a sense that things were bad in the neighborhood, so it was better not to get out. Or he would be someplace and suddenly get a feeling that it was time to go, and he would walk away. In one instance he walked away and another person stepped into the space and was shot. If Michael had stayed there, he might have been shot instead. What led him to respond in this way is that he was feeling strange or negative energy forms, and they served to signal him that it was time to leave or stay away. In turn, by working with some of the energy techniques described in this chapter, he was able to develop a sensitivity to perceiving these energies.

Perhaps most of us do not experience such life threatening situations. But these kinds of sensitivities to energy can be applied in very ordinary situations such as a work or career setting to help you realize certain truths about things. Suppose you work in a bureaucratic setting. You might think someone is being very nice to you, but maybe in reality they do not really like you and when the opportunity comes they will give you the shaft. But if you become sensitive to these psychic and spiritual energies, you may be able to pick up what the person really feels. You can possibly do this because underneath the person's outwardly friendly exterior, his negative attitude towards you will be reflected in a projection of negative energy towards you. If you are sensitive to these energy forms, you may be able to pick that up.

Perceiving and Working with Personal Colors—Exercise #6

One final consideration that is important to basic seeing is the use of personal colors. Each person has his own personal color or vibration, and when you tune into other people you can pick that up. As your sensitivity increases, you can also pick up the colors of other people who might have been in a particular area before. If you are out somewhere and you suddenly pick up the image of lots of red, perhaps a person who was there before had a red energy or aura around him.

One way to discover your own color is to notice what color you see when your eyes are stressed, because your own color appears under this condition. For example, when you look at something very bright or see a bright flash of something, the first color you see when you react to this is your personal color.

To see your own personal color now, look at a bright light. You can turn on a light in a dim room and look at it, or shine a flashlight in your eyes. After you look for a moment, close your eyes and look away. Now notice what afterimage or color appears.

Try this a few times. Commonly you will see the same color each time. When you get this consistency, you know this is your personal color. You will probably feel very comfortable with this color, as if it belongs to you.

Using Personal Colors

Note that your personal color is different than your working colors. As previously noted, these colors tend to be white, blue and amber, and these are the colors that typically appear around your staff or other power object when you work with it. In some cases, you may have the same colors as your own, but often you will not. So make sure you recognize these distinctions when you try to work with colors and interpret what they mean.

One advantage of being aware of a person's colors is you can use this to better understand the person by interpreting what those colors mean to you.

Or you may be able to pick up that a person has been someplace if you sense that color in the area, as previously discussed.

Commonly, when you first meet someone or come into an area very near him, sometimes referred to as "coming into their air space," you will pick up his colors in this way. At first you will pick up a whitish yellowish light that is around him. But then, as you tune in more closely into this person, you will pick up his resonant colors which surround that whitish yellow light or are intermingled with it. It may take some time to pick up this information about someone when you are first learning to see energy, since you may often just see the whitish yellowish light if you see any aura at all. But gradually, if you keep working with this, over time these colors will emerge too. And after a while, you will be able to see them even when the person is not present, such as when you go into an area where he has been, or when you try to pick up some information about that person psychically by focusing on a mental image of that person and seeing what sensations, images and colors come into view.

You can also use your own color to affect your mood. If things are bothering you or you are in a difficult emotional crisis or experiencing a lot of pressure, you can use your resonant color as a source of strength. The way to do this is to visualize that color around you, protecting you and infusing you with its strength. So your color becomes like a protective shield around you or an image you can turn to as a way of strengthening yourself.

You can gain more power for yourself when you do a ritual or work on projecting energy by radiating your own color. The way to do this is to see the energy you are sending forth suffused with your own color. That will intensify the power of the energy you are sending out.

The Relationship Between Your Own Energy Level and the Use of These Techniques

Since the process of seeing and projecting energy involves working with energy, you can do this more effectively when your own energy is in a good, high place. On the other hand, if you are not in a place where you can really concentrate and focus because you feel ill or tired or otherwise distracted, you are not going to experience things as intensely or at all.

If you are in a very low energy state, there are techniques you can use to build it up. But sometimes you are so tired and your energy so down, any build-up is not going to work. As a result, if you do not have and cannot build up the energy to be with it or concentrate, you are not going to be able to visualize things or sense things or feel things, or direct your energy as you would if you felt perfectly fine.

The best way to deal with this problem is to first try to build yourself up. To do this, consciously acknowledge that you are in this low energy state, and then visualize your personal color or some other image of strength or power. Or perhaps visualize your negative energy being poured into a bag, and then you tie up that bag and throw it into a fire, so all that negativity is destroyed. This kind of imaging should help you get out of a negative space so you feel energized again.

I have seen this process work in a group also. Once Michael took a group of us out in the field, and one of his associates did a ritual in which he asked the rest of us to think of the worst negative images or feelings we had right now. As he suggested: "Think of the worst thing that happened to you in the last week." Next, he asked all of us to project that negative image on him, and he imagined that negativity coming into a bag. He took that bag and imagined throwing it into a fire, and then saw that negativity totally destroyed. It was a very intense experience for him because he had all of this negative energy heaped on him, and then he had to destroy and transform it. While he was doing all of this mentally, everyone could actually see this energy transformed, for it appeared to form into a ball of grayish energy hanging in the air. Then it rose up like grayish, misty smoke. Finally it evaporated into the air. All eight of us in the group saw this happen.

Using Your Power of Seeing and Working With Energy to Make Things Happen

In summary, there are all sorts of things you can do with seeing and working with energy. It is up to the creativity of your own imagination. And the more you work with your seeing and these energy techniques, the more you can do.

The way to start is by learning how to see and project your energy. You can use various power tools to help you do this. Then you can start using your ability to see and project energy to create the images of what you want to happen in your life. Once you have this vision you can start feeding energy into it, either your own energy or the energy you call up from outside yourself in order to make this vision happen. For example, you focus on someone calling, and then he does. You concentrate on getting a job you want, and then you do. You imagine a relationship you want and send out your energy to get it.

These techniques have worked for shamans from time immemorial. Now you can learn to use these techniques yourself and make them work for you.

Chapter Three

Controlling, Directing And Gaining Information From Your Dreams

The Power of Dreaming

Dreaming can be used much like the seeing process to gain information and insights about yourself and others, to peer into distant places and future times, and to make changes in yourself, in others and in events. The major difference in the two processes is that seeing involves more conscious control and the use of your intuition in a wakeful state. By contrast, in dreaming you are using your unconscious when you are asleep or in a near sleep state to perform these activities.

The two processes reinforce and complement one another. If you do not get information from one channel of knowledge, you may get it from the other. Or if you get the same information from both channels, you can be more sure of its accuracy. By the same token, you can seek to have an impact on changing yourself or your environment by either method, or if you work on effecting this change through both channels, your efforts will be even stronger and therefore will more likely be effective.

The Use of Dreaming in Shamanism

The use of dreaming to gain insights and have an influence on daily life has a long history. Traditional shamans have used it since time immemorial to give them knowledge and help them make predictions and heal, much in the same way that they have used other tools for the same purposes. For example, they have used dreams as omens of the future, much like they have looked to everyday occurrences, plants, birds and objects for a sign of what is coming next. Many shamans have used active dreaming like a magical ritual to have an effect on the outcome of a situation.

One of the most cited examples of how traditional peoples have used dreaming is the Senoi, a tribal group living in Malaysia. According to many psychologists who have reported on this group, the Senoi make their dreams a regular part of their lives. When the Senoi have a dream, they talk about it with others, and they try to interpret what it means because they believe it has powerful insights about what is happening in everyday life.For example, if a person has a dream about a tiger, and he is afraid of it and runs away, this suggests the person is frightened about something, if not the tiger itself, then something the tiger symbolizes. Further, the Senoi believe that when a person has such a frightening dream, this indicates that the person should work on overcoming this fear by confronting whatever it is he is afraid of. One way to do this, they believe, is by working on confronting that thing in one's dream and changing the dream's outcome. To do this, they seek to have such a dream again, but this time their goal is to actively control it so that fearful image is overcome. When this happens, they believe the person will similarly be able to overcome what he fears in everyday life.

In contrast to this use of dreaming, we tend to use dreams today more as a way of understanding ourselves than for any other purpose, and we tend to forget the many other purposes of dreams. But if we start working with dreams in these other ways, we can capture their power and use them for a variety of purposes.

Some Ways You Can Use Dreaming

How can you use dreaming in your own life? I will describe a few major ways here and then discuss them later in detail after explaining how and why they work.

First, you can use dreaming to learn about yourself. You can gain insights into who you are and what you want. Secondly, you can use dreaming to direct your attention to certain areas of your life that you want to work on, and then you can use your dreams to change yourself or events you do not like. Thirdly, you can gain some advance information about the probable future that lies ahead, and if you wish you can use your dreams to help move you in that direction or to change things. You can learn about others through your dreams and affect your relationships with them also. In short, your dreams can be mobilized as a tool, much like your abilities to see, think, feel and know things, to improve your everyday life, whether you want to get a better job, have more satisfying relationships with others, control your weight or whatever you want.

To achieve these effects, you need to be able to use the appropriate active dreaming techniques in order to get more in touch with your dreams, use them to obtain information and control, and manipulate them to achieve your goals. Then you can use these techniques to make your dreams more perceptive by guiding them to get more information from your unconscious or higher consciousness. And you can make your dreams more predictive, by teaching yourself to be more receptive to insights from outside sources of knowledge.

There are two basic ways to empower your ability to use your dreams. One is by developing your ability to be receptive and gain more accurate information in this way. This is the mode of essentially just looking at your dreams carefully and seeing what they are telling you about areas where you want information. For example, this receptive mode can be used to gain the insights you want to know about yourself, about others or about what will happen in your life.

The other approach is to take an active role in guiding or directing your dream. In this more active mode, you can consciously ask yourself a question and seek out information from your dream on something you want to know about, and you can project your will into your dreams to make other things happen as well. Suppose you have to make a decision such as what job to take. You can direct yourself to dream about a job, which will give you an answer to your questions.

The Power of Knowing You Can Do It and Practice

Many of these techniques for dream control may sound strange and unfamiliar. By believing you can do it and by practicing, you will find you do have the power to actively gain information from your dreams and influence them in various ways. Like many other people, I found this the case at some dream workshops I attended some years ago. In each case, I found I could make my dream do exactly what I wanted, just by directing my attention accordingly. And in each case this occurred at a time when I normally did not dream very much or at least remember my dreams, because I was very busy and was not paying much attention to them.

In the first case, the workshop leader asked us to merely pay attention to our dreams and remember them. He told us to remind ourselves before going to bed that we would have dreams and would remember them, and after I did this unconsciously, this is exactly what happened. Though I had not remembered a dream for months, that night I was aware of my dream. But afterwards, when I shifted back to a state of inattention, I barely had dreams again.

In the second case, a few years later, the results were more dramatic. This time the workshop leader, after explaining the conscious dreaming process of the Senoi, told us how we should do it ourselves. "Just remind yourself as you are falling asleep that your consciousness will remain awake and alert when you have a dream so you will be aware you are dreaming. Then, observe your dream as it occurs, and if it goes in a direction you do not like, you can step in and change it." Again, I consciously gave myself these directions as I drifted off to sleep, and again I found I could do it. I saw my dream unfolding like I was in a movie theater watching it, and I was aware that as the projectionist, at any time I could change the reel.

At a third workshop, the leader showed us how to program our unconscious to bring forth a certain kind of dream. "Just tell yourself again and again before you go to bed that you will dream about a certain subject and ask yourself the questions you want to know at that time. Then, when you go to sleep, pay attention to the answers you get." And once more I found that this programming process worked. I wanted to learn about what job I should take next, and that night, right on cue, I ended up having a dream about working on a job. I did not get a clear answer, but I was certainly amazed that I should dream about a job just as I had requested. As before I had not had any dreams I could recall for months, but now once I thought about what I wanted, I was able to dream the dream I wanted.

Thus, my own experience each time made it quite clear that these techniques can work. Yet, to use them effectively, you also have to practice. You have to consciously pay attention or work on controlling your dreams or asking for information. Otherwise nothing will happen and your dreams will slip away. As I found myself, the few times I consciously thought about my dreams, I gained the kind of experience I sought. But once I stopped trying to control the process, I once more had only occasional random dreams.

So you do have the power to influence both whether you have dreams and what you dream about. And you can intervene in your dreams too. But you have to do this actively to make it happen. You need to practice, just like any skill, if you want to master your ability to tap into and control your dreams. You have to practice doing this regularly to make this skill your own. With this practice, you can take control of your dreams.

How Dreaming Can Affect Everyday Reality

Dreaming can have this impact on everyday life, just like your everyday life can influence your dreams, because the two are part of the same reality continuum which ranges from the deep unconsciousness of ordinary dreams on the one hand, to the alert awareness characteristic of the active waking state. At times, one may be more in one state than the other, but these different levels of reality may also exist simultaneously, so that as you experience something in the waking state, your unconsciousness will be receiving or processing information too, as it follows its own dynamic.

At times these two levels of consciousness may go on separately, as if they are in parallel but distinct channels. But then, at other times, they may interact with one another, so that you may consciously tap into your dream images while you are doing things in everyday life, or alternatively your dream experiences may influence what you are doing in your waking state. The result of this situation is you can use your experiences in real life to get information on your dreams, and you can use your dreams to impact on your life. In some cases, you will find that some of your dreams are much more powerful than others in giving you information or having an effect, and as you become more sensitive you can tell which dreams have more power.

For example, people who claim to be psychics often report having these dream images come to them with information they can use to guide their lives or provide insights to others. But generally they only tune into these images from time to time. It's like turning on and off a television screen at different times. You need to balance out the times you watch with getting everyday information as you go about the routine of everyday life.

Many people go through life unaware of these other levels of consciousness or reality which may exist simultaneously or offer insights if only people are aware. Even if people are aware they exist, they may tune them out. A key reason this occurs is because children are brought up to disregard or devalue this other world. At first, children tend to be very much in touch with this reality. They have rich images in their imagination and may believe they can talk to spirits and all sorts of fantasy creatures. But soon they learn, typically by first or second grade, that one is not supposed to recognize or communicate with such things because they are not there. So people learn to turn this level of consciousness off. Sometimes it can get shut off completely, or at other times it is pushed down away from our ordinary level of awareness. But in either case, a person can learn to start these processes going again or tune back into them by pushing aside the veils of ordinary everyday consciousness. Then it becomes possible to look at the other reality that exists if we tap into it on the level of our unconsciousness or higher consciousness, or reach it through our intuition and our dreams.

One way to think of this relationship is to think of this reality or consciousness continuum divided up into three little boxes representing three levels of reality.

Higher Consciousness

Normal Awareness

Physical Reality

All of these levels exist at the same time, and your awareness can shift from one level to another.

The top box represents the area of the unconscious or higher consciousness. This is the level you enter when you work with altered states of consciousness or dream projections. It is the level where you can get in touch with the forces and energies of nature and perhaps contact spiritual beings or self-created constructs representing aspects of your higher self.

The middle box represents the level of your rational consciousness or normal awareness. This is the level of consciousness that picks up and responds to everyday reality.

And finally, the bottom box corresponds to your physical awareness of material objects, forms and sensations. It is represented most characteristically by your sense of touch, smell, movement and feeling.

Your normal awareness in the middle acts like a kind of monitor or channel selector which determines what state you will be in at any given time, or whether your awareness might focus on a level of consciousness that operates between channels to pick up more than one at the same time. For instance, in your normal state you can program yourself to have a dream unfold in a certain way, or you can change the focus of your consciousness. This shift in consciousness will affect what information you are receiving from this higher realm, from the everyday world, or from the lower physical senses. You always have the choice of options by moving from one box or level to the other and, if you wish, you can pull in information simultaneously from different channels, though one may be much stronger than the others. It's like tuning a television channel and increasing or decreasing the brightness of the color or the volume of the sound.

As an example, when you are in a room you may be in the presence of different levels of energy, and you can pick these up by changing your focus of attention. Normally, you will be in a state of wakeful consciousness and see everything from this perspective. In this state you will be separate and apart from your environment. It's a state of being neutral and detached. As you pay more attention to the physical level, you will feel things like the play of the air in the room, the level of the temperature, a sense of lightness or heaviness depending on the atmosphere in the room.

On the other hand, you can direct your attention away from such levels to get into a more meditative or dream-like state, so your unconsciousness or intuition can pick up the normally unseen energies that are there in the form of images, thoughts, knowings and undefined feelings. The more you work with these processes, the more you will be able to switch levels and be aware of the parallels between picking up information through hypnotic and meditative states and through dreams.

I had this kind of experience with parallels when I first started designing games. It started with thinking about creating them in an ordinary waking state and organizing some meetings of people who wanted to play games. Soon after, I began having random dreams in which I would see people playing a game or see the image of a game board. In the next stage, a friend of mine worked on hypnotizing me so I could gain more control over these dream processes. At first, he would go through a long, elaborate process in which he would take me down in an elevator to a toy store where I would see new games. After a while I no longer needed to have someone direct me through this process. Instead, I could take control of moving into that state almost immediately from my conscious waking state. I could simply tell my consciousness to shift and it would, and I would experience a kind of waking dream. Much like the dreams I had once had of games at night, now I would simply watch and the images of people playing a game would unfold apart from my conscious control. My consciousness was in charge of my watching, observing and remembering. Also, it suggested the topic for the dream. But then my unconsciousness would take over, and it was in charge of what happened in the dream. When that dream ended, I could reconstruct it with my normal waking consciousness and later translate it into a physical reality.

Typically, the waking consciousness is able to discern the difference between these different levels of reality. But sometimes these cloud together in your mind, so it is not really clear where something is coming from—another example of this close connection between these levels of reality. For example, sometimes you may have the experience that you have done something before, because the place, the people or what you did feel familiar. And then suddenly you are not sure. Did you really do it, or did you just dream you did it? Or maybe you remember saying something or having someone give you some information. But did you say it or dream you said it? Or did someone tell you? Or did the information appear in a dream? Sometimes you really cannot tell. But in other cases, you may get some feedback later that helps you decide. For instance, you are positive someone said something to you or you told someone to do something, but the other person declares you had no such conversation. Perhaps the other person forgot, or maybe you were having a dream. As you get more discerning, you will be better able to tell the difference.

You will also be better able to distinguish between the recollections you have from the waking and sleeping dream. The key difference is that these waking dreams occur when we are conscious and are usually aware we are having a dream. Then, if we wish, we can more readily intervene to stop it or change it. When we have sleeping dreams, until we learn how to control them, our conscious part is normally asleep, so we don't really know what is happening in the dream until we wake up and remember back. But in both cases, we can sometimes think the dream really happened when we were awake. And in both cases we have the ability to tell the difference and to recognize the circumstances of the dream.

It all comes from gaining discernment and learning to be more aware of these different levels of reality and when we are operating at a particular level or choosing the level in which we want to operate; in turn we choose that level by tuning in the channel.

Perhaps another way to think of this tuning process is like setting a receiving device or screen to pick up very soft notes of sound or very small particles of energy. As we go up the scale to ever higher levels of unconsciousness and become more in contact with the altered states of reality that open the doors to the level of the higher self, intuition and spiritual beings, the energy particles become even finer. So we need more subtle and refined instruments to pick it up, and correspondingly, we need to do more work on training our mind to do this through meditative states and dreams. As we go down the scale and focus on the world of everyday reality, and then on to the solidity of the physical world, the energy particles become correspondingly larger, so they are increasingly easier to pick up through our ordinary consciousness or our physical senses, like taste and touch.

Numerous spiritual, metaphysical and shamanistic groups make these distinctions. In fact, some of them have very elaborate schemes describing these planes of existence. One common approach is to describe all of these energies in the universe as coming from one source of unity, sometimes described as God. As it comes from this source, which is like a point of bright white light, it is at the highest level of refinement and lightness. As it radiates out and moves further away from the source, it gains more and more solid material form and becomes heavier and heavier. So eventually you are able to see it in your ordinary waking state. But with proper training, one can learn to become more discriminating in his seeing when awake or in his dreams, so that he can see into these smaller spaces of reality, then pick up information on these higher levels.

The shaman warrior path is one way to do this. Then you can use these higher insights gained through dreams and altered states in the various ways discussed in this book.

The First Step of Paying Attention

To begin the process of getting in touch with your dreams so you can gain information from them or control them, you have to first pay attention. You need this awareness to better remember your dreams, to discern when your dreams are important or predictive, and to determine how to best intervene in and influence your dreams.

You have probably experienced the effects of paying attention to your dreams yourself. If you are very busy and do not have time to think about your dream life, you are likely to not remember your dreams at all or only experience them very vaguely. If you consciously think about wanting to have dreams and remember them and take some time in the morning to make note of any dreams you have, you will probably find you are having and recalling more dreams.

That has certainly been my own experience. I have gone through cycles where I was very busy with all sorts of everyday things, and did not pay much attention to my dreams. I have felt at times that I did not really want to be bothered by having a dream and taking the time to write it down. At those times, I had no dreams at all. But consistently I found that when I did something to break the cycle and pay attention to my dreams again, my dream life suddenly became very active. This happened whenever I signed up for a dream workshop and the leader told us to pay attention to our dreams. It happened again when I went on vacation and put aside my everyday cares and concerns. In this case, I had opened up space again in my life for these dreams to come in and that's exactly what they did.

Once you start paying attention to the unconscious part of yourself, you will find that part of you responds. It's like you have turned on the channel, so a picture will soon appear.

Learning to Be More Discerning

Once you start paying attention and being aware of your dreams, you can start developing a sense of discernment so you become observant about the different qualities of your dreams.

A key aspect of this discernment is to pay attention to the difference between random and special dreams. The random dreams are basically ordinary dreams in which you process the everyday images and experiences you have had over the past day or so. Usually, such dreams are built around fragmentary images or thoughts which do not have a great deal of power or impact for you. It's like flipping casually through a newspaper or weekly newsmagazine and noticing what happened.

Special dreams feel special. There is a quality about them that makes you want to pay attention. The dream may be more vivid visually; it may seem more immediate and real; it may seem to have some special symbolic significance; it may contain some powerful new information, or it may seem to be precognitive in that it is telling you something about the future. Whatever this quality is, you will feel the dream has some special power— that it is calling out to you to notice it and do something in response to it. It is hard to define this, because you won't get this information about the dream on a rational basis. You will simply sense that the dream has a special symbolic quality or compelling power so that you will feel the dream is very important.

The process is much the same as when you are using your seeing and pick up something that seems significant on an unconscious level. You may feel like you are experiencing some significant event in your life; you may sense you have picked up some significant information; you may have a strong feeling of knowing something is going to happen, or you may have a powerful vision of the future. In this case, you are using your waking consciousness to guide yourself into the altered state of consciousness where you can see. But the information you get can be the same as you get through dreaming where you have released your unconscious mind while you are still asleep.

So by being more discerning about your dreams, you can pick up when they are more important and when they are not, just like you discern these distinctions when you see. At times you will feel very certain that your dream is about something that is very important or is about to happen. At other times you will feel it is more symbolic, and at still others, you will recognize it as something that is not very important at all—just random thoughts and images. So start noticing these differences and in time you will be better able to make these important distinctions.

Keeping a Dream Log

One of the best ways to learn to pay attention and develop this discernment is by keeping a dream log. This dream log will also give you vital information you can use in understanding and tracking your dreams.

Just keeping the log will encourage you to be more aware of your dreams and remember them. If you have a dream log by the side of your bed and remind yourself before going to bed that you are going to record any dreams you have during the night in this log, it will signal your mind that you think your dreams are important. Thus, you will be more likely to have or remember a dream.

You can keep this log in several forms. Probably the most common way to do this is to keep a notebook and write down your dreams. But if you prefer, you can use a tape recorder and record them. Then later, if you wish, you can always transcribe them. Some people prefer to simply draw or paint their dreams, rather than express them in words. Use the approach that feels most comfortable for you, or use a combination of approaches.

In any case, it is ideal to devote a little time in the morning when you first wake up to recording your dream, because this is when it is freshest in your mind. Also, you may find that even if you think at first that you did not have a dream, but spend some time trying to retrieve one, you will suddenly realize that you did in fact have one. The process of trying to think of it will evoke a series of images and thoughts, and often one of these will suddenly bring back the dream, sometimes in fragments that you must struggle to pull together, sometimes like a complete story now clearly laid out in front of you. I have had this experience many times. I will look at my dream log in the morning, thinking I have not dreamt about anything at all. But then I will focus on the sheet of paper in front of me anyway and let my mind go. And often I will recapture a dream in a few minutes.

In some cases, you may wake up in the middle of the night remembering a dream; if you wish, include it in your log. This can be especially valuable if it seemed to be a powerful dream. Or if it seems trivial, perhaps just let it go and go back to sleep.

If you wish, you can program yourself before you go to sleep so you remember to wake yourself up if you have a dream. As your ability to program yourself gets better, you can guide your unconscious to distinguish between those dreams that are important and worth waking up for and those that are not. While it can be important to capture these dreams you may get by with recording them when you wake up. It is also important to find a balance between remembering to record your dreams, and waking yourself up too much so you disturb your sleep.

One good way to achieve this balance is to use a tape recorder rather than a notebook for in-the-middle-of-the-night dream memories. This way you can simply describe your dream into the recorder while you are still lying in bed and then go right back to sleep. This process is less likely to wake you up as much as sitting up and writing something down. Also, you can speak faster than you can write.

As you go through the process of remembering your dreams in whatever way, you will find your dream will often turn out more detailed. For example, the dream can be very fragmentary when you wake up, but as you write you may suddenly have the experience of remembering more than you did at first. Sometimes, you may at first only remember the last part of the dream. Or maybe the ending may be much clearer than the beginning.

But as you write or talk out or draw your dream, you may find the first part of the dream starts to come back in reverse order. You may also find you start making logical connections, so the fragments of your dream make sense. In the dream state, we often dream in fragments or our images shift quickly in time or space from one setting to another. But once we work on remembering, our conscious mind can have trouble with all this vagueness. So our logical mind will try to put the pieces together in a meaningful way so these random pieces of data make sense.

Once you have the basic information of the dream, there are a number of things you can do with this. First, you can use your dream records to refer back to later on, when you have a recollection of something happening and are not sure whether it really happened or was just a dream.

Secondly, if you have a dream that seems predictive of the future, you can check out its accuracy and determine whether it was really predictive or not. If you do this for a series of dreams, you can tally up your batting average on your power of prediction through your dreams. Also, if you have some dreams which were predictive and some which were not, you can examine those dreams more closely to see if there were some differences. In the future, you may be better able to determine which of your dreams are more likely to be accurate. For instance, your more accurate dreams may be more detailed or more intense and they might have been accompanied by a feeling of knowingness. Whatever their quality, by checking, you may be able to identify this. With this improved knowledge of your dreams' accuracy you can better decide when to follow your dreams based on what they are suggesting will happen in the future.

A third way you can use your dream records is to look for recurring patterns. These can give you some insights into yourself and who you are. Or you may find that these patterns change as you effect changes in your everyday life. I know one woman who used to have recurring dreams about her mother telling her what to do and controlling her life. Her mother was a very dominant and controlling person, and even though she lived five hundred miles away, the woman felt she had to listen when her mother told her to do something. However, as her dreams suggested, she was disturbed about this control her mother appeared to have over her life. When she worked on making her own decisions and standing up to her mother, the dreams of her mother taking over stopped. She no longer felt under her mother's control, so her dreams no longer showed this.

Similarly, when you review your own dreams, you will get insights into what is happening in your life and what you should do to either keep things as they are or make a change. Your dreams will serve as a kind of weather vane or barometer to let you know what is happening and what lies ahead. Then you can use that information to stay on course or shift, depending on the pattern you observe in your dreams and the pattern you would like to create in your life.

Some Parallels Between Dreaming, Other Unconscious Processes and Working With Energy

As you start thinking about your dreams to remember and record them, you may notice that dreaming is much like other unconscious processes that give you information or which you can direct to influence what happens. There are strong parallels between dreaming and automatic writing and painting, since in all of these activities you release the control of your conscious mind and let your unconsciousness go, though you may start with some initial conscious direction. In ordinary dreaming, of course, you are asleep. But when you do automatic writing or painting, you enter into a quasi-dream-like state where you go into a semi-trance that is much like the hypnotic state of deep relaxation that precedes ordinary sleep. Then, you open yourself up to your higher self or your unconsciousness, which then directs your writing or painting.

Sometimes it can feel like a spirit-guide or being is directing your writing or painting, since whatever you are doing is not consciously controlled by you. Instead, it's like someone is talking to you or through you, and sometimes it can help the process to imagine that there is this being communicating with you. For then you may find it easier to listen and respond to directions if you see yourself talking with someone who has some identifiable form or personality rather than just disembodied voices.

Dreams can operate much like that. You either consciously trigger them or they may start happening on their own when you let your conscious control go as you fall asleep. Like the unconscious communications you get through automatic writing or art, they can give you information either in the form of thoughts (which are much like the ideas of automatic writing), or images (much like the pictures you produce through automatic art).

When you learn how to do more active dreaming you will discover it can be much like working with the energies of nature in the field. When you work with these energies within or outside of yourself, you start the process off by consciously planning what you intend. Then you work to guide yourself into a meditative dreaming kind of state in which you can project your energy to direct activity or open yourself up to be receptive to sensations, perceptions and other information. In the same way, you can project your energy or be receptive in your dreams.

The most usual mode of dreaming is the open, receptive state. But in active dreaming you can set the stage for your dreams to create the same kinds of projections you do otherwise in a meditative, trance-like state. You have a little less control over the process in dreaming, since you are in a deeper state of unconsciousness. But since you are, you can create even more powerful, symbolic images. For example, when you are working with energy in the field, you can use your imagination to call forth spirits and beings and all manner of symbolic images and thoughts. You can program your dreams to operate on this level too.

The more you work with dreaming, the more you will become aware of the parallels between these two levels of consciousness—the state of dreaming and the projection of your energy into altered states of reality, which is the basis for the magical or energy-changing event.

Interpreting Your Dreams

It takes a little more work to actively guide your dreams. It is easier to start by interpreting them. To do this, look at both what the dream is most obviously about on the surface and also at the symbols of your dream. The surface of the dream is the overall story line —the events and images of the dream. But the symbols are the meanings and themes underlying these events and images. They are the thoughts and feelings you have about what you are seeing and experiencing and the reasons you think and feel this way.

These dream symbols are very personal, because everyone will have their own meanings they attach to these symbols. At one time, people used to think there were certain standard symbols. The Freudian psychologists developed a whole catalog of meanings in which they suggested that certain symbols had one meaning, while other symbols meant something else.

Perhaps there were certain commonalities of meanings when Freudian students of psychology grew up in Victorian times, because there was a much more rigid culture, in which people's lives were more strictly patterned than today. So people would be more likely to attach similar meanings to similar images and thoughts, and they would be more likely to have dreams based on commonly shared experiences.

Today, most people have personal idiosyncratic meanings for the symbols in their dream. Someone else may be able to help you interpret the dream because there are certain universal images and symbols which may have common meanings for people, because we all come from the same culture. A bird may suggest freedom or flight, while water may be associated with purity and peacefulness. But any symbol may also have some special and unique meanings for you. If you have been brought up near the ocean, the image of water will have one set of meanings for you as compared to someone who has been raised in a desert. Thus, while someone who has studied dream psychology and has spent a lot of time interpreting dreams may have certain insights into dream meanings because they know a little more about the subject, they still may not know about the personal idiosyncrasies that have influenced your own dream. That comes from you.

Each person should interpret his own dreams in terms of what it means to himself. Suppose you have a dream about someone else. You may pick up some images and associations with that person that come about as a result of the meanings and symbols you associate with that person, as well as the meanings and symbols that person wants to convey when other people relate to him. When you look at such a dream, it is important to distinguish between whether the symbols you are picking up are occurring because they are something the other person is sending out to tell others about himself or whether they are symbols of your own projection that have special meaning to you.

Be aware that dream symbols can be interpreted on a lot of different levels, and the more you work with your dreams, the more sensitive you will become to these different levels of meaning. If a person has an injury in your dream, you may pick this up on a concrete physical level and soon after you see that person with the injury. It's like you are picking up something about this person, and it shows up as an image of this person in your dream. But you might also dream about this person being injured in a more symbolic way such as having a loss of some sort, or maybe you might see an image of this person suddenly fragment or scatter in your dream. This symbol could have many different meanings, so its up to you to interpret what it means to you, and as you get more sensitive and get more feedback on the relationship between your dreams and what is happening in the real world (such as the dream image of your friend and then your friend turning up with an injury), you will be better able to understand your dreams' meanings and be more accurate in relating these meanings to real events.

This attention to meanings can give you important information about yourself. Suppose you have a dream about yourself when you see yourself approaching some sort of danger. That might suggest that you have to pay more attention to yourself and watch out because if you do not do something differently, you are going to be in either physical or emotional danger.

When you think about your dreams, look for such symbols. They are a way in which your dream is telling you something or giving you warnings or suggestions. The dream may do this in a symbolic or shorthand way, because it is sometimes too difficult to confront the actual event or experience directly. Instead, the dream smooths over the information it wants to convey to you so you can deal with this data in a way that feels comfortable to you. Then, if you are ready, you may see the meaning immediately or if the realization is too heavy or powerful for you to confront right away, the symbol gives you a protective coating or barrier that stands in the way. As you feel comfortable, you can gradually see the meaning of it.

This gradual process works like this. Suppose you have a dream about falling into a hole. This might occur because there are certain difficulties that you cannot look at right away. However, the hole might be a way of alerting you that you should start to pay attention to something. So the dream serves as a way to prepare yourself to look at the possible danger ahead a little more closely, although it does not let you know just yet what it is because you aren't fully ready.

At the same time that you should pay attention to symbols, also be aware that everything in your dreams may not necessarily be a symbol, because often you are merely processing and reflecting on the experiences of the day. Sometimes you may notice that your dream revolves around a particular object or event. Then, if you think back to the last day or so, you may realize that your dream has focused on some objects or events you have recently encountered. At times, these objects or events may have been selected because they have some special significance. In that case, it can be helpful to think about any associated meanings to help you interpret the dream. But at other times, these scenes and images fall in the category of random dreaming. You are just recollecting recent events that are of no particular importance; they are just passing through your mind because you experienced or observed them recently.

It is a matter of discernment, which is a skill that will come with practice. When relevant, consider the symbolic meaning of your dreams and use these meanings to better understand what is happening in your life, get insights about other people and events, or make decisions and predictions. At other times, just note the image or event in your dream and then pass on. This way, as you become more discerning, and you will not only be better at interpreting these dream symbols and meanings, but you will know when not to interpret them.

An Exercise in Interpreting Your Dreams—Exercise #7

Use your dream log as a basis for interpreting your dreams. Preferably use a written dream log for this purpose. The following exercise is designed to get you in the habit of interpreting your dreams over a weekly period. You should continue to do this on a regular basis whenever you have a dream or after a week or two of accumulating dream accounts.

Begin the process by consciously reminding yourself that you will pay attention to your dreams that night. Then, keep your dream log by your bed, and make it a point to write down your dreams in the morning or if you should wake up with a dream memory during the night. If you do not immediately remember anything when you wake up in the morning, focus on your dream log for a few moments and possibly something may come back to you.

Then record your dream as you would normally. Afterwards, review the dream and think about what it means to you. Are there any images or events that might have a symbolic quality? If so, what might they represent? Write down any thoughts, images or impressions these questions suggest.

If you have had a previous dream in the last few days, review that too. Note your previous thoughts, images and impressions, and notice if there are any recurring symbols or themes.

Do this for at least a week or perhaps two. You will find that by doing this you will be more likely to have dreams, and your dreams will become more vivid and rich in meaning. You will also be better able to interpret this meaning and understand your dreams.

Programming Your Dreams to Dream What You Want

Besides being receptive and paying attention to the dreams that come to you, you can take an active role in creating the dreams you want by programming yourself to dream about specific things. You can even control the dream you create in this way so if you do not like what's happening in it, you can step into your dream and change it. But that is the next step which involves lucid and directive dreaming, which is discussed next.

The way to do this programming is to sit down and take some time consciously focusing on what you want to dream about. Preferably do this before you go to sleep, although you can do it at other times during the day. The process works much the same way that you can consciously direct yourself to have a daydream on a certain subject or otherwise guide yourself to do automatic writing or painting on a certain topic. In this case, your direction to have a dream about something is somewhat further removed in time from the dream itself, and the direction is somewhat less direct since it has to cross over two bridges rather than just one. In the case of daydreaming and automatic writing and painting you are sending your directions from the conscious to the unconscious state, but you are still in a state of wakefulness in both instances. However, in programming your dreams, your directions from the conscious must not only trigger the unconscious, but they must move from a waking to a sleeping state. Thus, your programming directions must be even stronger if they are to succeed. When they do, the result can be extremely powerful because you are evoking a response from the deeper reaches of your unconscious, and this deeper part of you is more difficult to reach when you try to get a response in a strictly waking state.

As an example of how this works, suppose you want to have a dream about flying. You would work on consciously telling yourself while in a meditative state that you want to do this when you go to sleep. The more powerfully you give this suggestion, the more likely it will work. Often, particularly when you are just getting started in programming yourself, you will have to give the suggestion again and again. But as you do this more, the power of the suggestion will build up until it has acquired sufficient power to trigger that dream.

Creating the Right State of Consciousness for Programming Your Dreams

The best way to do this programming is in a meditative state where part of you is actively in control and aware you are meditating and directing the process, while the other part of you is openly receptive to your active commands. It is generally better to do this while you are sitting up and alert rather than when you are lying down, especially when you are in the process of going to sleep, because you are better able to stay in active control in an upright position.

Also, it is best to do this as close to sleep as possible so that the command is fresh in your mind. You can also build up the intensity of this command by giving it to yourself several times during the day. This will reinforce any suggestion you give yourself before you go to sleep. For example, as you sit on your bed in the morning, you could tell yourself, "I'm going to have a particular dream tonight," and you could tell yourself this as you sit down to lunch or dinner or as you are riding in a car or a bus. As long as you can take a minute or two to get into this meditative state of mind and give yourself the inner direction to have the dream, that is all you need.

Practicing Your Programming—Exercise #8

Once you learn how to program your dreams, you can use this ability to dream about anything. You can ask yourself questions you want answered, dream about something you are trying to make a decision about, like which job to take, or dream about someone you want to get insight about.

The following exercise is designed to help you have a dream about something you want to dream about. It is best to do it at night, while you are sitting on your bed just before you go to sleep for the reasons explained, though you can do it at other times. Preferably assume a comfortable cross-legged position or place your feet firmly on the floor, and hold your hands up and out in front of you in a position of open receptiveness.

Then pick something you would like to dream about, and in this meditative state tell yourself, "I'd like to have a dream about this, and I will remember this." Then say it over and over to yourself a few times. "I'd like to have a consciously controlled dream about this and I will remember this."

Meanwhile, as you say this to yourself, continue to see the object, image, person, event, idea or question you want to dream about in your mind's eye. Then, say to yourself that you will either remember this when you wake up in the morning, or that you will wake up at the end of the experience and record your dream.

Continue to repeat this to yourself until you feel you have given yourself enough support for what you want to do, and then let go of this projection. If you are doing this on your bed just before you go to sleep, get right into bed and go to sleep with this thought fresh in your mind. Or if you have done this at another time, be sure to remind yourself of your earlier suggestion just before you go to bed. When you wake up in the morning or during the night, be ready to recall your dream and record it.

Try to do this process at least once a night for a week until you get used to the process of dream-programming. Supplement it with some added suggestions during the day if you want. As with dream interpretation, you'll find that the more you do this, the better you'll get. The more likely you will be to have a dream and the more likely this dream will be about what you want.

Projecting Yourself Into Your Dreams to Control Them

A third way you can use your dreams to get the information you want or produce effects or changes in your life is to actually step into your dream and direct it while you are dreaming. This is a process which is sometimes called lucid dreaming, and it basically involves being aware while you are dreaming so you can influence and control that dream. It is like telling yourself that you are going to monitor and watch your dream while it is happening, so you know what is going on and can use this knowledge to decide what you want to do. To be able to do this you have to be able to keep a little conscious part of yourself awake to serve as this watcher and director.

Another way to look at this process is to see that you are functioning on two levels of consciousness at the same time. On the one hand you are conscious, and on the other you are dreaming. It is as if two parts of you have split apart so that your unconscious is having the dream while your conscious is aware that you are having it.

Normally, your conscious is merged with your unconscious when you are dreaming, so you are not aware of this separation. You do not feel like you are watching your dream as an outsider or have any control over it. But if you train yourself in a certain way, you can learn to keep that conscious part of you awake while you are dreaming. Then, that little part of you can take note of what is happening in the dream, and if something happens which it does not like, it can say: "I don't like this," and change it. Through this process you can, in effect, become a director of yourself and your dreams.

This can be a hard state to get into because it is so easy to slip from consciousness to unconsciousness as you go to sleep. Yet it is possible with concentration and practice. For example, I did this once when I took a class on using this technique, and I gave myself the appropriate suggestions. That night I was very aware I was having a dream and what was happening in it, and I was aware that I was aware and could change it if I wanted. But then I stopped trying to do this, and for a long time I could not do it again, because I did not pay attention. Later, when I worked on maintaining this conscious control again, I was once more able to do it.

Others working with lucid dreaming have had a similar experience. The more you concentrate on preparing yourself to have a lucid dream before you go to sleep, the more likely you are to have these conscious and controllable dreams, although at times some people may have such experiences without any training. You have had this kind of lucid dream experience if you have ever had a dream where you suddenly realized that you were dreaming and that you had a choice of which decision to make so you could control the outcome of the dream. You know there are options in the dream, and you can choose between one course or the other, so you can guide your dream. Such experiences are rare, but if you have had them you are especially receptive to this process. By training you can increase your ability to have the experience again on a more consistent and controlled basis.

The lucid dream state opens up a flood of images and possibilities that well up from the unconscious. In our day to day lives we commonly go along in a routine way, not aware of the choices every moment that are possible. It is more comfortable and efficient to simply go along with our usual habits and routines and proceed through much of the day on our inner automatic pilot. But when we get into a more unconscious state through whatever route— dreams, meditation, etc.—then many choices may be presented. When we maintain our point of consciousness or awareness, so we can see this, then we can consciously select the options we want and therefore have the power to choose. Through that choice we can guide and direct the unfolding of the dream, just as the person in meditation can pick and choose and direct that experience too, as long as he keeps that conscious control.

In fact, it is possible to make the process of dream control a regular part of your life. Earlier I mentioned how the Senoi use their dreams to get information and insights. The Senoi also use this lucid dreaming process. They have learned how to manipulate the outcome of their dreams. Suppose a person has a dream about a lion or tiger threatening him. Not only may he use that information to recognize a fear he must work on or program himself to have a dream where he is not afraid, but he may also seek to have his dream about these frightening lions or tigers again. However, this time he will seek to step into that dream with his conscious awareness and change the outcome, so in his dream he shows no fear and masters the lion or tiger. By changing his dream through conscious intervention he can change the same experience in his everyday life.

Similarly, by separating your consciousness from your dreams, you can remain aware of what is happening and direct or change your dreams to produce corresponding outcomes in your life.

How You Can Control Your Own Dreams—Exercise #9

One way to develop this power of dream control through lucid dreaming is to give yourself instructions when you are in the very relaxed hypnogogic state that precedes falling asleep. One set of instructions should be of the topic or question you want to dream about. You can tell yourself you want to dream about a particular person, object, place or event, or you can ask yourself a question. And secondly, you should tell yourself that you will remain awake in your dream and be aware of what is happening. Then, if you wish, you can change the direction or outcome of your dream.

The reason you want to be in this hypnogogic state when you give these instructions is because you are on the border of consciousness and unconsciousness. It is like you are giving yourself conscious suggestions, but your unconscious is very receptive to picking these up. So this is a very powerful time to make a specific request and you are best able to influence your dreams when you are on the edge of unconsciousness in this way. However, you will often find it is very hard to give these instructions at this time as you are going to sleep. But with practice and discipline, you can learn to do this.

The reason it can be a very difficult process is because there's the pull of your sleep that is keeping you from staying alert as you both give instructions and then shift into sleep. You need to have a strong willpower to stay awake while you are going to sleep. In my own experience, I have been able to do this a few times, though at other times, with less concentration, I have lost control of it. So the process takes practice. But the more you work with this, the more you will be able to do it.

What to Look For In Your Dreams

Once you are able to stay aware in your dreams, concentrate on paying attention to what you observe first. Later, as you feel more comfortable with this process, you can work on making choices and directing and changing your dream.

A good way to begin looking is to pay attention to your surroundings. Notice details and try to make any indistinct or fuzzy dream images you see more solid. Sometimes when you see objects in your dream, they may have a very flimsy, fuzzy look. But if you look at them more closely, you can make them more solid. Sometimes, too, as you look at objects they may vanish or change shape. But again, if you take control with your conscious mind which you have projected into your dream, you can make those objects more solid and strong. If you see a fuzzy red or pinkish shape, you can make it a firmer, brighter red. Or if you see shapes that are shifting and moving around, you can stop them and control them.

Besides visualizing something becoming more solid. you can actually do something to make it more solid. For example, if you see a doorknob which doesn't look very firm in your dream, you can reach for it again and experience it being hard in your hands or perhaps turn the knob and open the door. It will firm up that way.

Besides looking, you might also from time to time remind yourself that you are awake in your dream, so that you do not slip over into unconsciousness. Rather, you want to keep that separation between your conscious/awake self and your unconscious/asleep self by having your conscious part keep telling you occasionally: "Yes, I am awake, and I'm really dreaming."

Once you feel comfortable with being observant and staying alert in this lucid dream state that combines dreaming with waking, try to make choices and changes. First, be aware of all the options you have, and consciously make choices about where your dream should go next. Think of yourself as a stage or screen director, and you have control over the script.

If you find things in your dream that you do not like, or things which make you feel uncomfortable or afraid, actively intervene to make them change. And be aware that when you do this you are not only making changes in your dream, but you are also making changes, through the power of your dream, on your life as well.

The three dream processes we have discussed in this chapter — interpreting your dreams, programming them and projecting yourself into your dreams—are powerful techniques for shaping your life. In this chapter, we have concentrated on discussing how these techniques work and how dreams can intersect with daily life. In the following chapter, we will look more specifically at how you can apply these techniques in various situations. We will also look at how you can use another powerful method in which you share your dreams with others or use dreaming to help or influence others.

Chapter Four

Using Your Dreams
To Shape Your Life

Once you have learned the techniques described in the last chapter for understanding and influencing your dreams, you are in a position to use your dreams to affect your everyday life. This chapter is designed to illustrate some of the ways you can apply your dreaming to help yourself or help others. Once you start thinking of the applications, you may come up with more possible uses for dreaming yourself.

Gaining Insights About Yourself

One of the most common uses of dreams is to learn more about yourself. The easiest way, of course, is to simply let a dream happen in the ordinary course of events. Then, you review the dream to see what it is telling you about yourself. In some cases the dream's message will be fairly obvious, since the dream clearly relates to a familiar situation or setting. But at other times, you must search the dream more closely and pull out symbols and meanings to learn a little about yourself. When you do find such symbols and hidden meanings, look to your own associations with the images you see. Sometimes you may share common symbols with others because you come from the same background or from the same society where people share common values, beliefs and expectations for behavior. But also your symbols may draw on your own idiosyncratic personality characteristics and experiences. Hence, whenever you interpret your dreams, it is important to tailor that assessment to your own reactions and meanings in response to the dream.

Waiting for a dream to just happen so you can interpret it can sometimes take too long. You may not have dreams or remember your random dreams well enough, or the dreams you do have may not seem relevant. To gain insights about yourself, about what you want to do, or what you should do next, it helps to remind yourself to have a dream, or to guide your dreaming so you will dream about what you want to know.

To have a dream of any sort, simply give yourself reminders before bed that you will have a dream, or have a dream log nearby so you can record what you dream. Also, the presence of the dream log will help to remind you to dream. Likewise, any activity or ritual that focuses you on the act of dreaming will help to trigger a dream.

If you want to have a dream about a particular topic such as what job you want, what you really want to do with your life, or what this person is really like, take some time before you go to bed to consciously program yourself. As discussed in the last chapter, tell yourself while in a relaxed state that you will have a particular dream or pose yourself a question that you want answered. Then, you can let your conscious self go and leave it up to your higher self to respond however it wishes by giving you its message in your dream.

This programmed dream process is particularly good to use when you have tried asking yourself a similar question in your waking state and have tried to let your higher self answer in automatic writing. But sometimes this may not work if you are doing it consciously, because your rational mind may be too involved in the process, with the result that you may feel blocked. Your unconscious process cannot get through, even when you use the seeing techniques previously described.

But sometimes programming your dreams can work, because when you dream you are much more in touch with your unconscious processes than when you seek to see. Thus, by letting your dream answer for you, you may get insights you could not get otherwise.

Think of your dreams as an alternate way of getting information about yourself. You can learn much just by paying attention and interpreting the random dreams that come to you. And you can seek to learn even more by pre-programming your dreams so you dream about what you want to know and ask your dream for the answers you seek.

Look to Your Dreams for Information and Advice on What Will Happen

A second way to use your dreams is to get information about what is likely to happen in the future and what you should do. Again, you can use dreams in this way by either monitoring the dreams you do have or actively programming yourself to have such a dream.

In some cases, the dream may give you a very clear vision of what might happen and suggest that you take some action in real life if you want that outcome to occur. For instance, suppose you are thinking of moving somewhere else, and you are not sure whether to move or where to go. But then you have a dream where you see yourself in a new city. If you are having a positive experience in the dream, this could be a good sign that you are ready to move and should go to the city in your dream, assuming you can identify it. On the other hand, if you are having bad experiences in your dream, this could be a warning not to move.

In other cases, your dream insights about the future may be much less clear. Instead, the dream may just be suggestive of future possibilities, and you must read between the lines to decide what is best to do based on what these dream images mean to you. One man who frequently had predictive dreams about what he should do in the future had a dream about a good friend he was thinking of moving in with. The two of them were flying in a helicopter over San Francisco, when it crashed into the bay and began to sink. The man felt he had a choice in the dream: "Do I go and save myself, or do I go back and try to save my friend as well, though this will be riskier for myself?" Ultimately, after some questioning, he decided to save himself, and then he saw his friend bob up to the surface too on his own.

In thinking about the dream, the man felt it was predictive and he read it as guidance about what to do. As he explained: "I feel the dream was telling me something about whether we should move in together. I feel we have a lot together, and that is why we were together in the plane. However, the dream also seemed to be pointing out that we need to break away, we need to be more independent of each other. That's why I didn't choose to save my friend, and he was able to save himself." Thus, having had the dream and interpreted it in this way, the man decided the dream was telling him not to move in with his friend, and he decided to follow his dream. Later he felt the dream had been right. They both had a need to be freer, and the dream was pointing to that.

Your dream can sometimes give you information about something that has just happened while you are dreaming. In this case, it is helpful to check out the dream to see if it is accurate. Then you will have a better sense of when you can trust your dreams to give you valid information in the future. Later, you will be able to develop the ability to use your dreams as a kind of early warning signal when you need that kind of information.

Suppose you have a dream about a broken vase. Then if you get up and look and discover it has been broken, you have had a predictive dream. Or if you dream about someone in a particular location, check out if he or she is there. One man, who had many dreams of this type, had one in which he dreamt that a friend of his who was staying upstairs in another room had gone someplace else in the house. When he woke up, he checked and found out his dream was true.

Another woman, who sometimes painted her dreams, had a particularly dramatic experience with these predictive dreams. When she was in college about twenty years ago, she had a dream in which she was walking down a hallway and then up some stairs to visit the father of her boyfriend. At the top of the stairs the door was closed. She noticed that there was blood pouring out from under the door and cascading down the stairs. The scene impressed her, and a few days later she painted the scene. She soon learned that her boyfriend's father died on the day she had the dream.

So these powerful predictive dreams can sometimes be very accurate. Accordingly, when you have such dreams or program yourself to have them, check them out for their accuracy and use them for guidance in understanding what has or will happen that you may not know about now. Then, you can use this information to help you in personal planning and in making choices which will affect what you do.

Creating and Dreaming About The Goals You Seek to Achieve

A third technique is to program your dreams so you dream about something you want to happen. This is a particularly good approach to use when you want to change something that is currently happening in your life. It helps when you are doing other things in your life to create that change. By working with your dreams you help to reaffirm or reinforce anything you are doing on a more conscious level. It's like giving you that extra bit of motivation and inspiration you need to succeed, and your dreams can help you clarify your goals so you can better focus and move towards them in the everyday world.

To a great extent, using your dreams in this way is much like the process of directing your seeing so you visualize what you want to happen and help to make it occur. In seeing, you are consciously visualizing things and creating goals to make those things come into your life. You can do the same thing on the unconscious level with your dreams. You start by directing your dreams so that at night, on your unconscious level, you can visualize the same kinds of things you might see with your seeing. By doing so, either on the unconscious dreaming level or the conscious seeing level, you can contribute to having these things happen in your life. You have added one more level of energy towards working to get what you want, and that added reinforcement will help you get this.

Making Your Goal a Reality—Exercise #10

To make one of your own goals a reality, review the technique for programming your dreams described in the previous chapter. Then, before you go to sleep for the night, think about the goal you want to have. Get in the comfortable meditative state as described, where you are seated and alert, yet very relaxed.

Then, think of a goal you want to achieve within the next few weeks or months. As you do, tell yourself again and again that you want to achieve this goal, and see yourself having already attained this end.

With this image in mind, say to yourself, "I'm going to have a dream about my goal. I will see myself achieving it, and my dream will give me some ideas about how to best achieve this goal. I know I will achieve this, and I will gain this achievement in my dream. And I will have this dream tonight."

Say this message over and over to yourself for a few minutes while you are in this relaxed meditative state. You want to get this impression etched firmly in your mind, so you will be more likely to have such a dream.

You may not always have this dream the first time. But don't let that concern you. Just keep repeating this same message to yourself over and over again for about eight to ten minutes before you go to sleep each night for about a week, and you will very probably dream about your goal. Yet whether you do or you do not, you will find the process itself will contribute to achieving it, just like your dream. The dream will act as one more reinforcement and a very powerful one to help you attain your goal.

Making Changes In Your Life and Overcoming Fears

Besides dreaming about what you want, you can also use your dreams to get rid of what you do not want. The way the process works is that by changing your dream content you can change what happens in your life.

The way to use this process is through lucid or manipulative dreaming during which you actively step into your dream to change it. In this case, a little conscious part of yourself stays awake, so you remain aware that you are dreaming even though you are asleep. If you see something in your dream which you do not like, you can move your mind consciously into your dream and make that desired change.

In the previous chapter, I described how the Senoi use this process to change everyday events. If a child has a dream about a lion or tiger threatening him, the Senoi encourage the child to work with that image and use programming so he has another dream on that subject. Using projection, the child can go into that dream, so he can influence the outcome. If he has any trouble with that lion or tiger, he can send it away or stand up to it, and thereby show in his dream that he has mastered the lion. Since this represents symbolically a mastery of something in his life, the child will find this dream experience will carry over and he will better be able to show this mastery in encountering everyday events.

You can treat your dreams in the same way. If you have a dream that is frightening for you, you can change the dream. To begin, look at the dream to see what it is telling you about your own life. Then, you are ready to work on having the dream again (through programming) and changing it (through projection). At the same time, you can work on changing what it is that you do not like in your life and see in your dream.

You will find that the support you get from thinking about and changing your dream will help you change your life in the same way. It is like you are reinforcing the process of visualization that you do with your seeing, and likewise reinforcing your thoughts and feelings that you want to change or get rid of old fears. Your dreams have a special power to help you do this, because they operate on your unconscious level. Therefore, through your dreams you can send yourself an even more powerful signal that you are determined to make a change or eliminate a fear.

Become the Person You Want to Be

Another use of active dreaming is to become the type of person you want to be. It is an extension of using your seeing to imagine yourself with the personality traits or image you want. But now you are making the transformation on an even deeper unconscious level.

What you do to use your dream for personal transformation is to begin by consciously imagining the image of the person you want to be or the personality traits you want to acquire. Then, in a meditation state before you go to sleep, program yourself to have a dream about yourself with those characteristics. If you want to be a more forceful, stronger person in general or you want to be able to be more assertive with the people who put you down at work, you would meditate on having a dream where you will be stronger and can stand up to people.

The result of this process is you will give yourself reinforcements on the dream level of the kind of person you want to be. At the same time, you can use the same sort of process on the waking level through seeing. The effect is to strengthen the new image you want to acquire and change the way you act.

Bring Yourself Into Balance Through Your Dreams

You can also become more balanced in your life through your dreaming. Suppose you experience an imbalance between the inner you and the outer you, where you have one public persona, but the way you feel inside is very different. A good example of this is the person who may appear to be very outgoing and aggressive, but inside he is really very insecure and shy, so his outer appearance is largely a front. Through your dreams, you can bring these disparate parts of yourself into balance.

The way to do this is by finding out more about yourself and programming yourself to have desired dreams. Then you can become more in tune with who you are and feel more of a connection with both your inner and outer parts. Suppose you fee very strong and assertive inside and you have firm opinions, yet you cannot express yourself very well and you come across as being very shy with people. One way to work with your dreams to change might be to concentrate on bringing that assertiveness out in your dreams so there is more of a balance between the quieter outer self and the inner self that wants to express itself more openly. As your dreams start expressing your desires, you will feel more balanced, and these changes will be reflected in the way you feel and act in everyday life.

Whatever the circumstances, if you do not feel quite comfortable with the relationship between the personality you are expressing to others and the one you feel, and if you find you are behaving one way because you feel you have to behave that way but don't feel connected with yourself inside, you can mobilize your dreams to help you change. The first step is to have dreams to get some insight into where the imbalance is. You can gain this information by either observing the dreams you have or asking yourself questions and programming yourself to have such dreams. After having discovered the imbalance, you can focus on having dreams of the traits you want to develop. Then you can change your personality so that you feel more balanced because you now feel more of a connection between your inner and outer self.

Learn About Others Through Dreaming

Dreaming can be especially useful for learning what someone else is really like because you can pick up normally hidden information about that person on the unconscious level. A person may seem very nice and quiet on the surface, but when you dream about that person he or she may appear to be really hard or tough or perhaps even sneaky in your dream. So that may give you some insight into what that person is really like underneath his or her outer veneer.

The process is much like what happens when you pick up some feelings about someone you meet in everyday life. You may meet a politician or business person at a party who comes on as very friendly and likeable. Yet, there is a part of you that says this person is really insincere and does not mean what he is saying. Or alternatively, you may hear rumors that you should not trust someone. But when you meet this person, you have a very strong feeling that this person is very straight and trustworthy after all.

These kind of disparities between what the person seems to be and what he is often crop up, because many people are very protected in their outer image. They can deceive a person into thinking they are who they appear to be. They can become so good at playing a particular role that they become similar to a con man though they can use that appearance to the good (to assume a leadership position, though they feel insecure inside) or to the bad (to dupe you into giving up your trust and your money when they have no intention of keeping any promises they have made).

In some cases, if you are aware and perceptive, you may be able to pick up cues that let you know a person is not all he seems. But at other times, people are so good at playing their altered roles that they literally become that role, and you cannot tell what is going on underneath. A recent film, *House of Games*, illustrates how people can become such masters of the art of conning that others looking for the con will not even see it and be duped, despite their careful observation and predisposition not to trust.

Even if you cannot pick such information about what is really going on inside a person in everyday life, your dreams might get through to that level. Again, it is because your dreams are operating on the unconscious level. As such, they know no conscious barriers. So they can tune in to the person you want to know about directly on the unconscious level.

You may have such dreams on a random basis. For instance, after you have met with someone, you may happen to have a dream about him. But you can also actively choose to have such a dream by using the process of programming already discussed.

Interpreting the Dreams You Have About Others—Exercise #11

When you do have a dream about someone else, sometimes you will get the information about him in a fairly realistic way. You may see this person involved in some activity in the real world, and perhaps you may be together in this dream. At other times, you may pick up symbols associated with that person, and you have to interpret these symbols to realize that you are actually dreaming about that person and getting information about him. As an example, you might have a dream about an animal and you happen to associate that animal with a certain person or type of person in your life. So your dream is giving you information on a symbolic level if only you recognize the meaning of the symbol. In turn, the reason for the symbol, according to many psychologists, is that it may be too threatening to confront this truth represented by the symbol directly on the unconscious level in your dreams.

On the other hand, sometimes a symbolic dream may have nothing to do with a particular person. Rather the image, say of an animal, has a more generic meaning, or maybe it isn't a symbol of anything in that particular dream. You are just seeing that image because something during the day reminded you of it, and now you are just randomly processing images from the day.

Therefore, in interpreting your dreams about others, as in interpreting any dreams, you need to be discerning, particularly in determining the meaning of symbols so you can recognize whether they are coming from outside you from the person you are dreaming about, whether they have only general meanings, or whether they are personal symbols with other special meanings for you. As you work with these dream images more and more, you will increasingly develop this ability to discern as well as to have dreams which bring you the information you want about another person or about other things you want to know about.

The following exercise will help you to both have dreams about others and interpret them.

Use the usual programming procedures for generating a dream. Pick the person you want to know about, and as you meditate before going to bed, put up an image of this person in front of you in your mind's eye. Then, tell yourself again and again, you are going to have a dream tonight about this person. And if there is anything special about this person that you want to know, ask to have this question answered in your dream. For example, you might tell yourself something like: "I want to have a dream about the person I have recently met, Jim Davis, because I am thinking of starting a business partnership with him. I want to know if I can trust him, and I want to have a dream about that."

In the morning (or if you wake up remembering), record your dream. If it is directly about the person, look at what happened in the dream and examine the relationship you have, if any, with this person there. Note if there are any images or symbols associated with this person. Then think about what the incidents, relationships, images or symbols mean. What do they tell you about the person or the question you have asked?

If you have a dream which outwardly seems to have nothing to do with the person or the question you have asked, still look at it closely. Maybe it is telling you about this person in a symbolic way. Examine this dream in light of this possibility. Consider the associations and meanings for the events or images in this dream on the basis that they may be giving you inside information about this person. Then, if there seems to be a connection and the associations and meanings do make sense when applied to that person, continue examining the dream in this light. On the other hand, if this connection does not appear to exist or seems forced, let the interpretation go, realizing that this dream may not have anything to do with the person or question about which you want information.

Continue to program yourself to have the dream you want over the next few days. Through repetition you will increase the likelihood that you will have such a dream. When you do, you can use the interpretation process described above.

At the same time, by going through this process of programming yourself to dream, you will increase your general awareness about this person or question. So you may find you are picking up insights you did not previously get on the seeing level too. For example, while you are meditating and trying to program yourself to have a dream about this person, you may suddenly have a vision about this person which reveals a deeper truth. If this happens, pay attention to your conscious insights and visions. For though you are conscious, you are getting these insights and visions welling up from your unconscious, and they will offer you inner truths just like your dreams.

Contacting Other People In Your Dreams

Another way to use dreaming is to contact or communicate with others. It can be a way of tuning into others to receive signals from them or send signals out.

Sometimes you will pick up this kind of information randomly, but with practice you can learn to increase your ability to do this on a more regular basis and when you want. Many people report dream coincidences which can occur as a result of this process, although coincidences can occur for other reasons too, such as incidents that trigger dreams which correspond to events in real life. One of the most common examples of the dream coincidence is when you dream about someone and that person calls you shortly thereafter. It is as if you have sent out a signal to the person in your dreams which has triggered a call, or perhaps the person has been thinking of calling you, which has triggered your dream. In either case, the dream may be the result of some unconscious communication.

You can also specifically send out or pick up messages in your dreams just as you do with seeing. You can program yourself before you go to sleep to see if you can contact a person in your dreams. One reason for doing this might be if you have lost touch with someone and do not know where he is. But by focusing on this person and dreaming about him, you may send out a signal on the unconscious level which that person might pick up and then contact you. Or, perhaps you have had an argument with someone and have left each other with harsh words. You may feel awkward about contacting that person directly, but hope that person might contact you, and you would also like to smooth over and restore the relationship again. You might focus on contacting that person through your dreams to ask him to contact you, and you might program yourself to have a dream where your relationship is full of good feelings. The other person might pick up these messages or your feelings on the unconscious level and respond in a positive way.

When you do seek to influence people by active intervention with your dreams, it's important to be aware of ethical considerations. These will be discussed in more detail at the end of the chapter, but basically, you want to be sure you have the permission to enter and influence their dreams. It's like you're coming to them seeking to be a guest, and you need to be sure they are willing to welcome you. If you feel the person may not want you there yet, don't go.

When you do program yourself to have dreams in which you are going to influence the dreams or actions of someone else, include in your programming a statement that you want to do what you wish, but also want to be sure you have permission. You want to influence the person to contact you or change their feelings about you or whatever; but at the same time, you want the person to do so freely. You are just making the suggestion through your images and dreams; then it is up to the person to respond freely.

Sharing Your Dreams with Others

You can also work on having mutual dreams with others. This occurs when you and another person share the same kinds of dreams, or you seek to project a dream to another person or receive one he sends. It is a way to develop a closer relationship together.

Sometimes you may find the process of sharing similar dreams with someone may happen when you are very close to that person. You may get so tuned in with each other that you just naturally start doing this. At one workshop a married couple reported doing this regularly. As the husband explained: "My wife and I frequently dream each other's dreams or get into each other's dreams. And sometimes we will both want to have a dream about something, and that night we'll both dream about that."

The wife gave a few examples of dreams they had shared. In one case she was dreaming about rattlesnakes jumping over a fence, and her husband was having a dream about something else. Then, she explained: "All of a sudden he had rattlesnakes in his dream, and they had nothing to do with it. So then in the morning he mentioned his crazy dream, and when he did, I said: 'Hey, those were the rattlesnakes from my dream.' He was happy to hear we were having the same images in our dreams."

She also described how they sometimes planned out their dreams together. They would begin by making an environment, like setting a stage, then they would have a dream involving that setting. As she described it: "Sometimes we make an environment, and then we both dream. For example, we're on the desert, and there are some Indian pueblo-type buildings around. It's like setting up the stage props in our imagination. And then we both dream about being there and doing something in our dreams together."

You can share your own dreams with another person, and with some practice you can develop this ability. One way to do this is to plan with someone that you are both going to share the same kind of dream. Decide on the environment, setting or topic you want to dream about in advance. Then, when you go into the meditative state to program yourself to dream, you should each give yourself similar directions.

If you already know someone well, you will be more likely to do this mutual dreaming since you have already established a close relationship. But you can develop this skill with anyone, whether it's someone you don't know well or at all. Simply work out your desired dream arrangements in advance and later on share the effectiveness of the results. In your preplanning, you might agree to something like this: "Okay, we're going to meet in our dreams, and we're going to have a dream about such and such, and it will occur in such and such a place at such and such a time." Then you can plan to get together later and describe what happened in your dreams. Numerous people who have worked with this process have found that it works.

You can also use this process to work out problems with another person if you have not been able to resolve the matter on a conscious level. In this case, the process works best with someone you are already close to such as a spouse or a lover. The way to use the process is for you and the other person to decide to have a dream about the problem situation in order to come up with a solution. You can then discuss and negotiate the problem on an unconscious level to resolve it. Some people have found this process has literally produced a breakthrough for them. They were not able to solve their problem by discussing it consciously, but they were able to come up with alternate ways of looking at the problem and resolving it in their mutual dreams.

Mutual Dream Projection

Another mutual dream technique that is less common, but possible with some practice, is dream projection. It basically involves projecting yourself into someone else's dream to see what they are dreaming about, and someone else can do the same with you. Or you can try to pick up someone else's dream projections. The rattlesnake dream described earlier is an example of this situation.

You can, of course, use this technique with anyone, although it is much harder to do when the person has not already arranged to do this with you and is not expecting you. It also raises the ethical considerations mentioned earlier about invading someone's unconscious personal space. As mentioned earlier, when you try this projection unannounced, it's a little like going to visit someone without an invitation, and they may not want you to come in. In fact, they may actively screen you out.

If you work out agreements to do these projections with someone in advance, you will find it easier to gain access since you have permission, and the person is receptive. Also, you can check out your experiences afterwards to assess your accuracy and become better at using this technique.

You can work with these projections in three different ways.

1) *You can both be dreaming.* One person may have the dream, and the other may pick it up. Also, the first person may do some active dream projection so that her dream imagery ends up in the other person's dream. In either instance, one or both dreamers pick up the images or events from the other's dream. One person is actively projecting his dream and the receiver is simply tuning into the other and picking up the dream images. The rattlesnake example previously described is the perfect example of the type of projecting which can occur without anyone specifically trying to project or pick up information in their dreams.

If you want to work on doing this consciously, you can concentrate on programming yourself before you go to sleep to travel into the other person's dream and pick up information. Also, you can tell yourself that you will be receptive to another person who wants to pick up some information from you.

Often you may find it easier to do this process if one of you concentrates on projecting and the other on receiving. Afterward, when you both wake up, share your dreams to see whether there are any common images or symbols in what the receiving person or the sender may have dreamt about. If so, this suggests that the receiver may have been picking something up, and the sender was successful in what he was trying to project out.

It is also possible to do this process where you are both concentrating on projecting and receiving. But when you compare, it is less clear who was sending and who was picking up. In this case, you may be more likely to find parallels in dream images and symbols. But it will be harder, if not impossible, to determine the dream content's original source.

2) *You can project yourself into someone else's dream while you are awake and the other person is asleep.* This process is much like projecting your energy consciously when seeing to travel somewhere else. It is like mentally visualizing yourself traveling to the person's home and visiting that person. The big difference is that you are trying to travel into the person's dream and therefore pick up what is going on in his unconsciousness which is much harder to do.

The way to do this is to get into a meditative state while the other person is sleeping. Use your seeing to focus in on this person. Begin by seeing the person lying there asleep, and let your consciousness tune in like an antennae on what that person is dreaming about. As you do, pay attention to any images or scenes that suddenly flash in front of you. Often they will be very fragmentary or even symbolic. But they will help to give you some insights into what is happening in the other's dream. Should you get a blank or just blackness when you try to focus, this could indicate that the other person is not having a dream or that you are not yet picking anything up.

It can take time to develop this skill, but again, practice helps. Also, be sure to get feedback from the person who is dreaming. Then you can check out your images or lack of images to learn how accurate you are in picking anything up.

3) *Lastly, you can work on projecting your dreams to someone who is awake.* Or alternatively, if you are awake, you can work on picking up someone's dreams. As an example of this, Michael reported that several people in his group experimented with this and reported some notable hits. One time a member of Michael's group, Gene, set up a time when he would go to sleep, and he concentrated on sending his dream out so Michael could pick it up. Later, around the time Gene was dreaming he was an eagle or a hawk, Michael happened to look up in the sky and saw a hawk flying around. It seemed unusual because it kept circling overhead. When Michael described his experience later, Gene told him about the dream.

In the same way, you can set up a time when you hope to have a dream. Then before you go to sleep, concentrate on having a dream and projecting out that dream image so the person who is receiving can see it. If you want to select a certain image or topic to dream about, focus on dreaming that, although be aware that if you do this advance planning, the receiver may pick up from your advance programming as well as from the dream. In any event, let the other person know approximately when you are going to be doing this so he can pay attention to what he notices then. Afterwards, compare what you dreamt and what the other person experienced. For added accuracy, you can both write down your own accounts separately and then compare them. If you wish, include as accurately as you can the time of your dream and the time the person reported similar images. This way you can get even further validation for the process.

As you will find, your hits using any of these projection techniques will increase over time. In Michael's group, the people who experimented with these methods became quite accurate over time as they practiced on a regular basis. In some instances, they got to the point where they could literally plan to have dreams at will, and then commonly the receiver would be able to pick up what the other was sending whether either was dreaming or awake. As Michael explained, one reason everyone did so well is that they were all quite close and did this frequently so they developed intuitive insights into each other.

While you do not have to actually know the person to use these methods, it definitely helps. The more you know about the person and the closer you are, the more you can do this. And the more you practice, the more this will make a difference too.

Experimenting with Dream Projection—Exercise #12

Here is an experiment you can try to develop your ability to use dream projection. One person should concentrate on dreaming, while another concentrates on dropping in for a visit or projecting thoughts to the person who is dreaming.

Arrange with your partner in advance who is going to do what and when you are going to do this. One possibility is to do this before you both go to sleep for the night, or schedule a special time, such as an hour or two in the afternoon when one of you will go to sleep and the other will concentrate on mental projection. It helps if you can make any last-minute contact about the experiment over the phone, so the dreamer will not know what the other person is wearing or doing before trying to dream.

If you are the dreamer, before you fall asleep focus on being receptive. Tell yourself that you will be open to welcoming the other person in your dream and to receiving whatever images or thoughts he projects.

If you are the person who is doing the projecting, concentrate on seeing the person who is dreaming and going to visit him. Get a clear picture or any thoughts or images you want to send, and focus on sending them to the dreamer. If you are both doing this experiment at night before going to bed, concentrate on these thoughts and images for about ten minutes before going to sleep. Let yourself go to sleep with these thoughts and images still in your mind. Or if you are doing this experiment at another time when the dreamer is going to be sleeping and you are going to be awake, focus on these thoughts and images during the time the dreamer is seeking to dream.

If the dreamer has any dreams, he should try to be as observant as possible during the dream (using such techniques as described in lucid dreaming), or afterwards, he should try to recollect as much as possible and write it down. For example, if you dream about the other person, notice what he is wearing, where he is and what he is doing. Or pay attention to any images or symbols in your dreams. Notice the details of events and scenes as closely as possible.

Afterwards, you should both compare your notes and experiences. Notice when you find parallels between what the dreamer was dreaming and what the other person was projecting and doing. You will find as you practice, the dreamer will be more likely to have dreams and will be more likely to be receptive.

Helping Others With Your Dreams

Still another way to use your dreaming is to help others by projecting your dream energy to help them. The process works much like doing a ritual to send healing energy to someone, or using your seeing in meditation or prayer to focus on seeing that person get well. The key difference is that you are doing this while dreaming and are thus sending out your energy from a deep unconscious level.

Some traditional shamans use this technique in their own healing practices. They dream about the person being well in order to hasten his cure. Many members of Michael's group had some successful experiences with this process too. In a few cases a member of the group was having problems with an illness. So the group did a few things to help. First, they had a group ritual in which they sent healing energy to the person. Secondly, some of the people in the group who were skilled in dreaming had dreams in which they sent their dream images to the person who was ill to try to help him.

Later, after the ill person was well, they did some checking to see if in fact there seemed to be a connection between what they were doing and the healing that occurred. And it seemed there was. In one case, when they did the healing ritual one day and the dreaming the next, there seemed to be a parallel between what they were doing and what the ill person experienced when he was in the hospital. He reported feeling a sudden infusion of energy around the time that the group members were doing the ritual and another burst of healing around the time a few people were concentrating on dreaming about him being well, although at the time he did not know what anyone was doing. It would appear that he was receiving the energy that people were sending out, whether in ritual or in dreaming. And this healing energy seemed to help him get well because in a few days he was up and about and soon out of the hospital.

You may also be able to pick up information in your dreams that may be useful in helping another person see what may be wrong so he can make some changes to help heal himself. Most commonly, however, this technique works with people who are close to each other, so they are already sensitive to each other and more able to pick up deeper information about the other on a more unconscious level.

One woman in one of my workshops reported that she had a gentleman friend who had a sleep disorder and other personal difficulties. So one day she told him: "I'm going to go to sleep and come visit you in my dreams and see what is going on with you." The man gave his permission, and that night she had a dream about the man which reflected his problem in symbolic form. As she described it: "In my dream, there was this great barren plain, and there was a hole. It was a deep hole. It was a kind of hole that went down and down, deep into the earth. I was walking towards it and I was just about ready to go down into it, and all of a sudden my friend was pulling me out of it, and was preventing me from going down into that deep hole."

The meaning of the dream was at first unclear, but soon, as we discussed it, the dream seemed to shed some light on his problem. The man was very protective of himself and closed off from others, yet he had this deep, dark side to his nature and he was very afraid of himself and afraid to show this side to others. He felt very anxious in his relationships with people, because he was afraid of opening up and letting go and possibly losing control of himself. The dream suggested that he needed to begin looking at this part of himself so he could understand, manage, and tame it. At the same time, he needed to open up and trust others more so he would feel more comfortable with himself and others.

In the same way, you may be able to have your own dreams about people you are close to who are troubled, so that you may be able to help them if they wish.

Using Your Dreams to Resolve Conflicts

Another way you can use dreaming is to resolve a conflict you are experiencing within yourself or with someone. And again your work with dreaming can parallel what you do on the level of conscious visualization through seeing.

The way to use dreaming this way is to program yourself before going to sleep to dream about the problem situation and come up with a solution. You may not have been able to work things out on the conscious level, or you may feel very uncertain about what to do. But through dreaming, you may be able to tap into some very basic truths which give you the solution you need.

Suppose you are having some problems at work with your boss, and you aren't sure whether to make a move to another job, stay put, change fields, or what. Perhaps your dreaming can be used along with other techniques to advise you what to do. You might use your seeing to visualize yourself working together more harmoniously with your boss. Or, you might program your dreams to come up with a resolution; then, you can look to your dreams for insights and cues. For instance, if you suddenly have dreams about traveling or moving to another city, that could possibly be a clear sign that it's time to change jobs.

Another way to seek to resolve conflicts is to program your dreams to send healing and loving energy to the person with whom you are having a conflict, just as you might similarly send the person such energy in a conscious visualization. This kind of programming will help change your dreams and your feelings towards this person, and in turn it will help change that person's attitude towards you.

You can also use your dreams, much like your seeing, as a source of information about a person or a situation so you can better find out what is causing the conflict. Such information might not be immediately available to you if you just look on the surface because someone wants to keep the conflict hidden or is not aware of it. But you may be able to pick this up on the unconscious level. In this case, you simply program your dream to give you information on what is causing the conflict and pay attention to what your dream indicates. If you are continually having arguments with a lover or spouse and these are triggered by something that does not seem very consequential, it may be that there is some hidden reason triggering the problem and a dream can reveal it. As an example, let's say after programming your dreams you have a dream in which your spouse is arguing with someone else who has stepped into your place. That might suggest that on a deeper level you remind your spouse of another person, and at times that reminder triggers your spouse's anger, so he takes it out by arguing with you. Having gained such an insight from your dream, you can bring the topic out in the open and discuss it and perhaps resolve the conflict this way. It's a way to supplement your other conflict solving and information gathering tools, and often it will successfully work for you.

Resolving Ethical Considerations

Once you start using your dreams or your seeing to contact, influence or help other people, there are a number of ethical considerations that arise. It is important to use these skills ethically because they open up doors into looking into and affecting other people and you want to be sure to use these in a positive, benevolent way. Otherwise, if you start doing psychical damage to others, you will find the negative energy you put out will ultimately come back to hurt you.

Because these techniques give the ability to see or step into places which are normally closed, it's also important to see yourself as a guest and make sure you are welcome or have permission, because you do not want to intrude in places or spaces where you should not be. It's really a question of respecting another's privacy, just as you would like others to respect yours.

As you become more experienced in working with seeing and dreaming so that you are better able to enter other people's dream spaces or waking spaces, ask for permission before you contact someone, influence them to do something, or try to help them. For example, when you program yourself to do some dream traveling or use your seeing to peer into someone's everyday life or his dreams, express the thought that you would like to do these things and that you are asking for the other person's permission to let you get this information or let you in. Approach these activities in a spirit of common curtesy. Of course, if you make prior arrangements to meet with someone psychically or enter his dreams, you know everything is fine in advance.

Keeping Unwanted Influences Out of Your Dreams

As you become more aware of your dreams and more sensitive to unconscious processes generally, you may find you are also more sensitive to the influences of other people affecting your own unconscious processes and your dreams. In some cases, you may like these influences, such as when someone is projecting helpful, healing energy to you, or you may have made an arrangement to be receptive to someone's energy such as in a dream projection experiment.

At other times, though, you may not want those influences and you should be aware of when they are present, such as when someone else is projecting himself into your dream. Then you can do things to stop that interference.

The way to tell when someone else is interfering in your dreams is through discernment. Sometimes it will be very obvious, such as when you see that person in your dreams and you feel disturbed by what that person is doing. At other times, the person's influence can come into your dreams on a more symbolic level, but it has a feeling of being foreign to you. So you need to pay attention, and when you are not sure, ask where this dream is coming from.

Even people who do not work with their dreams may sometimes have the experience of outside interference. An example of this would be the woman's dreams described in Chapter 3 concerning her dominant mother.

However, dreams like this about someone's influence you do not want are generally a cue that you should do something to change that situation in your life. Then, once the situation opening you up to such outside influences is changed, the dreams influenced by this person's interference will generally go away. For instance, the woman who felt too influenced by her dominant mother began to stand up to her mother, and gradually, as she felt her mother had less influence over her, her dreams changed too. As she commented: "Suddenly I didn't have these heavy dreams anymore where I felt like my mother was overwhelming me and taking over my life or pushing me out of the house and things like that. Instead my dreams became more calm and peaceful."

Thus, one way to change your own dreams to get rid of unwanted influences is to look at the situation in your life that may be producing those dreams, and then take some action to change that situation.

A second way, which is especially useful if you cannot change the situation, is to set up some protection for your dreams in advance against that influence. You can do this when you are programming yourself to have certain kinds of dreams before you go to sleep, or when you are giving yourself instructions in the lucid dreaming state. At this time you can tell yourself to guard against this influence. Simply tell yourself that if this person or the images associated with this person try to come into your dreams, you will send that person or those images away.

Thirdly, if you feel the influence coming into your dreams is particularly powerful, you can do a ritual of some kind to send the energy coming into your dream back to the sender and keep it out of your dreams. Michael did this when he had a conflict with someone he knew and this person began trying to project negative images into his dreams, so that Michael experienced a series of nightmares. According to Michael, he knew at once where the source of these nightmares was coming from, since he had a serious feud with this person whom he knew was very experienced in working with magical and energy techniques.

So Michael did a series of rituals to send this energy back. He set up a protective magical circle and lit some candles. Next he visualized all of the negative energy the man was sending him formed together into a tight black ball. Then, calling on the help of some protective guardians, Michael sent the energy back. After this his own nightmares stopped and later he learned that the man who had tried to harm him in this way suddenly ran into a series of difficulties himself. He lost his job, was ill for several days and had some financial problems as well. As Michael told me: "He got his negative energy back in kind, and as a result, my own dreams were now free of his negative influences."

If you do such a ritual it does not have to be anything elaborate. You don't even need to use anything physical, like the candles that Michael used, and you don't need the magical circle. Basically, you should do any sort of ritual which has meaning for you to intensify the power of what you are doing. Magical circles, candles and ritual words can be one way to do this, but you can also create your own ritual which has power for you. In whatever ritual form you use, you can draw on the powers of nature represented by the energies of air, earth, fire and water both within and outside yourself to increase your power to get rid of the influence you don't want and send it back to its source and its sender.

Using Your Dreams to Feel Good that Day

You can also use your dreams to set the tone for your day and feel good. If you have had a pleasant dream, take a few minutes after you wake up to savor that feeling of peace, benevolence and calm. Also, you might record the dream and then for a short while you might think about it and mediate on it and consider how you can take the imagery or events you have had in the dream and apply them to your day.

On the other hand, if you have a dream with any negative experiences or feelings, such as a scary or frightening dream or one that deals with something that causes you anxiety, you can get rid of these feelings which can carry over. One way to do this is by using a cleansing technique to brush the dream away and cleanse yourself of any lasting effects. As you think of the dream, imagine yourself putting your hands over your head and shake the negative energy away. You can do this mentally if you want, or if you wish, shake this energy away using these motions physically as well as envisioning the negative feelings being gone.

Return to the Dreams You Like

Should you have a dream you especially like, you can also extend the experience. If you wake up and feel this kind of pervasive glow that comes from having just experienced a very enjoyable, intense dream, you can go back into that by returning to your dream space again. It's like continuing the dream instead of waking up and going on from there.

I have had a couple of dreams where I have done this. They were both about flying, and I felt like it was such a powerful real experience that I was actually flying. It was more real than a usual dream, and it was such a good experience that I wanted to go back and experience it again. So I went back into it and did this.

When you do go back like this, you probably will not have quite as intense an experience as in the original dream because you are somewhat awake now and you won't go back into as deep an unconscious state. But it still will be very pleasant. In my own case, when I went back into my dreams, I dreamt about flying again, but now it was on a more peaceful level, whereas before it had been tremendously exciting and exhilarating. The main reason for this difference is that now I was more like an observer seeing me flying, whereas before I had been really flying in my dreams or at least that was my experience of it.

To make this dream return, just savor your dream while you are lying down for a few minutes, and consciously see it continuing. Gradually you are likely to slip into sleep, and as you do you will often continue the dream. If this does not happen, at least you will have had the experience of savoring and enjoying your dream. As you attempt this more often, you will be more likely to re-experience the continuation of your dream.

Explore in Your Dreams

Another way to use your dreams is to visit and explore new places, much like a tourist goes on a visit. A good way to get this process started is to set up an environment where you are going to go in advance, and then program yourself to travel there in your dream. You can do this on your own, or you can use this as something to do in mutual dreaming, and plan where you are going to go together.

Michael and the members of his group experimented a great deal with this technique and took all sorts of journeys. Often they went to visit places they had never seen before, and sometimes these were fantasies of places that didn't really exist in everyday life, such as faraway imaginary planets or places existing on another dimension. To begin the process they would set up some basic guidelines or structures for their trip and the place they were going, and then go explore it. They might decide in advance that they were going to another planet, to a space in another dimension or to a world of a certain color; then they would program themselves to have that dream. As Michael described it, the process is a little bit like being a traveling anthropologist. And it's a way to play with and have fun with your dreams.

Get Insights About the Future

At times your dreams may tell you about the future too. Nothing in the future is fixed, so you are really looking at a probable future. But your dreams can help give you insights into what is likely to happen, so you can better prepare for what lies ahead or take some action to make that future more or less likely.

Let's say you are planning a trip and you dream about getting stranded somewhere on your journey. This can be a signal that you should be more cautious about how or where you are traveling, so you may be able to avoid being stranded.

Just like you can program other dreams, you can program future dreams too. This is a particularly good approach to use when you are planning to do something that is very important. Or if you have a major decision to make, you can plan your dreaming around that subject to help you decide. Just tell yourself to dream about yourself in the future setting, and see which setting your dream seems to prefer, or look at what happens in each setting. When you review your dreams later, you can consider which possible outcome you prefer.

Also be alert to random dreams you may have about the future and notice what they are telling you. How can you tell when dreams are about the future? Often it will be quite obvious when a dream is set at a future time. But in other cases you will often get a sense of this future orientation when you think about your dreams. It's like a subtle signal, warning or inner tug to look ahead. Experiencing this sense of future time is part of the process of becoming more discerning, and when you do have a future dream, there will be a sense of knowing—and knowing that you know.

Look to Your Dreams for Enlightenment and Teaching

You can additionally use your dreams as a source of enlightenment and higher truth. Commonly, dreams are filled with everyday reality. They often process the bits and pieces we experience daily in the mundane world, so at times they are like a random trash collector for the detritus or happenings of the day. Yet just as you can program your dreams to provide you with all sorts of information and insights, so you can look to your dreams to become a source of higher teachings. One woman who came to my workshops described how she often invited the spirits who knew more than she did to come into her dreams and give her knowledge.

By the same token, you can call upon any teachers or guides that have a special wisdom for you. These can be real people who you think are wise, such as the leader of a spiritual group. Or if you prefer, call on spiritual beings that you consider helpful, such as a guardian angel or spiritual guide.

The process is much like what you might do on the conscious level where you are seeking a higher spiritual help, such as using automatic writing or communicating with a spirit guide. In this case you are getting your information on a deeper unconscious plane, through dreaming.

One way to program yourself to get this information is to ask your higher self to speak to you in your dream about anything you need to know (i.e., What is my larger purpose in life? What should I do to become a better person?). Or if you feel more comfortable about getting this information from an outer source or from your higher self in a personified form, ask for the teacher you wish to learn from to come into your dreams and give you information. If you are asking for a specific person or being to come in, put up an image of this individual and focus on it as you ask for guidance in your dream.

After your dream, look for both direct messages and for messages contained in symbols and metaphors as a source of the information you need to know.

Keep a Balance Between Your Dreams and Everyday Reality

One final note on working with dreams. It's important to work with your dreams on a regular basis through paying attention, programming, and consciously directing your dreams, if you want to stay closely in touch with them and use them as a continuing and reliable source of information. Otherwise it's too easy not to have dreams at all or not be aware that you have them. You get caught up in the everyday world, and the influence of your unconscious slips further and further away.

If you do work with your dreams regularly, you want to avoid the opposite imbalance of getting so much into your dreams that you feel they are starting to take over your life. If that becomes the case you should cut back. You don't want to pay so much attention that things get out of hand and you start to feel unsure of what is dream and what is reality. The ideal situation is to maintain a balance between the two. In most cases, people are more likely to be busy and involved in everyday reality, so they don't want to pay very much attention to their dreams.

Spend enough time each day to stay in touch with your dreams, perhaps about 15-20 minutes each morning writing them down and about 10-15 minutes at night programming yourself to dream. Also, take some time now and then to review and interpret your dreams, maybe 5-10 minutes in the morning when you write down your dreams, or set up another time each day or a few days each week to do this. And if you are doing special dream experiments at other times, just do this occasionally.

After you have gleaned the information and guidance you need from them, let your dreams go and get on with the day. This way, you should be able to attain a good state of balance so you both stay in touch with your dreams and use their insights to help you take charge of your life. It's a winning combination, and you will find your dreams can be a source of both inspiration and guidance in helping you better enjoy and work with each day.

Chapter Five

Projecting Your Vision To See Into Other Places And Events

Another powerful way you can use your ability to "see" is to project your consciousness into other realities which are either happening simultaneously or in the future. Then you can experience what is happening at other places and in future times. Sometimes it can be difficult to determine whether you are seeing the present or a possible future, since your vision of one can blend almost imperceptibly into the other, and as you observe, you can see present events play themselves out into future time. The process used to project into another place or into the future is much the same. However, with these qualifications, this chapter will focus on the nature of the process of projection and how to use it to project into other places at the present time. Then, Chapter 6 will deal with how to apply this ability to project in everyday life.

The Nature of Consciousness Projection and How It Works

The process of consciousness projection is called by a number of names—geoteleportation, seeing with the mind's eye, creating a waking dream. It operates a little like having a directed daydream. Basically it involves going into a semi-conscious state in which you consciously project your unconscious or inner or higher self to another location or time, so you can observe whatever it going on there. After you are there, you let your unconsciousness freely observe.

   You may already be familiar with the experience, although you may not be aware that you have done this. You may have had an experience such as the one a woman reported at a workshop. She was in a trance-like state one day when she experienced herself suddenly visiting her daughter's house in New York. She had never been there before but all of a sudden she saw the house the daughter lived in and she walked around it as if she was actually there. She even noticed what lights were on and off. After she came back from what was a very intense experience, she called her daughter and described the experience she had just had. She told her how the house was furnished, and as she commented: "I was even able to tell her which light was on." And she was correct.

Using Conscious Control to Project Yourself

The way the process works is that you use your conscious mental control to enter into a kind of waking dream state in which you usually let your body relax completely, while your consciousness remains alert. Once you are trained you can do this in an up and around waking-state too.

Once you trigger this waking dream, this enables your higher self to leave your body and project itself into another space or time. The process is a little like going into a trance-like state although you are not going into a deep trance where you are no longer conscious of what you are thinking or saying. Instead you are in an altered state of consciousness in which you are consciously aware of and observing your inner or higher consciousness, which you can see or sense as a single point of consciousness inside your head. Then you can direct this point of consciousness or higher self outside of your body wherever you want to go, unless you encounter barriers or blocks, and you can travel either to other places in the present or in future time.

Perhaps one way to think of this is that you are traveling on the level of the soul or spirit so that while your ordinary consciousness remains behind, your spiritual self is off traveling. This conception of the process has had a long history which goes back before recorded time. Many primitive peoples have believed in the possibility of soul travel and they have suggested that when the mind goes off in dreams at night this is one form of the soul traveling out of the body. Some have also used the process to help them in day to day activities by doing such things as projecting their consciousness ahead of themselves to search for game when out on a hunt.

Experiencing the Sensation of Being Outside of Your Body

A major characteristic of this process is you feel like you are literally outside of your body. In this respect, the projection process differs very much from the experience of simply imagining or visualizing something happening far away or in the future. Instead, you actively experience your inner self or consciousness as being there. You observe from this vantage point outside your body rather than from inside it.

You may have had somewhat the same experience when you lie down and are in that half-waking/half-sleeping state that comes just before falling asleep or waking up. At this time you may sometimes feel your body vibrating or you have a floating, drifting sensation. Suddenly after this you might experience a sense of rising up outside yourself looking down at yourself. Sometimes this experience can happen spontaneously when you are not even thinking about it.

Also, you can control the process so that you can experience it on greater or lesser levels of intensity if you do this on the light level. On the light level you may be very conscious that you are projecting yourself, and that you are doing it more on an intellectual level where you are essentially an observer who is aware of what's around you. Alternatively, you may be able to do this on a much more intense level where you are still conscious, but you are more involved in sensing and feeling everything around you as well as simply perceiving things. It may be a little more difficult to achieve this level of much deeper involvement, but when you do, the experience will have a much greater feeling of immediacy. It is like the difference between watching as an observer and feeling you are actually there.

Differences Between Conscious Projection and the Dream or Trance State

The conscious projection state does have some similarities to the experience of directed or lucid dreaming and to the trance state, in that you can get similar types of information through each process. In all of these states you can travel to other places or into future time to observe what is happening. However, the nature of the process is quite different.

The key difference is that in conscious projection you're awake and you have more control over the process. In dreaming you may begin before you go to sleep by giving yourself suggestions that you are going to do certain things or go to certain places. But after you have programmed yourself you let the dream go and your unconscious takes over. Or if you are using lucid dreaming, the conscious part may still be there observing your dream but you are still asleep. In conscious projection it's more like the hypnotic experience where you know you are in an altered state but you can direct it. As a result, as I've experienced in hypnosis, when you want to change your focus and look at something else you can do so consciously. Your conscious parts steps back and lets the unconsciousness go.

Likewise, the process is quite different than being in a trance because you are aware you are outside your body and are projecting yourself out there. As a result you can get back into your body when you want. Sometimes when people get into a trance, they literally lose control of their body. I've seen films of some of the dancers in Bali who go into a trance state through dancing. In this state they don't have the slightest idea of what they are doing and they continue dancing in a very excited frenetic way until they drop to the ground and pass out. When they wake up they have no recollection of what has happened. In the conscious projection state, however, you will normally remember what you have seen as well as being consciously aware while you are seeing it.

Getting Relaxed to Induce the State

In order to get into this state it's a good idea to be very relaxed and find a time when you can either lie down or sit quietly, so you can completely concentrate on sending your consciousness out. You can do it at other times, even when you are walking around and participating in other activities by maintaining a split consciousness. But until you learn to be in full control of the state and can both stay in charge of projecting yourself and doing other things at the same time, it's better not to try this.

A key reason it is preferable to get in a relaxed, comfortable state is because you are trying to separate your consciousness from yourself. So if you are in motion, you may find that you suddenly lose control of what you are doing in the everyday world because, while you're trying to function in this world, part of you is off trying to do something else.

You may have even had this kind of experience yourself, where without any planning you drift off and have projected your consciousness somewhere else, though often, since you have not intentionally projected yourself, you may not be aware you are doing this or where you are. I have sometimes had this experience while driving. Typically, what happens is I have been driving for a while on a freeway or otherwise open and straight stretch of road. Then, I will go into this very foggy state where my eyes go out of focus and I am both looking at things and staring off into space. Suddenly I'll catch myself, and I'll be back in the car and everything will be back in focus.

Needless to say, you do not want to be in that kind of out-of-body place when driving or doing other important everyday things because your reaction time will be affected, and you may not be able to react quickly enough when you need to do so. You can, of course, continue to do things in this state because part of you is on automatic pilot, so you may be able to carry out whatever you are doing for a while. But if something happens you need to react quickly, and you are not really in an alert enough state to do that.

In fact, you may sometimes have the experience of suddenly going off into this state, but then snapping right back, because you have to be back to take care of everyday events. At the same time, you may be drawn into this kind of projection because you are in a situation where you don't want to be. So you space off and drift out, but very quickly, you snap right back.

One woman described a typical experience that happened to her when she was at school. She was in math class and was not particularly interested in what was happening. So for a moment she let herself go, and suddenly she was above everybody's head. Then, just as suddenly, she felt her math teacher looking at her and in another moment, when her teacher called on her, she had come right back. Essentially what happened is she didn't like what was happening in her classroom, so a part of her had said something like: "Well, I don't really want to be here," and so for a short time, that part of herself went off. However, moments later the conscious part of herself that was still there in the classroom and still somewhat aware picked up that she was off someplace else and needed to come back. With that realization, the projection was broken and she immediately returned.

Because of this split consciousness phenomena, the snapping back experience may sometimes occur when you go off while involved in some everyday activity and suddenly realize you need to be back. Also this experience can sometimes happen because whatever you encounter when you project yourself may seem a little scary, since you are not in control of the process but are just drifting off into it. So you're not sure where you are going or what's going to happen out there. Thus, you snap back.

When you get started in using this process it's best to be in a relaxed state, either lying or sitting down when you do projection. This way you can freely let your consciousness project outside of yourself without your having to worry about mundane concerns. Also, this relaxed state will help you focus and develop the concentration you need to get past the point of snapping back, so you can consciously project your unconscious or inner self with the clear intention that you want to do this and there is nothing to hold or call you back.

Staying Awake When You Relax and Project Your Consciousness

Just as there can be the danger of snapping back when you are not deeply enough into projecting yourself or encounter everyday interferences, you may also encounter the opposite hurdle of falling asleep when you get so relaxed and into the experience that your consciousness totally lets go.

One way to deal with this is to have some kind of awakening trigger you can use, so if you start to drift off to sleep you have programmed yourself to use your trigger to wake yourself up again. Perhaps train yourself to use a motion of your hand, a click of your foot or some other gesture to tell yourself: "No, I don't want that to happen. I don't want to go to sleep."

Another way to stay awake is to sit up while you try to get into this relaxed state for projection. This way your body itself is more rigid and controlled and will help you stay alert. Also, if you start to drift off to sleep, your body or head will start to lunge forward, and that will wake you up.

Maintaining the Proper Balance

However it works best for you, the type of state you want to maintain in order to have an optimal projection experience is one in which you are both in consicous control of the projection at the same time that your unconscious is off having the experience. You want to be relaxed and yet in charge so that you can consciously project and direct your one-pointed consciousness or higher self to leave your body to go where you want.

Normally, you can best achieve this state of balance between sleep and wakefulness needed for this experience by getting relaxed, yet staying consciously awake and alert. However, once you are comfortable with the projection process, you can do this while you are doing other things. This is because you are not in a deep trance and are instead having what is much like a waking daydream. Once you can learn to maintain a state of split consciousness, you can go about your everyday business while a part of you travels off somewhere else. The process works much the same as when we split our attention while doing everyday things, such as talking on the phone, while watching TV or having a conversation while driving. However, in this case, you are not doing two things on a conscious level. Instead, one part of you is operating in normal consciousness, while the other part is engaged in the conscious projection of your unconscious higher self. So the process can be tricky.

With practice you can do it and learn to balance all of the various levels of consciousness necessary to consciously project yourself, whether you are relaxed or functioning in the day to day world. Start with being in a relaxed state to learn how to control this projection process first. Then you can work on applying it in other everyday situations.

The Purpose of Conscious Projection

Why use conscious projection? The practice can be very valuable for a number of different purposes. I'll describe them very briefly and generally here. Then, I'll explain how you can start doing conscious projection yourself, and afterwards detail some specific applications.

First, one general goal of this technique is to obtain knowledge and see things. You can use it to gain knowledge about events that are happening around you or what people are doing. You can then use this information to make decisions or change your own behavior accordingly.

Secondly, you can use this technique to perceive what you do see more accurately. Many of the projection exercises and experiments are designed with this goal in mind. An example of this is when someone projects her consciousness to see a number someone has written or a drawing someone has done in another place. Often when you first use projection the images can be somewhat fuzzy or lacking in detail. But when you work with numbers and simple objects, that can help you focus in to see more clearly.

Conscious Projection to Go to Another Place

When you use conscious projection to go to another place or observe an event happening somewhere else, you can begin by creating a picture or image of the scene you want to go to in your mind. The process is much the same as that used in the remote viewing experiements where some people are sent to a certain site and then try to send back a projection of where they are. Meanwhile a receiver somewhere else tries to pick that up. The key difference here is that someone is not off in this particular location where you are going mentally while he or she is trying to project any information or images to you. So you're not getting any additional source of stimulation. Rather, you've got to get wherever you are going on your own.

A good way to begin after you get in a relaxed receptive state and project your consciousness wherever you are going is to allow whatever images you receive to come through. At first these images may be very smoky or fuzzy, and you may not be sure exactly what you are seeing. But concentrate on it anyway and see if you can tune in that picture. It's like you're picking up a picture on a television set, where at first the station is not really clear. Then you tune it in a little better. Once the image clears, look closely and notice where you are.

You will find that this process of looking closely and tuning in will help to clear up any images, no matter what kind of seeing process you are using— projecting into other places, into future time, into the past or even into imaginary landscapes or scenes of your own creation. I had this kind of experience when I attended a class on reincarnation. The teacher led us in a directed experience in which she told us to visualize ourselves going back in time, and then she asked us to land somewhere. Once we did, she asked us to look around, notice what others were wearing and how we were dressed, and so forth. At first things were somewhat foggy and misty. But then they cleared.

If you start looking at the surroundings around you wherever you go, you will find that everything gradually clears up if there is any haze and you'll soon see things in much more detail.

How to See When You "Travel"

Once you project your consciousness and get where you are going, the key to really seeing is paying attention. Some of the things to pay attention to are: Are you in a city? Are you in the country? If you are in a city, which city are you in?

It doesn't matter whether you have decided exactly where you are going in advance or not. Sometimes you might just say to yourself: "Well, I'm going to travel and see where I land," but you are not really sure. Other times you might have a particular location in mind, such as saying to yourself: "I want to travel to New York," or "I want to go to see my friend in the country." It may be easier if you have a particular destination in mind when you start, but when you are not sure you can simply be receptive as you travel out and you can go to whatever location comes to mind.

After you project yourself to that place and have a general sense of where you are (i.e., in a city, in the country, in a town), then look around. Get a sense of what's on the street, who is around you, and what people are doing. Ask yourself, are there crowds? What time of day is it? And so forth. Ask yourself questions as you observe and see what you notice. It's a little bit like being on a tour that has just arrived at a location. You look out of the bus window or get off of the bus, look around and see what's there.

As you look, try to get as much detail as possible and that will help you gain more clarity and an even more intense sense of immediacy of being actually there. If you are in a street, notice what particular street, and think if you have been on this street before. See if there are cars on it. To get all of this detail, ask yourself some of these questions consciously. Then look to your unconscious for the answer. It may even add more questions, too.

Focus on keeping your conscious, observing part active in the process. By triggering yourself to look more closely with your conscious part, you'll get more information than if you just look around and hope that something comes in. Essentially, your conscious part helps to focus you a little bit more, and you will start getting more accuracy. It's a little like keeping your energy focused by using a slingshot or a laser beam to hit exactly the target you want. By contrast, if you use a shotgun or a flashlight, your energy is scattered all over the place, and the impact of any hit will not be as strong or clear.

The key is to concentrate and focus. Then what you want to see will come in more clearly and you'll see much more detail. You'll feel you really are there, because the images you see will be so strong. You won't feel like just a way-off observer.

Stay in this observer role when you first start looking on your travels. Just view the scene as an observer. Later, after you are more skilled and feel more comfortable in looking, you can try to experiment with communicating and talking to any people you happen to meet where you go. But initially, it is easier to just go to the location and look.

A Technique You Can Use for Projecting Yourself—Exercise #13

The following technique is designed to help you project yourself to another place. In it you will imagine yourself traveling as a point of consciousness along a laser beam to your destination. However, you can also project yourself without seeing yourself as a point of consciousness or projecting along a laser beam. Rather, this technique is basically just a way to help you get where you are going, and the more you do projection, the less you need a particular visualization or ritual to get you there. Instead, you can simply project yourself to wherever you want to travel and be there almost instantaneously. It's like you think: "I'm there," and you are.

But until you can do this, this technique will help you get from here to there. You can use the following instructions for general guidance. Or if you wish, record them with a tape recorder, and then play the tape back to yourself when you want to project, until you no longer need the tape.

Start by getting relaxed. You want to calm your conscious mind. So focus on your breathing. Experience your breathing going in and out. You feel very comfortable, very relaxed.

You know you are going to stay conscious. If you feel yourself drifting off to sleep, use some kind of trigger, such as maybe raise your finger or snap your fingers together. You want to do something to stay alert and awake.

When you feel comfortable, imagine your consciousness as a little white point of energy and see it as something you can project out of your head.

Now, if you wish, see your point of consciousness located at the beginning of a laser beam, and notice that this laser beam is projecting out of your head. See your consciousness traveling along this beam and essentially becoming one with this beam.

When you are ready, start scanning with this beam. Direct it to briefly focus on the places that you might want to go to. You can direct this beam near or far. You can even go around the corner or maybe someplace else in your own city. You can visit the house of somebody you know or if you prefer, direct the beam even further, to another city, another town, out in the countryside. Move it around and just scan.

After a while, you will find that there is a place out there that you are interested in going to. Once you do, let this beam of your consciousness focus on that. Then, project this little point of your consciousness out along this beam. So you can travel along this beam in your consciousness and go to this location.

Just look around when you get there. Start by asking yourself some questions, like... Where are you? Are you in a city? A country? What city are you in if you know?

Look at the buildings or walls around you. What are they like? Are there any people? Do you notice what they are wearing? Are there people moving around? If so, get a sense of their energy.

Ask if you are moving fast or slow. Also, be aware of the time of day. Is it morning, afternoon, evening? Notice the colors around you also. Be aware of what you're wearing, what other people are wearing. Maybe notice the temperature. Is it hot? Cold?

Take a walk around where you are. If you see any doors, if you feel comfortable, you can open them. Feel very safe wherever you are. Go explore. If you see some stairs, you can go up them if you want. Notice if there are any decorations around you.

If you are on the street, notice any cars. What do they look like? Are there any other kinds of vehicles? And if you're on a street, maybe there's a newspaper. If so, you can pick it up, look at the headlines. Notice if

*there's anyone you know or someone who reminds you of someone you
know.*

*And then, just ask some of your own questions. Take a few minutes to
do this. Just ask and observe...*

*When you feel ready, you can return to the point where you started. To
do so, imagine your consciousness getting back on this beam and imagine
this beam being pulled back, back into your head. When you feel ready,
come back into the room and open your eyes.*

Developing Your Own Travel Guide

The previous guide for projecting yourself is one possible guide you can use.
Also, you can design your own travel guide if you prefer, if it's more
appropriate for where you want to go or if you want to ask other kinds of
questions. You may need a little practice with the process through directed
traveling first. But then feel free to break out on your own. You might think of
this process of developing your guide as similar to what you might do as any
traveler embarking on foreign travel. You might start off going on a
preplanned tour. But once you feel comfortable traveling, you can create
your own itinerary.

In creating the previous guide, this is essentially what I did. I travelled along
the beam in my own consciousness and when I arrived where I was going,
which happened to be New York, I proceeded to ask the questions and
notice things as outlined above, except instead of just saying them to myself I
said them aloud for others to use as a guide to wherever they were, too. I
wasn't in the same place, but the general questions could be used in other
locations as well.

You can readily do this yourself by splitting your consciousness so that
part of you is giving instructions about where to go and what to look for, and
the other part of you is looking at things. It's easier of course to simply travel
and look when someone else tells you what to look for, or to already have a
plan in advance so you pay attention to certain things as planned. But you
can learn with practice how to create you own trip, and then you can get as
creative as you want in what you look for or see.

In fact, you may need to do this in some locations since the previous guide
is designed primarily for traveling to a city or town. But if you go to the
country, to someone's house, take a voyage at sea, or go to other places, it
helps to devise your own map to guide you along. You'll get much more out of
the trip and "see" much more than if you just go and leave what you see to
chance. By actively creating your own list of things to look for you can focus
more clearly, pay attention better, and observe much more.

Things to Look For and Experience

Some of the things to look for in projecting yourself have already been discussed in the previous guided projection. For example, these include things like:

What are the immediate surroundings like?
Who is there?
What are people wearing?
What are people doing?
What time is it?
What is the temperature like?
What season is it?
Are there cars on the streets? What kind?
What are the buildings like? And so on...

In addition to observing you can also feel and touch things. When you do, you will feel more involved and a greater immediacy than simply observing. You can start to feel textures or the warmth and coolness of something.

The next step for even more total involvement is to begin interacting and communicating with the people who are there.

Avoiding the Major Problems in Projection

The three main problems you may encounter in conscious projection is the tendency to drift off to sleep, the interference of your rational mind, and the possibility of critizing yourself, which is a special type of rational mind interference. Here's how to deal with them.

Avoiding the Tendency to Drift Off to Sleep

If you have a tendency to drift off to sleep, it may be a good idea to sit up while you do projection. Likewise, if you tend to drift off into a kind of blankness, where you find it difficult to follow directions or give yourself directions, perhaps sit up, too. This way, if you start drifting off to sleep or into this no mind state, your falling head will trigger you that this is happening. Also, you will be a little bit more alert because your body is holding you up.

It may also be better to start off by taping directions to yourself and listening to them while you have the experience rather than using the directions as a general road map of what to observe where you are going. This way, as you listen to the tape you will have something to control you from outside yourself, and you don't have to be the controller yourself. This outside controller can help to keep you awake and on target, since the spoken directions are right there. If you're your own controller, you have to make sure that part of you stays alert to give directions, in addition to keeping the part of you that listens and observes awake, too. Since it's harder to do both—control and be aware—if you are having trouble staying alert, perhaps try using this outside controller in the form of taped directions.

If drifting off or falling asleep is still a problem, you can always sit up and listen to a tape with directions. Then you will be even less likely to drift off or fall asleep.

Avoiding the Interference of Your Rational Mind

In some cases, you may experience some interference from your rational mind questioning whether what you are seeing is really happening. Or your rational mind may start to question discrepancies based on real time considerations or what you already know about (or think you should know about) the place you are visiting.

In one workshop a woman mathematician had an interference problem because she began to calculate what the real time probably was where she was going, and she thought it different from the time she was now experiencing. As she commented:

"I was having a really good, intense visualization—better than usual—until you said to notice what time it was. I was experiencing what I was seeing as midday. But then, when you said what time is it, I thought: 'Oh, they're eight or nine hours ahead of us, so it must be 5 or 6 o'clock in the morning.'"

Another woman had similar problems because she was seeing everything very bright and lit up, but she started thinking that it should be night and she wondered why she should be able to see. She found that her rational mind started intruding by placing objects in the scene, which she thought should be there, so it was difficult for her to simply observe. She kept thinking about what should be there and putting it there, and she kept wondering if what was there should be there or not. As she explained:

"I went to a friend of mine's house, just to check it out. But I had some difficulties with my rational mind because I knew it was not daylight right now in San Francisco, and yet the room I was seeing was in daylight, because I could see it better that way...Then, when I decided to check things out at my own house, I had a hard time because of my conscious mind. I think I was using logic to place things in my living room that would logically be there on a Friday night, like a Sunday paper. And I thought, oh, there's papers on the floor. And then I wondered, hmmm, are they really there. I mean, that's a typical scene in my living room and I thought maybe that's why I'm seeing it, but those papers aren't really there right now. So part of me kept asking about it and kept wanting to go home and check it out to see if the paper was indeed spread out all over the floor and everything else was there, such as the TV being on, like I saw it."

The way to deal with this kind of rational interference is to simply acknowledge it and then let it go. You may not be totally accurate initially, so don't worrry about it. The idea is to just be receptive and see whatever you see.

Avoiding Self-Criticism

Another way your rational mind can interfere is to lead you to criticize yourself if you are wrong. In this case, you may be hesitant to see more because you are afraid that the more you observe, the more chances you have of being wrong.

Again, if you experience this kind of feeling, simply acknowledge it and send it away. Accept the fact that you may not be totally accurate. Don't criticize yourself if you are wrong. Don't worry about whether you're correct in what you see.

Instead, just focus on having your conscious mind ask questions and remain open and ready to receive. Recognize that in time you will get better as you practice more and more with projection. And when you get feedback, use it as an independent source of validation. But don't let it discourage or lead you to develop a self-critical frame of mind. Your emphasis should be on perceiving and receiving, and gradually, through feedback, your ability in this area will improve over time.

Having a Smooth Trip

There are two other factors to keep in mind to promote a smooth projection. You want to keep a balance in how close you get to what you observe, and you want to keep the experience positive.

Maintaining a Balance in How Close You Get

Once you project yourself to wherever you are going, you want to maintain a balance between getting too close and not close enough. You want to be close enough to observe the people and events in the scene, but at the same time you don't want to get too close so that you get stuck in their space.

If someone is in a negative situation or is feeling in a bad mood and you are observing, you don't want to get stuck in that. In one projection I was on the streets of New York and I saw people having an argument. As an observer, I felt I could just watch and that's what I did. I stood far enough away so I felt a sense of distance. That's what you want to do. You don't want to get too close to something that you suddenly feel like you are being pulled into a scene that's going on. Sometimes it can get scary when you do and you may feel threatened. So it can be best to stay in the observer role, particularly when you are just starting to work with this process. This way you can be close enough so you can see what is happening in detail but, at the same time, removed enough from it so you feel safe.

Once you feel very comfortable and controlled in working with the process and are in a safe, positive environment, you can permit yourself to get even closer and perhaps get involved. An example might be projecting yourself into an enjoyable party or to a relaxed, placid scene on a beach. You feel sure you can let go and step into the scene. In this case, go ahead. Experience and enjoy. If you notice that the scene is changing and becoming less favorable (i.e., a storm blows up at the beach, an unpleasant character suddenly shows up at the party), get ready to pull back or remove yourself or return to the observer role.

Avoiding Negative Situations or Protecting Yourself to Encounter Them

Generally, you should also stay away from situations that are negative, unpleasant, or morbid, particularly when you are first doing projection. It's best to focus on going to places where good, favorable things are happening, so you feel comfortable and have a positive experience—such as going to the beach or a recreational place or going to the home of someone you like. If you go to places that are potentially dangerous, weird, or full of negative forces or situations, you may experience fear or other unpleasant emotions yourself.

One woman projected herself into a country experiencing political turmoil and famine, and she came out of the experience feeling somewhat jangled and depressed. In another case, some friends of Michael's, out of curiosity went to explore a cemetary, and they had some hair-raising encounters with some ghosts and evil presences they experienced in their visions. So generally, when you're working with this technique, stick to positive places.

However, recognize that at some times you may want to go to places where there is some negativity, and when you do, take the appropriate precautions. You might want to make such a projection if someone is sick and you want to sense what is happening to him so you can help him. Or you may just want to get some general information on the problems that are happening somewhere in the world.

Whatever the reasons, when you do go somewhere that seems dangerous, scary, or otherwise negative for you, stay in the role of an observer. If you should try to project any helpful, healing energy to better the situation, do so from outside the scene. It can help you feel more protected if you imagine a protective shield around you as you travel to this location or put one around yourself when you get there. For example, see a ball of white light surrounding you as you travel or protecting yourself from whatever is happening where you go. This way, even if you are in a negative situation, you can feel separate and apart, and you have a shield around you to keep the negative you are observing from getting in.

Getting Feedback

Getting feedback is important to help you develop accuracy in your projections. Generally, the more you try working with projection, the more accurate you will become, and feedback will help you sense your level of accuracy, so you can work on improving.

When you do get feedback, look for parallels between what you observed and what was actually present or happening at the time. In addition, if you were accurate, notice whether you had a sense of knowingness about that experience. Sometimes when you are right you will feel this quality of knowingness, which is like a mental twinge, tingle, or other hard-to-describe feeling telling you that you are in fact right.

What you want to do through feedback is to try to become more aware of this sense of knowingness and look for a correlation between how you feel when you are accurate and the accurate observation you have made. By looking for that feeling of knowingness in the future, you can try to increase your accuracy.

It's very hard to define how the process of becoming more accurate works, but increasingly, as you get this knowingness or intuition that you are seeing what's actually there, you will be correct. Then in the future, when you get this feeling, you will be better able to trust it because you will be more and more certain you really are right when you feel you are.

Chapter Six

Using Your Ability To Project In Everyday Life

Once you have developed your ability to do conscious projection, you can apply it in numerous ways to your everyday life. This chapter suggests some applications and also includes some exercises you can use to test and refine your projection ability. The following applications of conscious projection are merely some possibilities. You may find many other uses yourself.

Better Understand Another's Point of View and Feel More Empathy

One way to use projection is to project yourself into the eyes of another person, so you can get a sense of how he is feeling about something or is looking at the world. Then you are in a better position to interact with that person with empathy and understanding, which is a good way to improve your relationship.

To do this you can project your little point of consciousness into the person's head, so you are now looking at the world from his point of view. The process works much like a visualization in which you see yourself putting on someone else's head, so you can see and experience what he feels, except in this case you have projected outside of yourself into him rather than mentally incorporating him into you. So you remain a little more the neutral but understanding observer, and some people feel more comfortable with this than trying to step into the other person's shoes.

A good time to use this projection to understand someone is when you are going to get together to decide something or negotiate. Then you can better know where the person is coming from. Or suppose someone is going through a difficult time and you want to show your help and support. You might use projection to help you feel closer and more supportive of that person. In turn, the other person will feel an emotional lift from your aid.

When you do use this technique to get into someone's headspace or otherwise interact with anyone, you should be sure to be ethical. Make sure you are doing something he feels comfortable with and that you are not prying into any deep dark secrets. But otherwise, when you're basically an observer, these ethical concerns don't present a problem.

Pick Up What Another Person is Thinking About Something

A closely related application is to tune into what someone else is thinking about something or whether he is thinking about it at all. For example, one woman wondered if her mother who lived across the country, and whom she hadn't been in touch with in years, ever thought about her. They had had a parting of the ways and now the woman hoped they could get back in touch, but she was hesitant to make the first move unless she felt her mother was still thinking about her and open to being receptive. This tuning in might help her find the answer.

Using Projection to Trigger Someone Else's Thoughts

You can also use projection to trigger someone else into thinking about you—or even if you don't have that intention, your own projection may create that effect. People often have the experience of thinking about someone and imagine themself visiting a person, and then that person calls. Or similarly, you may think about calling someone you haven't spoken to in some time, but don't get around to it, and then that person calls you. Or alternatively, perhaps you do call and the person says: "Oh, I was just thinking about calling you."

These are all examples of the power of projection to have this triggering effect. It's like your subconscious is sending out a message to their subconscious on a subconscious level, and the result is that you trigger their thoughts or they may trigger yours.

Using Projection to Send Messages

An extension of this triggering process is to use projection to send out a specific message for someone to do something, not just think generally about you. In this case, the process tends to work much better with people who have developed their abilities in this area or have a strong, close relationship so they are especially attuned to one another.

One example of when you might do this is when you want to meet someone, but you have lost her phone number or can't remember it. You were supposed to get together and now you can't, or maybe you are going to be late. Sometimes you can use your projection to get the message through. Then, you can tell the person you have been delayed and ask the person to wait, or perhaps tell the person not to come to the particular place where she is supposed to be.

For example, Michael frequently used this with the members of his group when he had to change a meeting place, but couldn't reach the person. So he would project out this message to not show up, and somehow the other person seemed to know not to show up, too. Or sometimes even if the other person didn't know this consciously, his plans would change, with the same result.

I have frequently had the experience when someone will call me about a project that I don't want to do, but I feel I really can't say no. So I may agree to do it, but I also send out the message that I don't want this to happen. And repeatedly I have noticed that in such cases the person typically calls to cancel a meeting, postpones the project, or simply doesn't follow through or show up. In some of the classes I have had, I have sometimes felt like I didn't want a particular person to attend because he sounded very strange over the phone or I have met him and didn't feel he would fit in. Yet, since this is an open class, I haven't felt that I could say no. But then I have sent out the message not to come, and invariably I have found the person calls to say something else has suddenly come up so he can't come, or he doesn't appear. So once again, somehow my message seems to have gotten through.

Whether you know someone or not you may, through conscious projection, connect up on a subconscious level with others and get them to respond to your message. It may help to get the message through and get a favorable response if you know someone, because you are more sensitive to one another, but the process can work with anyone.

Anticipate What is Likely to Happen Where You Are Going

You can also project yourself into another setting, so you are better prepared for what lies ahead. In many cases, this type of projection involves looking at an ongoing event which is happening now and will continue into the future when you encounter it, or it may be that what is happening now is what will affect the future. However, don't worry about whether what you are seeing is happening now or in the future; we'll be talking about some techniques for looking specifically into future time next. But the two really merge together. So you may be getting insights into the present only, into the future, or into both.

In any case, the advantage of being able to travel to this other setting is that you can become more familiar or comfortable with the environment before you go there, or you can prepare for what is likely to happen.

If you are going to travel someplace as a tourist, maybe visualize yourself traveling there so you get a sense of what you need to bring with you and what might be likely to happen in the airport, so you are better prepared for this. Or if you are going to be going through customs, you can visualize yourself going through and imagine what the customs officers might be like and what you might say to them, so you are better able to get through quickly.

Likewise, if you are going to go to a place that you haven't been before, such as a cocktail party, performance, or some unfamiliar place, perhaps you can imagine who's going to be there and how other people are going to be dressed, so you can decide what to wear yourself and plan what to say or do. This way you arrive more prepared.

Obviously, in some of these examples you may be peering into the future a little. But at the same time you may be picking up activities that are happening now, such as if you are getting ready to go to a party while it is going on. So don't worry about whether your projection is into present or future time—just pick up the information you get and use it to help you prepare accordingly.

Picking Up Specific Information to Use in Planning

In some cases you may be able to pick up specific information, such as numbers, percentages, and facts you can use in planning. However, this is often an area where it is the most difficult to get completely accurate information or know it is correct, because often projection gives you more general information or only approximate results.

This is why it is generally difficult to use this technique for making a bet on a horse race or picking numbers for a lottery. Your ability to project is normally not certain enough to win regularly, although in some cases people do report having a very strong sense of seeing the result correctly, and they win.

The other issue that may sometimes come up in trying to pick up factual information is if you are trying to gain information you shouldn't have. One woman learning how to use the process wondered if she could use the process to see what was on a test her teacher was going to give her in advance, so she could then prepare her answer beforehand. In such a case one may be able to get a general sense of what someone is likely to choose, but when it comes to knowing exactly, this is like privileged information, so ethically it may not be appropriate to get it, and your subconsciousness may put up its own blocks to your seeing this.

The types of situations where this ability can be used successfully is in getting information to make everyday routine choices about what to do next. Some possibilities might be:

—You are looking for a parking place and aren't sure where to turn. Through projection you can scan the nearby blocks and get a sense of where a parking place might be. Then you can turn accordingly.

—You are looking for an item in a store and aren't sure where to go next. Your projection might help you sense where this item is.

—You are supposed to meet a friend and you have forgotten the name of the place, though you know the general area. Through projection, you can tune in on where your friend is.

—You have lost an object. Your projection can help you pick up where the item is.

You can also experiment with projection to pick up information as you pursue ordinary activities to help you develop this ability and become more accurate. Some practices which I have tried regularly from time to time are the following. In each case, after you do the projection, check to see if you were right and notice how you felt when they were right. The practices you might use are:

—As you arrive home, sense how many calls you got on your answering machine before you look at it.

—Before you check your mail, imagine how many letters you have gotten that day in response to a mailing you have done.

—Imagine how many people are at an event before you arrive.

—Picture whether there is a parking space ahead of you in the next block.

You'll find as you do this your projections will become more and more on target, and the information you get will be increasingly accurate. In turn, you'll develop your sense of knowing when you are right.

Sensing What Other People Like or Expect So You Can Respond Accordingly

Another way to use projection is to sense what someone is like or what he likes or expects, so you can adapt your own behavior to that person. Say you are going to a job interview with a person you have only talked to briefly on the phone. You can project yourself to that person's office, look around and see what that person is like. If the person and his environment seem warm and friendly, you can come to the interview prepared to act more informally. If you pick up that the person is more reserved and proper, prepare to act this way.

By the same token, if you have something important coming up and you feel like you need to make a good impression on someone, such as in giving a business presentation, you can use your projection to get a sense of the expectations of the person or group attending the presentation. You can then do the presentation in an appropriate way especially tailored for that person or group.

Sensing and Overcoming Resistances

Still another possibility is picking up resistances, sensing where they are coming from, and overcoming them. To take the job interview situation again, suppose you initially pick up that the person is going to say no. You might then combine your powers of observation through projection with your ability to project out new thoughts and ideas. Then you might focus on having the person you are going to meet be more receptive, and you might imagine what you might do yourself to make him more responsive to you. And then you might picture once again going to the interview, and this time you get a yes.

This process may not work every time, but it will increase your chances of turning what might be an initial no into a yes.

Also, if you feel someone is resisting and you want to talk to that person about something or you are involved in negotiating something, you might try to turn that resistance around. For this, perhaps picture this person calling you in your mind's eye, or picture him being responsive when you call.

This projection in present time may help to soften him up, so he is more receptive when you call, or perhaps he will take the initiative to call you. When you finally speak this internal work will help you know what to say so you are more likely to overcome any lingering resistance he feels.

Pick Up What is Happening to People When There are Delays or Problems

You can also get information through projection on what is happening to people you know when they run into delays or problems. Then you can use that information to better plan, be patient, or help the person.

Suppose friends are coming to visit and they are late and you're not sure what is happening to them. If you use your consicous projection to get a sense of where they are, you can plan accordingly to wait, postpone an activity such as dinner, or even send out some help. Michael described doing this frequently when he was expecting people, and was generally accurate. He'd project his consciousness and think: "Well, they're at such and such location and they're going to be here in about five minutes," and within a few minutes they would arrive. Commonly, within a few minutes one way or the other he would be right.

Getting What You Want Through Projection

Finally, you can use your ability to project what you want now in the present to get what you want in the future. The way to do this is to picture very clearly what you want and then focus all of your energy on achieving that. It's like setting up an image of your goal in the here and now, and then beaming your consciousness into that image so you infuse it with your commitment and your will. In other words, you're using your seeing ability to bend and shape reality by projection, whereby you clearly visualize what you want, and then you focus your energy on going after it and getting it both in your mental projection and subsequently in the actions you take.

At the same time, these projections can influence others who may contribute to your getting what you want, because others can pick up to a greater or lesser extent this projection of your energy. So if you want somebody to do something, your mental projection may help to trigger that person's decision to do it. Or if you picture something happening and you see a person saying no or otherwise standing in your way, that projection and any actions you take based on it may be just what you need to get that person to say yes instead of no or step aside so you pass through.

These techniques can be extremely powerful and have many applications to everyday living. And probably you can think of many more uses than those described here.

Developing Your Projection Skills Through Practice

To improve your ability to project with accuracy requires practice, including getting feedback about when you are right. One way to do this is by projecting yourself somewhere where you can subsequently check by asking someone who was there at the time of your projection, or you can go there later to see if what you saw there is true. For instance one woman at a workshop saw old newspapers scattered around the living room where she lived with a number of roommates. She hadn't put the papers there herself before the workshop, but when she returned the papers were there. When you get a hit like this, try to think back to how you felt when you did that projection and how that feeling might differ from another time when you projected yourself but didn't observe correctly. Such feedback will help you pinpoint what you feel or how you are projecting when you are on target, so you can repeat that process again—or at least you will better know when your projections are correct or when they are not.

You can work on developing these skills by practicing with objects. The principle here is to increase your ability to see accurately when you project by focusing in on something simple. You can target that and concentrate all of your energy on one particular subject, rather than having your vision more diffused as when you look at a whole scene.

One approach you can use if you are working on your own is to set up some objects in one room without looking at those objects. For instance, throw some dice behind a screen. Roll some cubes with numbers out of a bag while you are blindfolded. Or place some small objects in a bag, mix them up, and drop a few of them out without looking. Then quickly go into another room, get into an altered state of consciousness, project yourself, and write down what you see. Afterwards, go into the other room and check whether you were correct.

However, an even better way to test your accuracy and a more interesting way is to work with another person. You can take turns projecting yourselves to pick up objects. The way to work together is for one of you to select and arrange certain objects or pictures of objects in one room.

Meanwhile, the other should remain in another room. Then, when the objects are all selected and arranged, the person doing the projection can try to project and see these objects or pictures in the other room. The following exercise is designed to help you set up a joint projection practice.

Practicing Projection by Looking at Objects or Pictures—Exercise #14

You can use objects or drawings of objects in the following projection exercise, which I have used in my own workshops. It's best to use fairly simple objects or shapes, because these are easier to focus on and pick up than something complex. Thus, a strong graphic or geometrical image is good for this.

One person will then go into another room to choose the items and lay them out. Meanwhile, the other person (or persons) will wait in the other room. Then, if you are the person doing the projection, when the other person indicates he is ready you will project your consciousness into the other room and observe and make a note of what you see. After the person has selected a series of objects or drawings and you have done a series of projections, you can check your lists to see if and when you were correct.

If you are in an unfamiliar setting you should take a look at the room where the items will be set out, so you can focus on the objects as they are set out and don't have to imagine what the room looks like when you project yourself there. Instead, you can work to project yourself into a room which you already know, and then you can look directly at the object. So take a few minutes if you need to, to carefully look at the room where you will be going and commit it to memory.

As an alternative to choosing objects, a person might draw something simple. But in either case, the person should make a list of the sequence in which he is placing or drawing objects, just as the person projecting will keep his own list after each projection. The person placing the objects or making the drawings should also place them when ready in the same spot each time, to make it easier for the person doing the projection to go directly to that spot. Also, he should call out something like: "I'm ready." or "Okay," each time he has finished making the selection or the drawing. Then, the person projecting will know he can now project himself and observe what is there. He should then write down what he sees.

In summary, the experiment will go something like this:
1) The projector (person doing the projection) will look at the room where the selector (person selecting or drawing objects) will be making the selection or drawing. The selector will indicate where he will place the objects or drawing.
2) The selector will now go into that room and the projector will wait in another room.
3) The selector will choose or draw one object, place it in the designated

location, announce that he is ready, and write down what he is placing there.

4) The projector will try to project himself into this room and see what object or drawing is in the designated location. Then, he will write down what he sees.

5) The projector and selector will repeat this process several times (between three and five times is recommended).

6) Then the projector and selector will compare their lists, and the selector will reveal his objects.

The following is an example of the instructions I have used before beginning the experiment. You can use them if you find them helpful in setting up your own experiment and explaining what to do to someone.

For the following projection experiment, I'm going to go in the other room. I will have this board, and I will lay out an object or a card with a geometrical shape on it. And what I'd like you to do is to write down what you observe.

Now I'm going to give you each a sheet of paper, and I'll be doing five of these selections. Before I make each selection, I'll call out: "I'm doing it now," and then when I have finished making the selection, I will call out: "Okay, I'm ready."

Then what I'd like you to do is use the beam of energy technique or any other means of projection, and project your consciousness into this room. Just notice whatever you can, and write down an image or perhaps draw a picture of what you saw.

We'll do this five times, and afterwards we'll check your observations out.

After you have gotten this feedback, we'll try the exercise again and see if you have experienced any improvement in your accuracy.

Comparing the Results of Your Projection

The comparison process after each projection experiment is the key to your improvement. You can use it to track your accuracy and to note the awareness you have which is associated with success, so you can repeat that state of mind more often in the future and thereby increase your level of accuracy. Also, you can become aware of the state of mind or feelings you have when you don't score a hit or have an ambiguous result, so you can try not to have that in the future. The comparison process can help you fine tune your awareness, so you are better able to not only pick up things more accurately because you are more sensitive, but also you are better able to know when you know.

As you will find, this awareness of your own awareness or this knowingness of your knowing will come to you in different ways. You may have certain images, impressions, or sensations associated with the targets you hit, such as a momentary picture of a light flashing, a clearer image than usual, a more solid impression or feeling. The associations will vary for different people, and in the course of this feedback process you will discover the signals or triggers that best work for you.

Here are some of the descriptions of feelings or impressions associated with hits in one workshop:

"I just suddenly get a flash, and it would seem to be right."

"It seemed like in the first one (when I got a hit), I seemed to have gotten closer to it....It seemed like I was actualy turning the angles of it... But the other one, it wasn't...as clear." "I felt more clarity or more solidness to it, when I was closer or right."

Incidentally, your response doesn't have to be right on to be a hit. In some cases you may have a direct hit, but often you will find your impression represents an approximation, which seems relatively close. For instance, instead of a sphere you'll see a circle, or perhaps some semi-circular or curvilinear forms. Or perhaps if someone picks a square box you may sense there is some kind of container, but it is not square.

Regard your responses as falling along something of a continuum with the direct hits and complete misses at one end, and ambiguous responses in the middle. As you'll find, many of your responses may be closer to the direct hit end of the continuum and you should regard these as partial hits, even though not exactly accurate. So your first concern when just starting to do this should be to maximize both the hits and the partial hits. You can concentrate on getting closer hits later. The reason you don't want to be too critical in the beginning is you may discourage yourself by thinking you are wrong, when in fact you are picking up some information even though in a sketchy form. Your conscious projection will often give you only general information, so the perceptions you receive may not always be exact, but approximate.

However it comes to you, look for any differences in the experience you had when your image was either on target or came close to the one selected. In particular, pay attention to whether you have more of a sense of correctness or knowingness or a clear vision, which are common associations. Also notice any special images or associations which you may have with the hits.

It's important to look for these qualitative perceptions because the kind of associations you have with a hit and the trials which aren't hits will be different for different people. If you can pick up the associations that work for you, it will make you more sensitive and accurate in the future.

It's something like being a dowser. A dowser, who uses a stick, metal pointer, or other object to search for water, will similarly seek to learn how to dowse by getting feedback from the environment and from himself, so he can compare the differences when he is correct and when he is not. He then develops this sense of increased awareness and knowing so he can both pick up these very subtle movements coming from his dowsing tool and know when these are probably correct. Whatever he feels can be very difficult to identify in words. But it's like feeling an inner twinge or sense of sudden validity—a kind of "Yes, that's right" feeling. But exactly what that feeling is is hard to describe. Whatever it is for you, try to notice that feeling or intuitive sense of what is true.

Then, whenever you do this exercise again, pay attention to any impressions you get, no matter how subtle, and continue to check your accuracy until you get an intuitive sense of rightness. Often you may get very fragmentary kinds of images, but pay attention to those anyway, and sometimes those images will become clearer. Or later you may find even these fragments reflect a partial hit. So try to be very receptive to whatever comes, and recognize that it can take time to develop this receptivity and get this sensation of rightness. With practice, you'll become more sensitive over time.

Whenever you can, try these exercises with other people and get verification. This will help your sensitivity and accuracy improve.

Recognizing the Displacement Effect

At times when you make these comparisons, you will notice something that's called the "displacement effect." This occurs when you project yourself to pick up one thing, but you pick up the object or image which occurred just before or just after it in time.

J. B. Rhine and other researchers on ESP have found this effect is common in telepathy experiments. The researcher selects or concentrates on one card, and the other person tries to pick it up. But instead of getting that, he gets the card that is still face down and hasn't been turned over yet.

A reason this may happen is because you are anticipating what's to come or you feel impatient and want to get on to what's coming next. So you skip over what the person is trying to show you now and look at what he is going to show you.

Or alternatively, perhaps you pick up the previous image because you aren't paying attention to what the person is showing now. Instead you are trying to recheck again what he previously showed.

For whatever reason, this phenomena may happen at times, and because of this don't give up if you think you didn't get a hit. Instead, compare your projection results with images before and after the image you were trying to focus on to check for direct and partial hits. Count these as possible successes, too, and later you can work on targeting each image more exactly and reduce or eliminate the amount of possible displacement involved.

Getting Information from Other Channels

Another question that sometimes comes up in making comparisons is: What is the real source of the information obtained from projection? Are you observing the images through projection, or could you be picking up information from other channels? If you are doing a projection experiment with another person, maybe you are picking up that person's mental thoughts about the object he is placing, rather than seeing the object itself. Or maybe you are picking up information from both seeing the objects and sensing the other person's thoughts.

It can often be hard to tell on what channel you are getting information, particularly since all of these channels may be operating simultaneously even though you may be focusing on getting information in a particular way. Under the circumstances, it's best not to worry too much about which channel or channels are operating. Rather recognize that the more channels you have to get information, the more accurate you'll be. In the conscious projection process you are focusing on one way of getting information. But this is not to say you are not getting information from other sources. You may very well be.

Probably the best approach is to be accepting of the information you get wherever it comes from, although you may be concentrating on getting it from a particular channel. However you obtain that information, work on checking it out so you develop that sensitivity and sense of knowing which you need to pick up more and better information, better assess the information you receive and determine whether what you have observed or sensed is correct. This way you will see more and know more, and your accuracy will further improve.

Other Experiments You Can Try

You can also create your own projection experiments to practice with. In these cases, work with a partner and have one person be the sender or projector, the other the receiver or perceiver. Then switch. Here are some suggested approaches some people have used successfully.

Try wearing different clothes and the other person has to pick up what you are wearing. One person should be in one room with a variety of clothing to choose from and the other person should be in another room with the door closed so he can't see. The person with the clothing will put something on, and the other person will try to pick up what he is wearing.

Try projecting different mental images and have the other person try to pick up that image. This is possible because your ability to see when you project is not just confined to physical objects. But you can see mental thought forms or physical and symbolic representations of them, too. For instance, when Michael experimented with an associate, Gene in Los Angeles, Gene imagined projecting the image of a hawk to where Michael was in the field, and Michael looked up and saw a real one around the same time that Gene was doing the projection. So there may have been some connection between Gene visualizing a hawk, projecting it, and then Michael looking up and seeing one.

Try projecting an image to a person or group of people not involved in the experiment and see if they observe anything. The way to do this is to concentrate on projecting something when you are with one or more people who don't know you are doing this; then ask what they are thinking about or if they are seeing anything special. You could even do this while you are having a conversation with a person at a party or over dinner, or while you are teaching a class.

As an example, Michael was teaching a class on ritual techniques in the field, and before or during the class, he did some projections in which he imagined the energy taking the form of wolves. He didn't tell his students in advance what he was doing, but then, without Michael saying anything, some of his students noticed the wolves. Then he continued to maintain control over this projection, so when he stopped the projection and asked the energy forms that had taken the shapes of wolves to leave, they did, and the students stopped seeing the wolves or projections.

Using a Ritual to Intensify Your Projections

You can create even stronger, more intense projections by combining a ritual with your projections. This combination has this effect because through a ritual you can build up your energy and intensify your focus so that your projection becomes that much stronger and more intense. Since doing a ritual effectively involves some advanced techniques, I'll just mention the use of this process here.

Doing a ritual when you project can be especially valuable to get something you really want. The extra energy you create and the especially intense focus of a ritual can better help you get it. In one of his workshops Michael explained how he would do this when he wanted to get a job. He would go out in a field at night and make a circle or field of protective energy around himself. In this protective space he would ask for the help of the energies of nature. And in this intensely focused ritual state he would picture himself where he wanted to be, using the same kind of conscious projection discussed in this chapter. However, the process was more intense for him because he had built up a deeper altered state of consciousness by doing the ritual. And he found that it was more effective as a result. He pictured himself in the office where he wanted to work, went through the interview in his mind, and heard the interviewer saying yes. Later in real time he got the job.

The ritual process can help to make your projections more effective because you're using the ritual to increase the intensity of the energy you are putting out to get what you want. The ritual acts to increase the power of your energy while your projection selects the reality where you want to be.

At the same time, you should focus on believing that what you are seeking in your projection will occur without a doubt. You should express that certainty that you really know what is going to happen, because this is what you want and you have the confidence to see it through. So you know what you see and seek in your projection cannot possibly not happen, because you are going to make it happen. And the ritual, by increasing the energy you direct to this goal, makes it even more certain to happen, and this you know.

Chapter Seven

Projecting Yourself Into The Future

Projecting yourself into the future is much like projecting yourself into another place in the present. In fact, it's sometimes hard to separate the two processes because often when you pick up something about the present, it's easy to see that event continuing on into future time. You may initially tune into a series of events as they are happening now, but as you watch them unfold, time speeds up and soon you are seeing them occur in future time. However, while present and future may blend together as you seek information through conscious projection, this chapter is designed to focus more specifically on how to project yourself in future time.

The Theory of Probable Futures

When you do look into the future it is important to recognize that you are not pre-viewing a future that is fixed in time. What you are looking at is the probable future—or one of a number of probable futures. What this means is that in looking ahead you are seeing a certain event that may happen. However, all things in the future have different probabilities of happening. Mathematicians and statisticians, for example, are aware of the probablistic nature of events occurring, and assign different probabilities to them. It's much the same in picking up insights about the future. Certain things are going to be more probable than others in whether they happen, others less so.

When you look ahead this means what you see might happen, but then again, it might not. But since any given event is only more or less probable, that means you have the possibility of changing it. Or if a particularly powerful future event seems reasonably probable, you can prepare or adapt yourself to better deal with it, too.

Recognizing the Different Probabilities

The probabilities of the future events you perceive can range anywhere from something which is almost certain to happen to one which has little likelihood of occurring. But how do you know?

One factor is whether this is an occurrence which affects just you as an individual, or whether it involves a group, and whether that group is small or large. If there's only you involved, your own actions, thoughts, and feelings have a great influence in determining the probabilities, and if you want, you can readily alter your actions, thoughts, and feelings to make something more or less likely. But if the probability relates to a group process, the larger the mass involved, the more you or the number of people affected must do to change that particular outcome from happening. In other words, it's necessary to mobilize a sufficient critical mass to change the current probabilities to have a different outcome in the future. Similarly, a natural event may be more or less powerful and this level of power determines how much you need to do to change the probable occurrence of that event.

For example, if you look ahead and you see that a thunderstorm is likely, that is something you probably can't do anything to change, so it would be best to just prepare for the probable result. Or if you pick up information about a world event, you may have little power on your own to do anything, though enough people picking up this information may be able to act on it to change the likely future at a particular time. However, if you look ahead and see that you are probably not going to get a particular job that you really wanted, you can do things to make a change in that probable outcome by doing things now to make a difference. You then increase your chances of getting your job. It's something you have a good chance of changing if you wish, because the probabilities in this situation primarily depend on what you do.

As you think about the future, recognize that there are two major ways of thinking about the probabilities of events. 1) Certain occurrences or outcomes will be more or less probable, on a continuum of probabilities, ranging from 100% certainty to 0%—certain to not happen at all. 2) Certain occurrences or outcomes can sometimes be easily influenced by you or others, depending on the strength of that event and the number of people involved in creating it. The more powerful the event and the more people that are involved, the more power is needed to change its direction, whatever the initial probability of that event occurring.

What Effects the Relative Probability of Events

The probability of events is also affected by two main factors—the nature of the event and how near it is in time.

By their very nature, certain events are simply more or less probable than others. At times, we can know this by common sense. For example, we take certain natural events for granted, such as the sun rising in the morning and setting in the evening at a certain time. In other cases, we have built up certain expectations about probabilities as a result of history or previous experiences with that event. For instance, there is a certain level of probability that it will rain at different times during the year; there is a certain likelihood that one country or another will get into a war; there is a certain chance that a person may get married or divorced, have an accident, or get on a plane that crashes into the sea.

In some cases, we can have a fairly good estimate of how probable something is or there may be general agreement among some experts about what is likely. Some analysts may work out projections about the stock market or the state of the economy and have some degree of certainty about how likely they are to be correct. But in other cases, predictions are up for grabs—such as if Elizabeth Taylor is going to get married again or divorced. Whether an event is relatively predictable or not, you can still assign some estimated probability to it, based on your own sense of how likely it is to happen. Then you can take this into consideration when you look into the future and assess the likelihood of the events you observe.

Secondly, you should take into account the nearness of the event in time, as well as its nature, in estimating how likely it is. The closer something is in time, the higher the probability that it will occur as you foresee it, since there are less factors that can deflect it from its current path. But the further something is off in the future, the more likely the projected outcome can be different, because there are so many other events and influences that may intervene to make a change. If you do pick up that something is closer in time, you may have more of an ability to impact on it in the here or now than if it's way off in the future, because the farther off it is, the more other factors might have an effect too.

Because of these differences in the nature of future events and how close we are to them, the probability of these events can be very different. By being discerning, we can better estimate these probabilities and use these estimates in assessing how to react to the visions of the future that we pick up in projection. Recognizing these greater or lesser probabilities of future events is important, because it shows us that the future we perceive is not in fact fixed, and we have a greater or lesser opportunity to change it, based on the probability of the event in question and our own power to effect change, either individually or working with others who seek a similar change. As noted, some events are more amenable to individual change, others require a greater or lesser degree of collective action. In turn, some people have more or less power to effect change themselves or to mobilize others to join with them to make changes.

Recognizing the fluidity of the future and these ranges of possibilities is also important, because it will help you make decisions about what you want to try to change and what you want to prepare to go and flow with. Sometimes people can become very skeptical about future predictions because they don't realize that these predictions should only be taken as possibilities or probabilities. They think that what a person sees happening in the future is supposed to happen exactly that way, and then when it doesn't they say: "Oh, yeah. That didn't work," or they use this to argue that predicting the future is all a bunch of nonsense. But what they don't realize is that in seeing the future you are merely seeing a future which has a certain probability of occurring, so it's more or less likely to occur. So by being sensitive to the "probable probability" of this occurrence you can plan or respond accordingly, and you can work on developing this sensitivity through practice in future projection and in further honing your sense of discerning or knowing how likely a probable future is likely to be.

Your Relative Impact on Future Events

Besides assessing the probability of the events you pick up, you should also be aware of your relative ability to affect them. In some cases, when you are looking at events that concern yourself or a close circle of your friends, relatives, or associates, you may have a relatively good ability to have an effect.

But in other cases, you may be picking up events affecting larger groups or world events, where you really don't have much or any impact as an individual. Thus, while you can see into the future and sense what's going to happen, you may not have a lot of effect if you try to do something different as an individual or try to visualize that event not occurring. On the other hand, if you and a whole group of people similarly situated think about wanting a change and then this thinking leads to some form of concurrent or coordinated group action, then something different might occur, for now this group has initiated a kind of social or political movement.

Tuning into the future can be important for giving you that vision about what is likely and what is necessary to do to create change. But recognize that you will be more or less likely to do something about what you see, depending on the nature of the event. If you sense you can do something, do it. Or if you feel you can't, then perhaps simply plan and adjust. Again, as you become more sensitive to picking up the future, assessing the probabilities, and sensing the extent to which you can do something to change the outcome, you will better know what to do and will be more effective when you act.

Thinking About the Probabilities and What You Can Do

One way to think the probabilities of a particular event and the amount of impact you might have is to imagine a graph in which you look at what you can do in relationship to the probability of the event happening. The more probable the event and the greater the critical mass of people necessary to affect it, the less you can do. The less probable the event and the less power needed to change it, the more impact you can have. The graph representing this relationship might look something like this:

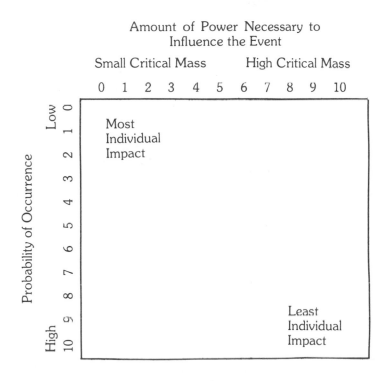

Amount of Power Necessary to
Influence the Event

Small Critical Mass   High Critical Mass

Perhaps another way to think about your impact on the probabilities of an event is to imagine the series of events you are perceiving in the future as like a series of notes of music which exist somewhere along the scale. The higher the note, the further the event is in the future. At the same time, each note is played at a certain level of volume or intensity. The tone of the note corresponds to the location of the particular event in the future. But the intensity of it corresponds to the concept of critical mass. The louder the sound, the more impact it has on everyone hearing it, the stronger its power. The softer the sound, the less influence it has, the easier it is to ignore. Just as the louder the sound, the more you must listen and respond to it, so the more probable the future and the greater the critical mass required to change it, the more you must adapt to it yourself. Likewise, just as you can ignore or change the impact of a softer sound by adding your own sounds on top of it, the more you can influence a future which is less probable or which requires less power to make a change.

The Source of Your Ability to Change the Future

Your own ability to influence the future to a greater or lesser extent occurs because everything you do has some influence on things, and the closer things are to you, the more you have an ability to affect them by taking some action to exert your influence. To better understand this process, you might imagine a series of circles around yourself. The inner circle represents the world of things that are most immediately around you, such as your home and family. Within this sphere you have the most influence.

Moving outward, there is a second circle that represents the world of your friends and associates. Now you have a little less influence because you are not so personally involved, and this sphere is more affected by many outside influences.

Even further out there are circles that represent the everyday world around you and the world of more distant world events. The further out the circles go, the less personal influence you have and the more you must simply adapt to the future events you pick up in these spheres.

Even though your influence may diminish as you travel outward from sphere to sphere, you still have some level of influence as well as the ability to pick up information about the future, because we are all connected to the whole web of things. In turn, by opening up your intuitive part and tuning into this web of connections on a deeper, unconscious level, you can sense what is going on. Then you can, as appropriate, take some action to influence that future reality, should you want to push for change.

In fact, these interconnections are what enable you to project yourself into other places in the present and into future time. Since all is connected in terms of time and space, you can project from where you are now to seeing other places and you can move back and forward in time. For the same reason, you can pick up information about other people and about world events, for everything and everyone is connected on some level. This connection derives from the fact that all things are part of a universal oneness or common core. Since everyone shares a little bit of that oneness which has existed over time and exists on this unconscious level of energy which underlies the material world, you can plug into this connection by going within and tuning into your own unconscious. Through conscious projection you can move along these pathways of energy connections from place to place and from time to time.

Perhaps another way to imagine this process is to think of the universe we live in as much like a rubber ball. It's like we're all little pieces of rubber within this ball. So if you push a little on one side of the ball it will move somewhere else in response to that presssure; and as little pieces of rubber within that ball, we can feel that pressure too.

Accordingly, if you make a movement of your own you will create a movement somewhere else in this ball, and if this is a very small movement this will, of course, just create a very small movement elsewhere. If it's a larger movement, the movement created elsewhere will be that much larger.

Again it goes back to the notion of the critical mass. As more and more people make movements in a certain direction, they will have more and more effect in changing things or reshaping the ball. And at a certain point their collective movements may cause the ball to move or bounce. So the question becomes for any given situation, what is the critical mass needed to move that ball. Every movement will have some influence, but then if very small, the ball will simply snap right back into its original shape or the ball will continue rolling or bouncing along as it is. But if the movement becomes strong enough, that may permanently affect the ball, so its shape could change or its direction might too.

Or think of your effect on the ball of life this way. You don't occupy just one ball, but a series of balls, representing these series of circles surrounding you, from the level of home and family to the larger community and the world around you. Your movements will have a certain effect on all of these balls, but they will have the most effect on the one that is immediately surrounding you.

At the same time, besides your movements there are also larger movements which represent the combined efforts of a greater or lesser number of people acting at once. These movements can occur on a small group, local community, corporate, national, or racial group level to encompass the overall movements of everyone in the world as a whole. It's like there are cycles within cycles of movements going on simultaneously, and at certain points they supplement one another or at other times they intersect in an opposition of conflicting motions. Together, all of these cycles combine to affect what happens, and the greater the combined impact in a certain direction, the more these cycles will affect the probable future in that way.

When you pick up information about the future, just realize it is like you are tuning into what is happening somewhere in the rubber ball. And then, if you wish you can either flow with what is happening, or you can make some movements to affect it and you may perhaps become part of the cycle of movements representing the actions of everyone else. The impact of these movements will depend on the combined power of those making them and the location and scope of a particular event in that rubber ball of life.

Experiencing the Effects of these Connections in Your Own Life

You have probably had many examples of how these interconnections affect what happens in your own life. A common example is when you make a decision to do something, and then suddenly all sorts of things start happening to facilitate your achieving that goal. For instance, people you need to meet to make your objective happen now come into your life. You encounter an article with exactly the information you need to know. You go to a meeting and someone tells you about some event or contact which will help you do a task you need to do.

It's as if you have sent out some energy by deciding what you want to do or what you need, and in turn people or events seem to respond to smooth the way. Possibly this occurs because your decision and sense of clear direction makes you more attentive to the appropriate opportunities, and perhaps now you go to greater lengths to go where you need to be or do what you need to do to be in a place where you will get these opportunities. Or perhaps this occurs because your decision is like a push on that rubber ball, so you push one place and the rubber ball, representing the larger world you are linked to, responds accordingly. So when you push for something you want, the ball pushes back and throws you what you want.

For whatever reason, the process seems to work so that our inter-connections with others seems to result in our getting just what we want and need at the time. I have experienced getting what I want just when I need it over the 20 year period that I have been freelancing. At first, the thought of being on my own was scary—no regular paycheck or security to fall back on. Just lots of open hours and my desire to get some work. Yet from the very beginning I always seemed to find a new project or a new client just when I needed one. When I was very busy I would think, "No more work, I can't handle anything else now." and nothing would come. But when I came to the end of one project and wanted others, someone would suddenly call with something to fill that space. Or if I wanted a backer or an assistant with special skills for a new project, I would just think about the kind of person I wanted, and he or she would be there, too.

So where did all these people come from? Some simply responded to a small ad or listing. In other cases, I made an announcement or put out a flyer at a meeting, and the very person I needed was there. And in very many cases, I would get a call from seemingly out of the blue, due to the referral or grapevine process, and the person would call when I had exactly that need.

When I decided to write some songs and wanted a musician to collaborate, I mentioned this at a small meeting and a musician was there. In another case, I was teaching a class on export marketing and showed off some of the games I had marketed about 10 years before. Why don't you design games again, someone in my class suggested, and within the week as I was considering this, I got a call from a man who was a partner of someone I hadn't spoken to in eight years. Together they had designed a game and they wanted me to be a consultant.

And more recently I found this happened again when I decided to do my next book on conflict management. I decided to do so after someone who read my sales book asked me to talk to her sales group about interpersonal conflict and competition. Soon after I made that decision, I went to a breakfast group and announced I was interested in talking to groups about this topic. One woman there immediately took me up on my offer, and after I spoke to her group this became the first chapter. At the same time, another woman who heard my announcement came over to tell me about a group which resolves conflicts in the community and has a training program on conflict resolution—exactly what I needed to write the book. Once I decided what to do, everything seemed to fall together, and the things I needed to do, the people I needed to meet, were right there.

Many other people have had much the same sort of experience. They open themself up to something they feel they want to do in the future, and all of a sudden the things they need come into their life. When I asked others to describe their own experience of this at a workshop, one woman commented:

"It's like once I decide to do something. I feel like there's a hand pushing me in one direction, and things related to that decision will come up again and again. So every time I turn around, it's like something to do with that decision is there."

Or as another woman put it:

"Sometimes I'll think about something the way I want or think it's going to be in the future...And then it all of a sudden starts happening...It's like everything I want or need is suddenly falling into place."

The types of events that occur in response to a decision or a desire for something can range from the very minor or even apparently trivial events to a much more complex, seemingly ordered up event. It's as if you say to the world "I want this" or "I want to do this," and then somehow that's exactly what you get.

For example, one man complained about having trouble with a bottle of glue; the glue kept drying out because the bottle lacked a rubber washer to create a seal between the bottle and the cap. A minor wish perhaps, but he was amazed a few days later when he passed a war surplus store and suddenly had a strong urge to stop and look for a seal for the bottle. He went in and there it was—exactly what he visualized. Or as he stated, "It was just as I had designed it, just within thousands of an inch. It went right there in the bottle. And afterwards I wondered, 'Did I create that washer?' It was there exactly when I needed it and where I felt it would be, and it worked fine."

In another case, a woman decided she wanted to meet someone she had been having trouble meeting at a workshop they both attended, and soon after she imagined what she wanted happening and she got just that. As she explained:

"I was taking a workshop on personal development and there was a man in the group that I felt was interesting, and I felt I wanted to meet him... Now one of the things we do at this workshop is to split into groups, and when we intially spoke at the meeting he seemed like a somewhat shy person, and so I found it difficult to talk that way...

"I really wanted to be in a small group with him as a chance to get more acquainted, and we only had one more day of doing this. So I imagined in advance being in a group with him, and when I walked up the stairs to the meeting it's very strange what happened.

"As I walked in, I saw that we were supposed to sign up to be in the group we wanted, and he had already signed in for Croup C. So I thought it would be really easy, and started to sign up for that.

"However, then the woman handling the list stopped me. She said there were already four people signed up for that group, and she asked me to instead sign in for Group B, with only three people so far.

"So I signed up for Group B, and I was feeling very disappointed for the next half hour as the leader was giving a talk to the whole group. I kept thinking that I really wanted to be in a group with this person, and now we would be apart.

"However, when they split up the groups based on the sign-ups, it was very strange. The leader asked people to go to different rooms, depending on which group they were in, and then he asked for anyone who wasn't sure what group they were in to check with him.

"And suddenly I got this strange feeling of uncertainty, and I went to check. I went up, and he said, 'Oh, you're in Group C,' and I couldn't believe it because I had remembered signing up for Group B. But then, I looked at the sheet of paper and there was my signature for Group C, even though I know they had asked me to sign up for Group B and I had.

"I discovered I had ended up in a different group, and it was the group I wanted to be in. And then, even more amazingly, after we formed into these groups we did a little role playing process in which two of us played the role of a couple talking to two social workers. And I was assigned to play it with this man I wanted to meet—so we were husband and wife.

"I could hardly believe what had happened. Here I had thought about being in the same group with this person, and at first I was upset because I thought I wouldn't be in a group with him. I hadn't expected that to happen. But then somehow I ended up in his group after all. It was so weird. I didn't really understand how it happened. But it did...like my thinking about it so much made it really so."

Many people have this kind of experience of pushing the universe, so to speak, and then it's as if the world responds and they end up getting what they want. They have to ask for what they want very clearly; they have to think about it, and that seems to affect the outcome in the future. They see what they want in future time in the here and now, and that process helps to create the future they want.

Differences in Abilities to Affect and Perceive the Future

Although everyone has this ability to influence what happens in the universe and to pick up information about what may happen because of these interconnections, people have differences their ability to do this.

First, some people are obviously more powerful than others. So when they make a decision, they are better able to exert the force to make it happen. Also some people can do more to lead or organize others to affect things and get what they want. Some people have more willpower or a greater sense of commitment, so they are better able to concentrate, focus, and see something through. And others have more skills and talents in a particular area. What happens in the future can depend on such qualities.

Secondly, it's also important to realize that your own goals for the future intersect with the goals that other people have. You may have a certain control over what happens through what you think and how you act in response to your views. But you are also intersecting with other people who have their own conceptions of the probable future that they would like, and they have their own skills, talents, and powers which they bring to the creation of the future. At times your desires for a certain probable future will operate in tandem, and that will facilitate the occurrence of that probable future for everyone. But if your goals are different, your relative powers will affect the outcome. It's like a balance scale. The greater the weight on one side in terms of the powers, abilities, and skills of the person or persons committed to a particular future, the more likely that future will occur as compared to one where the committed powers, abilities, and skills of those seeking that future are less.

And thirdly, some people are more sensitive than others in picking up what the probable future may bring and therefore responding accordingly to faciliate, deflect, or adapt to that expected future. In some cases, people have certain natural sensivies that they are born with, so they may have an advantage to start. At the same time, these are abilities you can develop, such as by working with the techniques suggested in this book.

Using Your Knowing to Sense What Will Happen

A key to being sensitive about the future is developing your sense of knowing, so you will be more accurate in picking up what the probable future is likely to bring.

Getting That Feeling of Knowing

The feeling of knowing is hard to define (though we'll be talking about it at more length in Chapter 9). It's basically just an intuitive sense that something is so, and when applied to picking up information about the future, it's an intuitive sense that something will most certainly occur. Very often that intuitive sense proves to be correct and you can further refine it to increase your chances of being accurate.

The way to do this is to notice when you have that very intense feeling of knowing that something will happen. Then, see if it does. You'll find that certain qualities of this feeling are associated with your being accurate, while others are associated with the event not happening after all. Since everyone is different and experiences this sense of knowingness in different ways, you'll have to check out the qualities of knowingness that are right on for you, and those which you experience when you are wrong. You can use the feelings associated with what's correct as your guide.

For example, I have had the experience of knowing which is associated with a complete clarity and feeling of calm assurance for me. I remember this happening very vividly once when I first entered the field of designing games, going back over a decade ago. I had designed one small puzzle, and I had a very intense feeling of knowing it was going to be accepted by a company. In fact, the feeling was so sharp and clear, that when someone from the company called to say they were going to produce it, I simply said: "Thank you. I was sure you would." It was so clear to me that the company was going to produce it; when they called, I already knew.

Testing Your Own Accuracy

When is your own feeling of knowing accurate? When is it not? To find out, you might try testing yourself to see how accurate you are when you have these feelings of knowing about something happening in the future. You can discover how likely it is that your feeling of knowing is correct by keeping track when something happens and when it doesn't.

For example, pick out some common event you can get some immediate feedback about, such as before you arrive home think about how many calls there will be on your answering machine. Or imagine how many people have written to you about a particular project. Notice how certain you feel about your future projections, and be aware of how that certainty feels for you. When you get home, check the results and notice the feelings associated with your hits and your misses.

Reaffirming Your Accuracy When Things Go Wrong

Another way to reaffirm your ability to know and to refine your accuracy is to notice what happens when you feel you know something but don't pay attention to that knowing. In the one case, you get a strong sensation that you shouldn't do something, but then you do it, or you feel very strongly you should act, but then you don't. In either case, the results can reaffirm your knowing and suggest you should follow it, because when you don't do so, things may often go wrong.

For example, one time I went to a convenience mailing company with a package to go to my agent in Europe, and I had a strong feeling that there was going to be a problem with this package. I felt certain it either wouldn't get there or there would be a long delay. And yet I pushed these feelings aside and went ahead with the mailng, because I was very rushed at the time and I felt like I didn't want to be bothered taking the package to another place. So I simply filled in the customs form and handed it to the agent, feeling these trepidations about what would happen, yet trying to ignore them.

Two days later the package came back to me because the agent had used the wrong customs form. So I had a confirmation about my reservations. Even so, I took the package back to this company for remailing, since the package already had $40 in postage on it and I still felt I had no time to take the package anywhere else. So I filled out a new customs form and sent it off. As it turned out, the package eventually did get there but there was a five week delay, and for weeks I carried around with me the feeling that the package hadn't arrived yet. But finally those feelings lightened, and right around the time they did the local representative of my European agent called to say the package had finally arrived. So the experience helped to serve as a confirmation for my perceptions that things were going to go wrong.

In another case, a man at one of my workshops reported that he had a strong feeling that he shouldn't go down an alley on a particular street. But he did anyway, because he was late and this was a shortcut. Unfortunately he was mugged, suggesting that he should have trusted and listened to his feeling of what would happen; now he pays more attention to what he feels.

On the other hand, people who have listened to these inner warnings have frequently found they were quite correct. Sometimes people have cancelled flights at the last minute because they had a feeling telling them "Don't get on that plane." And later the plane crashed. In fact, there have been some studies showing there were more cancellations on planes that crashed than those that didn't, suggesting perhaps some people may be listening to that sense of knowing and not taking the flight. The data is only suggestive, but it does support the value of learning to listen to your feelings of knowing about what may happen. At times this listening can be very critical. It can help you avoid some everyday hassles (like mailing a package that will get lost or delayed), and who knows, it may even save your life.

Michael, who developed many of these shamanic techniques, had numerous experiences like this when he was working with an ambulance company. The company went regularly to some very dangerous locations, so he was in a situation where it was important for him to pay attention to his feelings about what might happen, and sometimes he didn't listen and would soon discover that he should have. Or if he did listen, he would get confirmation that he would have experienced something negative if he did not.

In one case, as the driver was about to leave, he got a sudden feeling there would be danger ahead. But he pushed the feelings aside and didn't say anything. Later on that run, he and the driver stopped and encountered some men with guns who threatened them. In the end the men put down their guns and drove off. Had Michael said something, the driver could have changed their route so they would have avoided the potential danger Michael was picking up.

Another similar instance was described in Chapter 2 where Michael had a sudden feeling to "Leave this place right now, because something bad is going to happen," and he quickly moved away. A few seconds later, when somebody stepped in his place to get a newspaper, he was shot.

The feelings that you should or shouldn't do something because otherwise you may encounter danger or things may go wrong can often be quite accurate. Unfortunately, we often only realize this when we do or don't do what we shouldn't and the prediction comes true. Or perhaps we don't act but someone else does, and we see them suffer what might be our fate.

Trusting Your Feelings of Knowing

It is important to trust those feelings of knowing what will happen when they seem very strong and clear. You have to learn to be discerning (see Chapter 10 on how to develop this ability) because when you look ahead, your ability to know how accurate your vision is can help you decide what to do about the information you are picking up.

You have to be careful to discriminate, because when you think about the future you can imagine all sorts of probable and not so probable futures. So some of the things you pick up may be quite accurate while others are less so. However, the more you do this—the more you learn how to discern when your feelings are right on and get that sense of "Yes, this is accurate and this means I should go with this," or the sense that "No, this is just extraneous information I should ignore," and the more you will know what to do with the information you pick up.

Knowing Your Own Power to Influence the Future

You should also take into consideration your own power to influence the future, when you do pick up information about a probable future and think the information you are getting is reasonably accurate. This is important because sometimes you can influence things if you would prefer a particular outcome, but sometimes the other forces leading to that future are more powerful. So in some cases it may be fine to change things if you want to, but in other cases it may be better to leave things as they are. Or you may not have a lot of options since the future course is already set in motion. The process is a little bit like knowing where you stand and what your likely strength is relative to everyone else in playing poker. The good player knows when to play, when to fold, and when to hold. When you are playing from strength you can pretty much do what you want to shape the future. But when you're feeling weak relative to the forces leading towards a certain outcome, it's best to adapt to whatever you see coming or move out of the way. Otherwise, if you try to make changes when you don't have sufficient strangth to do so, you could experience a bad effect.

Michael and his friends experienced that kind of situation once when they were going to take a trip into the desert. They had all their ritual equipment with them and were feeling very powerful when they sensed that there might be a storm coming. They said to themselves, "That's alright. We're powerful shamans. We can go out there and not let it bother us." However, needless to say, the storm came up and they kept trying to use powerful techniques to make it go away, but nothing worked.

Sometimes you can lose sight of the larger picture. So you have to be aware that even if you have learned to work with powerful energies and have more control as a result of these techniques, you still have limitations and must recognize them. You sometimes have to recognize that a probable future is so likely that you cannot alter reality. It's like the case of encountering a storm. At times, you know it's about to break and then you have to take protection against it. It's not something you can confront or fight.

Learning to Trust Your Own Knowing About the Future

You also need to develop a trust in your own knowing about what will happen, so you don't let the beliefs and perceptions of others who may feel differently disturb you or distract you from what you consider a proper course. To take the storm analogy again, there are times when there are storm warnings but the storm may or may not come to the area. And even though most people are reacting with fear, their perception may not be appropriate. It may be fine to be prepared, but trust that inner knowing too.

An example of this occurred when I was back in New York. There were hurricane warnings and everyone seemed to be getting into a state of near panic. People were going home early from work; some stations had a running commentary on the storm watch, and cars were quickly heading out of the city or getting off the streets. Even the person I was staying with was becoming paranoid, since he kept trying to reach his girlfriend who lived near the shore to urge her to stay with him through the storm. And yet, despite it all, this concern with the storm didn't bother me. I had this strong feeling that we weren't going to get hit with the hurricane after all, so I tuned all the fear and paranoia out. I stayed inside to be sure, yet I felt calm and confident it would blow away. And it did. The hurricane simply hit harmlessly off shore.

So sometimes even though other people may become very upset about something, you may pick up that it may not happen. If that feeling is really strong, perhaps go with that. Leave yourself a margin of safety if necessary, yet listen to your feelings too. You may often be right on, even though everyone around you is behaving in a way that suggests you are wrong.

Tuning into the Present to Get Insight About the Future

How do we know what we know about the future? Sometimes we know because we have become more aware of what is happening in the present, and this present event will lead to or is a sign of a probable future soon to come. Sometimes we have this awareness unconsciously and we do not even realize that we are aware. Instead, this awareness translates into the feeling that we think something is about to happen. Yet, at other times we recognize what we are seeing and know that we know.

Sometimes people or animals get a strong sense that an earthquake is going to happen soon and then it does. In this case, they may get this feeling because they are picking up energies or changes in energies in the present which precede the earthquake, such as a barely perceptible build-up in tension in the earth.

Likewise, if you are really sensitive you may be able to pick these things up. When you do, you may think you are picking up something about the future, when in fact you are picking up some advance information that is going to translate into a future event. And then your own feelings or perceptions interpret that as a future event, too.

So, whatever your source of future information—a projection into the future or a more perceptive awareness of present events tending to produce a probable future—you can develop your sensitivity to perceive and know more. Then you can use that knowing to prepare for what lies ahead, make decisions about what to do, or go with what's happening, get out of the way, or work for change. The more you know, the better you can take advantage of that probable future and make the possibilities work for you.

Applying Your Knowledge About the Future in Everyday Life

Your insights into the future can be especially valuable in a number of key ways. You can plan ahead. You can become better aware of future trends. You can assess what is likely to happen and decide if that's what you want. You can overcome present fears that probably have no basis in future reality. You can adapt and flow with what's happening. You can work to change the probable future if you don't like it. Or if you do, you can work to increase the likelihood of its happening. More specifically, here are the kinds of things you can do.

• Planning Ahead

One obvious result of knowing what is likely to happen is you can plan for it. If you foresee a recession coming, you can save funds now to get through it. If you see your own job coming to an end, you can look in advance for another. Or if you foresee a future trend, you can perhaps take advantage of that knowledge to launch a new successful product catering to that need. And in your personal life, you can use what you pick up to similarly plan. For example, if you perceive that a particular road will be crowded on your way to a vacation spot, you can take another route. Or if you pick up that someone else will be at a certain event, you can likewise be ready if you want to meet that person.

Yet sometimes people might raise the question: Why look ahead to see what may happen if I'm involved in a situation where I have control and can already plan in advance? Why look into the future as an extra step? Why not start planning right now? One man raised this question at a workshop. He pointed out that he had often used treasure mapping to plot out what he wanted to get in the future, without trying to think about what the future was likely to bring first. He also wondered about how future thinking could help him rent his two apartments any faster than simply deciding the type of tenant he wanted to get and putting in an ad for that. As he stated:

"Why look and see into the future...If you do something like treasure mapping, you can ask yourself, 'What kind of tenant do I want?' and do all kinds of visualizations to focus on this tenant. You have a lot of control over that...So why do I need to look ahead and see what kind of tenant might show up?...Why shouldn't I just map out what I want and seek to get that kind of person now?"

In some cases, of course, advance planning can work just fine. You don't need to look ahead into the future, since if you do what you usually do (such as placing an ad for a tenant) the outcome will be fairly predictable (getting a few responses and renting the place as usual). On the other hand, looking ahead might give you some useful information which you can use in modifying what you usually would do now. For instance, in looking ahead, the man with the tenants might pick up that there is going to be a downswing in the economy, making it more difficult to get tenants in the future. So maybe he should change his usual requirements for month to month tenants and require a year's lease, so he is more likely to get a long-term tenant.

Looking ahead into the future can be a way of supplementing current planning. You can do this planning without thinking about the future, or alternatively you can take what you see in the future into account. If the results would be the same in both cases, you may not need to think about the future in doing your planning, so there's no need for that extra step. In other cases, the results might be significantly different, so that future projection might be very useful in helping you plan ahead—then you can take into consideration both what you know and want now, and what you pick up about the probable future that lies ahead.

It's up to you to choose the best approach for you. In some cases it may be more efficient to go ahead and set your goals and plan how you are going to go about achieving them. But in other cases, it helps to add another step to the process of thinking about what you want. So you can look ahead and see what's likely to happen. And then you can adjust your plans accordingly to take that probable future into account.

- *Becoming Aware of and Responding to Future Trends*

Another advantage of future projection is you can become more aware of future trends and shifts. This way you get the larger picture of what is likely to happen and you can take this into consideration in your current and long-term planning.

In some cases you can pick up this information just by reading the newspapers and being aware. Then you can get even further insights by combining this present information with the unconscious perceptions you pick up from projecting yourself ahead in future time.

For example, right now we appear to be in the beginning of a new shift in consciousness and values. There's a reaction to the materialistic values of the eighties, and a greater interest now in the more spiritual side of life. There's more interest in creativity. In many ways this swing parallels what happened about seven years ago when there was a shift to a more conservative economic philosophy, though now it's a more liberal swing. By projecting yourself into the future you may be able to get some deeper insights into where this shift is likely to go, and therefore plan for this probable future accordingly.

• Recognize Your Alternative Choices If You Let the Future Happen or If You Act

You can also use future projection to become more aware of your possible choices. For example, if you look ahead you may see one probable future occurring, if everything continues along just the way it is going now. Alternatively, you may see other possibilities if you think about the possible changes you might make now.

Take the rental situation described earlier. On the one hand, the man can look ahead and think about what is likely to happen if he doesn't do anything differently from what he usually does. In this case, if he is in a certain part of town and this is a certain time of year and he places his usual ad or notices, he is likely to get a certain type of tenant. And if this is a normally slow period, it is likely to take him a little bit longer than usual.

On the other hand, if the man looks ahead and thinks, 'This is not the type of tenant I really want; I'd like to get someone who is better, more stable, or will pay more rent', then he can think about what he might do to change what he is doing now, in order to change the probable future.

• Getting Your Information from Different Sources

When you do get this information about the future, recognize that it comes from various sources. When you project yourself ahead, your inner self or unconscious doing the projection essentially synthesizes it all together, so you get a holistic picture of what is likely to happen. The more information you have from various sources the more accurate you can be once you have developed your awareness and sensitivity.

You may get much of your inputs from the newspapers you read and the people you talk to. You may get it from the radio and TV. Using this information as a backdrop, you can project yourself ahead. Just let your mind go and see where it takes you, as you move ahead three months, six months, or whatever, to see what is happening in your own backyard or around the world.

As you think about the future, pay attention to what is happening now. It will help you be more accurate when you future project.

• *Overcome Present Fears by Assessing the Future Realistically*

You can also use your perception of the probable future to help calm yourself and overcome present fears that are not realistic. For example, one woman used to become extremely frightened when she traveled in an airplane. She had to go places so she continued to fly. But she would walk onto the plane in a state of extreme agitation, and when plane ran into problems, such as being tossed by a storm or encountering lightning, she would grow rigid with fear. When she started working with the future she learned how to calm down, since she realized nothing would happen to her and there was nothing to fear. As she explained:

> "When I got on an airplane I would be frightened to the point of panic... But then I began to think, 'No, now wait a minute, I have personally seen my own future and I'm not dead. Therefore, I'm not going to die today'...And as soon as I realized that, the whole fear just washed away. I felt free of the fear."

If you develop the habit of looking to the future and see a successful outcome, then you don't have to be frightened needlessly about something. You can come to realize that your fear is irrational; it has no basis in reality, and by having this larger picture you don't have to be afraid.

• *Adapting and Flowing With What's Happening*

Knowing about the likely future can also help you to adapt and flow with whatever is happening when you encounter a probable future over which you don't have much control. This is the kind of situation when you look ahead and ask things like: Are we likely to have a war? Is there likely to be a depression or a recession? Is the stock market likely to go up or down? You don't have much control over what will happen, because the individual decisions of so many people are involved. And you don't have much control over a powerful natural event, such as a storm.

But whatever you see, if you can sense the momentum of where things are likely to go, you can flow with it. The time to do this is when you sense that something is so inevitable, it is most probably going to happen. Just go along with it and accept it. It's like riding with the wave, rather than fighting it. And if you can sense where the swell is going to rise in advance, you can catch that wave and ride it like a good surfer does.

At times you can pick up that the outcome is likely to be inevitable if you continue to flow with things the way they are now, but there is still the possibility for change if you wish. So you can choose whether to go with the flow of events now in motion or to act to make a change. This kind of choice is often possible when you are picking up messages about a probable future in a social or work environment.

For instance, at work you may get some cues from other people that they like certain things you are doing, but don't like others. So if you keep acting that way and look ahead, you can see the inevitable outcome—either staying stuck in your present position or getting laid off when the time comes. If you choose, you can keep doing what you are doing and allow that probable future to happen and prepare accordingly by accepting your current position or steeling yourself to look for another job. Or you can choose to shift that future by altering your role at work, which will lead to another probable outcome such as a promotion, which is probably what you prefer.

By developing this sensitivity to probable futures you can either adapt to those that are virtually inevitable or choose whether to flow with or try to change those which are not; the successful shaman knows how to use power as appropriate to either adapt when necessary or to work for change. Also, being sensitive and discerning can help you know how to respond and what path to choose.

• Making Changes

Once you pick up information about the future that suggests that things are turning adversely or an event may occur which you don't want, you can think about changes to either adjust or alter the course of events. You can change yourself, the way you live. You can move. You can do things differently or do some different things. Suppose you see difficult times ahead. Maybe you could start saving or storing up food now. Or if you see a growing interest in spiritual things and are thinking of starting a new business, maybe this might be a direction in which to go.

The point is that your insights about the future can help you decide if and how to change in the here and now, depending on whether you expect that probable future to occur or hope to do something to change it.

• Influencing Future Events

In some cases you have the power to change the future yourself by looking ahead, considering the alternative futures, assessing their varying possibilities, and deciding what it is that you would like to have happen. You can then take the appropriate actions to try to influence the future to happen in a certain way. In this way, you can exercise some degree of future control, based on your own power and abilities, the probability of the future you want to affect, and the amount of effort needed to change it.

In other words, you often have the power yourself to change the future probabilities. You can do this when you pick up something about what's likely to happen in the future, and then in some cases, you can push that probable future in one direction or the other to make it more or less probable. Sometimes you may have that control yourself, though in other cases you need to join with a number of people to do this. It depends on the power of that future event and the critical mass needed to affect it.

One way to think of the process is to see observing the future as a little bit like being in a movie. You sit in the theater and as you look ahead, you watch a movie reel unwind. As the projectionist of this movie, you can decide if you like what's playing or if you want to change the movie and put on another reel. You can also decide if you want to speed it up or slow it down. You have all this control because, as the projectionist, you can control the projector and what films go in it. And you can speed ahead in the film to see what's going to happen later on in the reel; then if you don't like it you can wind that film back or switch the film. The film can be compared to your life, just speeded up in time. For instance, 15 minutes of film might be equivalent to 3 months ahead, 30 minutes to 6 months, an hour to a year. So you just take your film and fast forward it to some time in the future and decide what you want to see.

After you envision what might be probable, you have the power to help make that happen, so you can actively play a part in creating your own future. When you do, it can be difficult to tell whether you have looked ahead to see a probable future or whether you have thought about and planned now for what you would like to see happen. In other words, are you seeing a probable future that exists now, or are you, by your own imagination, creating a goal you want in the future? Whichever it is, it doesn't matter. In either case, by looking ahead to see the possibilities or imagining the possibilities now, you can work towards the one you want and make it more likely to happen.

I had that experience when I had to find a new place quickly. I had a month to month arrangement with my landlord that looked like it was going to go on forever, because my landlord was living in Hawaii and had no intention of returning to the house where I lived in Oakland that had once been her home. However, because of a series of unusual circumstances, she suddenly had to return. Briefly, what happened is I had rented a room to a student, and because of the extra car on the street, one of the neighbors called the Housing Authority. As it turned out, my landlord had illegally turned her house into two flats, and the area was zoned for one-family houses. The investigator from the Housing Authority soon found out this was the case, and somebody had to move. My landlord tried to fight the Housing Authority, but when she found she couldn't, she decided to return from Hawaii and move in herself. So suddenly I had a month to move.

But by looking ahead into the future, I found it easy to imagine where I saw myself living in the next few months. In fact, through this process, I perceived myself living in a certain part of San Francisco, and I even saw the block where I would live. Acting on this vision of the future, I proceeded to look in that area. Within a few hours I had found a new place. In fact, I drove by the place where I ultimately ended up living only a few hours after the rental sign went up, and I was the second person to look at it. The first people took the flat on top and I took the first floor flat. It was almost exactly what I saw in my vision of a probable future which I imagined about two weeks before.

Similarly, when you look ahead, if you like what you see happening, you can act to make that more likely to happen or make it happen more quickly. If you see a certain job in your future, you can start taking courses which will help you land that kind of job. Or if you are already taking these courses, maybe you can take more courses or finish the program you are involved in more quickly to make that future occur more quickly.

If you don't like what you see as a probable future, then you can think about what you can change which you are doing now to make that future less likely to occur.

The Power of Your Own Attitude to Affect the Future

Much of the power to influence the future yourself comes from your own attitude, which you can control. You can mobilize your attitude to help you get what you want when you see a probable future you would like to have.

As is commonly stated, by having a more positive attitude you can create more positive experiences in your life. I noticed this very dramatically myself. When I was growing up in New York, I came from a very negative environment. The people in my family always seemed to expect the worst to happen. So whenever I talked about things that I would like to see happen, I would inevitably be put down. My mother would say something like: "Oh, that's not going to happen," or "Why do you want to do that? Why do you think you can do it?" So there were many things I was afraid to try. I cut off many probable futures I wanted that way.

But after I participated in some spiritual growth programs, I learned that we can reprogram ourselves to think differently, and once I started to look at things in a positive, hopeful way, I found that all sorts of positive things started happening in my own life. I discovered new opportunities and I found I could do pretty much whatever I saw ahead and wanted in the future. I believed I could do it; then I acted on that belief in ways that would make that future even more likely. And the result was that generally the desired probable future occurred. As a freelance writer I would look ahead, think of a new project I wanted to do, and suddenly all sorts of things would happen to make that project possible. I would find the people or information I needed or I would find financial backers if I needed that.

Likewise, you have that power to create the future you want. It starts with looking ahead and imagining a probable future or perhaps seeing alternative probabilities. It may be that you are seeing something that is more or less likely; it may be that you are seeing something you want. In either case, you can take some action to increase the probability of that happening, and a key factor in the effectiveness of your action is your own attitude. Have a positive attitude and act with conviction and belief that you can succeed and you'll increase your own chances of doing so. For as you look into the future, what you see is never fixed or certain, only more or less probable. So you have the power to some degree to influence those future events.

Just think of your attitude like the fuel in a car. With the right attitude, you've got the fuel you need to keep the car going. In turn, when you see the probable future you want ahead, you can drive your car in that direction. And the faster you go, the more power you have. And the more other factors in your environment are favorable, the more likely and the more quickly you'll get there. The probable future you see just gives you the direction in which to go.

Chapter Eight

Working With Future Projections

Suppose you want to get some information on the probable future for yourself. The previous chapter discussed some of the basic principles involved in getting this information. This chapter describes how to use the technique of future projection to get information you can use in guiding your own life.

Getting and Using Information on the Future

A good time to use future projection is when there's something that you aren't sure about or something you want and you want to get some information on what is likely to happen. To get this information you simply look ahead—one month, two months, three months, or to whatever time period is critical for you. This will give you some insights into what is probable at that future time, given all the circumstances that exist right now, so you can decide whether this is a future you want or not. Then you can act accordingly to either influence it to happen or to prevent it.

When you do this projection it's important that you do not try to figure out what is going to happen logically. You may already have certain information about the situation and even certain desires about how you would like the situation to turn out. When you project, you can be consciously aware of this information or of your desires. But then you want to let these feelings go, so that in projection your unconsciousness or inner self pulls everything together in a kind of a synthesis as it looks ahead.

When you project into some period in the future, you should let go of your conscious mind and let the scene play itself out. As you see the scene happen you can decide if you want that thing to happen or not. If so, you can do what you can to make it more likely; if not, you can act to reduce the chances.

The Importance of Keeping Your Logical Mind Out of the Process

At times, when you do this projection process, your logical mind may try to interfere. If so, it's important to push it aside, because it can prevent you from getting the clear insights and the sense of knowing that you can get from your inner self or unconscious mind. Your logical mind can prevent the kind of automatic synthesis that occurs to pull everything together.

This interference can occur because your logical mind may start trying to analyze or criticize what you are experiencing, and that can short-circuit the experience. For example, one woman who began projecting to six months ahead suddenly found herself thinking about what month that must be and what would logically happen at that time of year ("Oh, that's May, so it must be warming up and we'll probably be thinking about our vacation then...."), and soon she was analyzing the future, not experiencing it.

What you want to do when you project is let your logical mind go and just get a rough sense of where you are as you look ahead. You don't want to worry about being totally accurate. Instead, what you're really trying to do is get a global picture or sensation of what things are going to be like at a certain time ahead. So you simply travel ahead to that time and get an experience of being there. You're not *thinking* about what it's like to be there. Rather you're *feeling* yourself there in the future in present time.

Projecting Yourself Into a Probable Future

When you project yourself into a probable future you can use any number of techniques to get there. A visualization of traveling ahead is one way, though you can also simply step into the future or feel yourself there.

You can also use any number of visualizations to step ahead—whatever symbols or images work for you. The following visualization is designed to suggest one approach, but feel free to adapt it or use other imagery that you prefer. You may also find that as you work with future projection you need less and less preparation to step into the future. So instead of having to use a visualization to get you there, you can simply think: "I'd like to foresee the future," and look ahead. But initially, a visualization or other form of preparation can help you get there. The following visualization is one possible approach you can use.

> To experience your own probable future, start by getting very relaxed. Then you can look ahead three months, six months, a year, two years, and five years, and notice the probable futures you see. As you'll notice, there are alternative possibilities, and as you pay attention to them, you can think about the possible changes you might make in your own life in order to bring about the probable future you most prefer.
>
> To do this, you can either lie down or get relaxed as you are sitting down. First, concentrate on just relaxing. Perhaps focus on your breathing for a few moments to calm down.

When you feel very relaxed, imagine yourself as a little point of consciousness. Then, as you prefer, you can imagine that a laser is projecting forward from your head in future time. Or perhaps see yourself getting on a train or going through a tunnel into the future. The further you go along this beam, along the tracks, or into the tunnel, the further you will go in future time.

To start your future journey, just imagine yourself projecting out along the beam, or along the tracks, or into the tunnel, and you'll notice there are little markings along the way. The markings say one month, two months, three months.

Imagine yourself going ahead and soon you arrive at the three month marker. When you do, look around and see what's happening. You have looked ahead in your own life three months, and you can see what is happening right now.

All you have to do is look to your right or your left, and you will see a movie screen or stage where this event is happening. Take some time to look and get a clear picture.

When you are done, get back on your beam or on the train or go back in the tunnel. Then travel further along this route, and this time get off at the marking that says six months. At this six month marking, see what is happening now. Again, you'll see a scene on the stage or on the screen in front of you. What you see might be a continuation of the same scene you just observed, or it could be another one happening six months from now.

Let that image of the future go and get back on your beam again. Or get back on the train or travel further down the tunnel.

This time, travel onward to a time one year ahead and get off there. Again see the stage, see the screen in front of you, and see some more incidents happening in your life.

Now let those experiences go and get back on the beam (or on the train or continue on through the tunnel). Now once again travel ahead in time, and now experience yourself being two years in the future. And again look at the screen or at the stage and see what's happening. Just let it happen, whatever you see.

We'll make one last stop. So get back on the beam again (or return to your journey on the train or through the tunnel). Again project yourself ahead even further into the future. This time, see yourself ahead five years, and again look on the screen or on the stage, and know that this is what is happening.

Now, get back on the beam again (or return to the train or the tunnel). Now what I'd like you to do this time is to realize you can go back and forth anywhere you want in time until you arrive at exactly the place you want to be.

Now pick out a particular space that you've already gone to before. It may be five years, two years, one year, six months, three months. Go back there, and look again at the stage or screen which you see there.

Looking at the stage or screen, call forth the image of the probable future you have already seen and recognize that this is just one probable future. There may be others which represent alternative possibilities.

Now take that one particular time and imagine other possible situations that are happening. You can see them unfolding now on the screen or on the stage.

As you watch, realize that you have a choice. For you can choose among the various futures that are more or less probable.

Imagine now that you are making that choice, and then think about what it is you need to do to bring about that particular future. Focus on the future you want. Be aware of the future you don't want. And think about the kinds of changes you need to make to make what you want occur. These could be changes in yourself. They could be changes involving someone else. There might be changes in your vocation, in your work, in your activities, in your way of life, or any number of things. Just start thinking about the kinds of changes you might make.

When you feel ready, get back on your beam (or return to the train or your tunnel). Let your consciousness be drawn back to the center of your head. Pull back your beam, or turn your train around or go back down the tunnel.

When you are ready, open your eyes and come back into the room.

Common Experiences in Conscious Projection into the Future

Different people may have different ways of doing these projections or they may gain insights about the future in different ways. This is fine. Use the images and channels for gaining information that work best for you.

In one workshop a woman visualized the laser beam as a measuring tape, which could snap forward and back. Instead of traveling back and forward along the beam, she simply pulled in and let out the tape.

Another woman didn't see things. Instead, she got impressions. In describing a visit to her house, she reported:

"I didn't visualize things. I got impressions, feelings like my house is real unsettled now...I talked to the landlord about some changes...And I thought about what it would be like in six months, about May or June. And I felt like it was a stable peaceful time. But I didn't see anything. I just felt like I was looking into outer space. It was very dark...And it just went on and on. I didn't see anything, I just got impressions of what my life would be like. I experienced the emotional tone of it, but not any pictures."

A man reported that he usually got a mixture of images and feelings. As he stated: "There have been some things I've actually seen, but I get more the emotional content."

Such differences are common because people have different ways of seeing or experiencing things. Some will get more visual information, others more feeling content, still others will be more likely to pick up information through hearing sounds or thoughts. You can train yourself to improve in any of these areas, but some people are more naturally gifted in a particular area.

Sometimes you will also have a strong sense of knowing when you look ahead, because some probable future will seem so extremely certain. If so, it just means that future is much more probable than others, and perhaps you should work on achieving that particular future. But like other futures, it is always subject to change, though perhaps less so than the probable futures where you don't get this knowing feeling.

Choosing Alternatives to a Likely Future

One of the most valuable uses of the previous technique is seeing what your likely future is if you keep going as you are going. Then you can use that as a point of comparison for examining other probable, but less likely futures, to see what you might have to do to change.

When one woman did this in a workshop, she saw ahead a fairly dull routine life if she kept doing what she was doing now. Then she saw a less likely but more desirable alternative, and she recognized what she would need to do to bring it about. As she described the experience:

> "At three months, I saw myself being in school and having the same girlfriends and working and puttering around on the same projects. In six months, I saw myself in Hawaii out on the beach, and not going to school. In two years, I saw myself with my kids. They're not there now, so that was nice. And in five years I found myself married and still going to school, and I felt it was all very boring.
>
> "When I thought about what I would really like, I was a movie producer writing wild scripts and having people help me do it. So the future I really want is being a movie producer and writing scripts and everyone helping.
>
> "And then I thought about the steps I would have to do. I thought about how boring and slow it is going to a regular kind of college. So then I thought about going to an artist's college, and I thought about the things that I would have to do.
>
> "So I realized I could passively go along in conventional school like I am now and follow the leader. Or I can do something else. I can't do both. I have to give one up and choose."

Through future projection, you can become aware of the different possibilities and can make decisions about what to do. In deciding, it is helpful to recognize that one possibility is more probable than in the others, since it is a likely outcome of patterns and trends which are already in existence now. So if you make a change, the probable outcome may be less probable. But if you put your efforts and intensity into getting it, that will increase the probability of the alternative happening. It's up to you to decide if you want to make that effort. Something which is a lot less probable now can happen if you make the appropriate change.

Prepare for the Unexpected

Sometimes when you do this exercise you may have some surprises, because you'll see something you don't expect. It may happen, and by seeing it now you can prepare ahead for that possibility or take some action to make it more likely to happen. One woman at a workshop reported:

> "I had some surprises. I saw the probable future, but it wasn't anything I expected at all...At six months I saw a whole bunch of Germans, a German family... And they were all lined up, and I realized this is a bunch of my in-laws, which I haven't met yet. And it looked like we were going to meet them in Frankfurt, so I realized we may be taking an unexpected trip."

Also, sometimes you may experience things being very spacey or undefined in the future because there is a lot of uncertainty about what may happen. In that case, it may be helpful to think about what you can do to make things more certain, if you feel uncomfortable with the uncertainties that lie ahead.

Dealing with Fears About the Future

Another issue that sometimes comes up is feeling some fear about the future. You may not want to look at something yet, or you may be disturbed by the uncertainty you see ahead. If so, pull back. You don't have to look at a probable future if you don't feel ready to look at it just yet. For instance, one woman described how she felt anxious and pulled back when she stated:

> "At first I had trouble seeing, because I got scared... Everything seemed so vague...And I had a lot of apprehension about looking two or five years ahead... I think that's why I used a retractable measuring tape to go into the future....It was like I wasn't quite ready to see that far ahead, and I could easily come back."

Recognizing It May Not Be Time to See Something Yet

At times you may not be able to see ahead, not because of fear but because it's not time for you to get that information yet. Sometimes this may occur because you haven't learned enough about something yet, or it may be that you have to have some other experiences first before you are ready to move on and see what other future possibilities are probable.

For instance, one woman had an experience in thinking about the direction of her future art career. She was working with creating visionary paintings and found she could not see the images of the future paintings she was likely to do, because the images had not been given to her yet. As she explained:

> "I kept saying, 'Okay, how's my work going at this future time'...And I could see that the paintings were done and they were fine... But I couldn't see the actual paintings because they were in the other room. They were in the gallery, and I couldn't go in there... And I couldn't, because when you look, it's like cheating... because they are prophetic paintings. So I haven't gotten the paintings yet...It's like they come to me through automatic drawing, and so therefore these drawings are given. But they haven't been given yet. So I can't see them...and that's why they're in the other room."

If this happens when you are future projecting, simply acknowledge that this is something you can't know yet and later, when the time is ready, just look again.

Distinguishing Between Your Logic, Wishes, and Your Intuitive Sense of a Future Reality

Another issue that frequently comes up in doing a future projection is what is actually real, and what is coming from your logic and your wishes.

It's important to realize that in interpreting your insights about the future that both of these influences are probably operating to shape what you see. When any psychic looks ahead into the future and makes predictions, he or she is taking into consideration, to some extent, what is really happening now. But at the same time, he or she is making an intuitive leap which goes beyond logically weighing all the alternatives to come up with an estimate of what will happen in the future. By contrast, the psychic sees in a complete, holistic way, in which everything comes together into a unified vision of what lies ahead.

Thus, your own projections may be grounded to some extent in the reality you are aware of. But your projection goes off from there as you make that intuitive leap.

A similar process occurs when you have certain wishes about what you would like to see happen. You may wonder if you are picking up a real external future image or if you are picking up something because you are really wishing it is so. In truth, you could be picking up either or a combination of both. On the one hand, you may be creating your future projection because of wish fulfillment—you want certain things to happen, so you project them into the future, and that's what you see. On the other hand, you may be picking up what really is going to happen, whether or not you want it to occur.

So how do you know? How do you distinguish between what your logic thinks will happen based on present events, what your desires want to happen so you see that occur, and what will really happen? How do you know when you're creating something through your logic and your wishes, or whether it's coming to you through your intuition?

Certainly it can be hard to distinguish sometimes and it takes some experience to pick up the differences. In time you will develop this knowing or discernment so you can tell. And often you will find it doesn't matter, in that your logic or your wishes are all leading to the same place, and the probable future you think will happen or you wish for is very likely to occur.

So as you examine what you experience in a future projection, it's probably best not to worry about the source of that information, for often what you are picking up is a synthesis of insights from various sources anyway (i.e., your logic, your wishes, and your intuitive leap into future time). Rather, learn to develop and trust your knowing, which will help you determine what's more probable and what is not, whatever the source of the information.

Distinguishing Between Daydreaming and Future Projection

The process of future projection is quite different than daydreaming about the future. In daydreaming you're basically just playing and imagining things, and often you know you're just fantasizing about the future without expecting it to be real.

In future projection you are trying to get a real experience of what it's probably going to be like in the future. You are seriously looking ahead to see what the future is likely to bring, rather than letting your mind drift, and perhaps thinking about the future in a casual, exploratory way. You are trying to get a sense of what is really probable.

The experience of the two processes is very different. In daydreaming you have a sense that you are just playing with your mind. By contrast, in future projection you're trying to experience really knowing that this is what the future is going to be like if you keep going the way you are going now, and you're trying to look at alternative probable futures that you might achieve if you make some changes. In future projection there's a different commitment, a different seriousness in how you are looking at the future. It's the difference between taking a vacation where you relax on the beach and learn basket weaving in Maui and taking some time out to really think about what you are doing with your life now and in the future.

Future Projection to Get Information on World Events

Besides using future projection to get information that directly affects you, you can also use future projection to get insights on world events generally. You can do this on your own or, if you wish, you can engage in a collective projection with others where you share and modify your visions.

When you do these future predictions, it's a good idea to keep a record of them, so that later on you can check back and see how accurate you were. When you do check, you may find that you had a greater feeling of certainty about your predictions that turn out to be accurate. This will help you pay attention to when you have that feeling of certainty in the future.

Also, note that sometimes shared group predictions may turn out to be more accurate. This is the case because the process works much like the Delphi process, which some futurists and scientists use in thinking about what the future may bring. In this process, a group of people make individual predictions about what they think will happen in the future. Then they get feedback on the predictions of everyone else in the group. After this, they get a chance to go back and make more predictions, and they can modify their original predictions based on what they have heard others say. The result is that members of the group often end up with a concensus of predictions that tend to be more accurate, because everybody has a chance to share their predictions and modify them according to what they have heard from others.

The following exercise is designed to guide you into the future so you can look at various world events. If you are working on your own, just pay attention to the instructions in regular type. If you are working with a group, add in the instructions in brackets. In either case, just consider this approach a guide, and feel free to modify it as you wish—or once you feel ready, just step into the future when you wish without using any guide to get you there.

Start by becoming relaxed and calm. What you'll be doing soon is making predictions. You'll hear that it's a certain time period, and you should experience whatever predictions come into your mind. (And then we'll share them). Then you'll make some more predictions.

For now, relax. Focus on your breathing going in and out. If it feels helpful to you, imagine yourself as a point of consciousness again and see it projecting outward along a horizontal plane. Or if you prefer, use any other image to see yourself moving into the future. Perhaps see yourself traveling down a tunnel into the future or riding on a train going into future time. Or perhaps you are turning on the TV news and hearing news of the future. Feel free to search your own symbol bank for images of the future, and use whatever symbols or images work for you.

I'll be giving you suggestions about certain places, certain kinds of events, to take a look at the future. When you do, if you feel you don't want to look at something, feel free not to look at it. Or if you feel very sensitive to any of the problems you may notice in the world, put up your own barrier to these, so you feel very safe as you look. For example, put up a white light barrier around yourself to keep any world problems you see out of your immediate world. So you can look freely, yet feel very protected and removed.

Now, if you are experiencing yourself at a point of consciousness, focus on that, and if you see a beam going out, then you can travel along this beam. Or travel out to the future in any other way you prefer.

Then imagine that you are stopping off along this beam or path one week ahead, and look around. You'll see a screen or stage, and on it you'll see some world event that is happening now. Know that you feel very protected and safe as you look, and if something feels uncomfortable for you in the future, just imagine the screen going blank or turn it off if you don't want to look.

Now take a moment to look and see what you see. Maybe you see a newspaper or a headline flash on the screen, or perhaps see yourself sitting down tonight to watch the world news on TV. However the event comes to you, just observe.

When you are ready to see something else, if you look around in the other direction you'll see another stage or screen and you'll see another event.

As you look at the stage or screen, you see an event that's happening in another country...Take a few minutes to watch the event...

And now you are seeing something that is happening in the entertainment or show business world in the next week. Perhaps it's a famous personality or a movie event. Take a moment to see it now...

(Now, what I'd like to do is for all of you to share. Stay in your altered state of consciousness, but say aloud what you have seen.)

Now get back on the beam or the path to the future again, and now see yourself projecting ahead one month. Travel ahead, and when you feel ready to stop and step off the beam or the path, look on the screen or on the stage. And as you do, see whatever the first event is that comes to mind.

As you look you see something that's happening in the medical or health field. Take a few moments to watch this event unfold.

Still watching the screen or stage, see some event having to do with business. Maybe it's a change in the economy, a new business that has started up, an old business that has done something new. Just see it happen now.

(Once again, remain in this state of consciousness, and describe what you have seen.)

For one more time, get back on the beam or path again, and project yourself ahead six months. Take a moment to move down the beam or path six months, and then look around and see the screen or stage nearby you.

First, see whatever comes up for you now. It's an event that could be happening anywhere.

Then you notice something happening in a place that's very warm. Take a moment to see what's happening there...

Lastly, focus on something that's happening in the government or politics. It could be something local, in your city. It could be in your state capital, or maybe in Washington. Maybe it's a new person being elected, a new law being passed, a new scandal. Just look and see whatever you see.

(When you're ready, stay in this same altered state and share what you have seen with everyone else. Take turns as you do.)

Finally, what I'd like you to do is get back on your beam or on your path. And just imagine yourself going back to where you started. When you are ready, open your eyes, look around and come back into this room.

Creating Your Own Guide for Making Future Predictions

You can easily create your own guide for making future predictions by directing yourself to look ahead at various intervals into the future, such as tomorrow, 1 week, 1 month, 3 months, 6 months, 1 year. Then give yourself a suggestion to look at various categories of events, and see what you see. As in conscious projection generally, let your mind go and be receptive to whatever comes to mind.

Some common categories and typical examples of what people often see in each are the following:

—natural events (i.e. storms, earthquakes, a dry spell)
—person-to-person events (i.e. celebrity achievements and activities, acts of political figures or crime figures)
—world events (i.e., wars, treaties, economic developments, foreign relationships, major decisions, world leaders, election results, conflicts between countries, etc.)
—social problems and concerns (i.e., the plight of the homeless, current trends in crime, health problems, etc.)

Keeping Track of Your Predictions

When you make predictions about the future, keep track of them so you can test your accuracy later, and perhaps note which of your predictions you feel are more likely to be accurate (either because they seem to make more sense based on what you know now, or because you have a greater feeling of certainty about them).

If you are doing this on your own, you can keep your own list. Or if you are working with a group, perhaps one person can guide the others in a group projection experience and then write down the predictions people make as they share. Also, in working with a group, notice if two or more people come up with the same prediction. If so, it may suggest that this prediction is more likely to be accurate.

You can experiment with looking into the future in a number of ways. For example, one way is to experiment on your own from time to time and make some short term predictions. For instance, during the day imagine what the TV news is going to be that night or the next day. Or perhaps use a projection to see what the newspaper headlines are going to be the next day or week.

You might also try to keep a future file. This way, when you make some predictions you can put them on cards and file them according to when you think something is going to happen. When that date comes up you can look at your predictions for that date or about that time, so you can see if your predictions are accurate.

Also, when you do make these predictions, it is helpful to pay attention to how certain you feel, and perhaps rate your predictions according to your sense of knowing. For example, if you feel strongly that something is probably going to happen, give it a 10. If you feel something less strongly, give it a proportionately lower rating. And if you feel something very unlikely, give it the lowest rating of all. In this way you are assigning probabilities to the predictions you make.

Then when you check these predictions out, you can get a better sense of not only how accurate you are, but how accurate you think you are when you initially make your predictions. When you check, you may be surprised at how accurate you are when many of your predictions come true.

You might even try to check out your accuracy in different areas of predictions by keeping your predictions separately by category. For instance, you might separate them in terms of predictions that refer to yourself, where you have control over what happens to some degree, and to events which affect you where you don't have any control. You might also keep separate predictions that refer to your environment generally, and those that refer to world situations. Predictions about well known figures and celebrities might be still another category. Then, when you check back in your file of predictions after the event is supposed to occur you can notice if you are more accurate in predicting certain things. You may find you are, particularly when you are making predictions in an area where you already have some background information or some control yourself, for then your intuition will draw on what you already know or on what you already want to do in making a prediction about what is likely in the future.

There are all sorts of ways you can experiment with predicting the future, and as you work more with making these predictions you will generally find your predictions become more accurate, too.

Chapter Nine

Working With Your Inner Voice To Know What Your Know

When you get insights about something that is happening now or in the future, the following questions may often arise: How do you know what you know? How do you know if the insights you are getting are true or not? This chapter deals with how to recognize this knowing and learn to trust it, and how you should use that knowing in influencing your actions.

Recognizing that Inner Knowing

People describe how they experience or recognize the feeling of inner knowing in various ways. Sometimes it's like a strong and clear inner voice talking to them; sometimes it is like a bright flash of understanding, sometimes a kind of aha, which is feeling accompanied by a feeling of certainty. But commonly it's hard to put this sense of knowing into words. There's just a feeling, vision, or voice that conveys the message very strongly: "Yes, I know."

For example, one man described his experience of knowing thus:

"Well, for me, I just know it. It's just a knowing... an ah-hah sort of thing...somehow, it feels...rock solid, and I know this is it."

When asked if he could explain this sensation further, he stated:

"It's like a sudden insight that is expressed in a lot of different ways...Another thing that characterizes it is you sometimes feel a very calm steadiness...And this feeling pushes through the conscious chatter you have and you suddenly see that this feeling is correct...It's like your mind is a subway...with all these people or thoughts rushing in and out... But you see the directions and you get on the train and you go in the right direction, and you have the sense that this is the train you want to be on, so you get on it, knowing you will get there very quickly. So you feel totally certain, and there is just this intuitive sense of knowing you're right, which is so hard to describe."

Thus, this knowing is a hard-to-define feeling or sense of rightness, and the more you become sensitive to the experience that you have when you are correct, the more you will be able to pick up when you have that feeling of rightness or sense of knowing about something. Then you'll feel more confident about that sensation and be better able to go with it and do what it suggests.

At times it can be hard to distinguish this knowing or inner voice from all the usual mental chatter or dialogue going on in our heads. This dialogue or stream of thoughts gives us all sorts of information of varying levels of accuracy. However, there is a certain intensity of knowing that accompanies the information when it is accurate and it is something we sense intuitively as correct.

Perhaps one way to think of this knowing is like listening to music, which has a greater power and intensity than what we ordinarily hear. By comparison, an ordinary note may be of the same tone but may sound very flat. But these special notes have much more texture, strength, and richness, so they sound fuller, more complete. In the same way, knowing compared to ordinary perception may seem more solid and powerful, too.

Still another way to think of this knowing is as a kind of a white sound, or pure sound, which you hear in your head. Others may characterize it as the Zen mind—a kind of one-pointed, focused, yet empty mind, which contains the truth. And still others may think of this knowing as a "gut sensation," which they feel in the pit of their stomach, rather than sensing that knowing in their head.

In short, there are many different ways of conceptualizing or describing this knowing. But in essence, it's a feeling or sensation that people have when they have an insight or intuitive understanding of something. It's like a little ah-ha reaction or a light flash of comprehension, or a strong feeling that grabs you to say that something is correct or true.

Verifying When Your Knowing Is Accurate

When you do get this feeling of knowing, how do you know it is accurate? How do you develop that sense of assurance that you can trust this inner voice or knowing?

One way is by looking for signs of confirmation that reaffirm what your knowing has told you is correct. For example, you sense something is going to happen; then when it does, that's the verification for your knowing. You can even do this with fairly routine, everyday experiences. Even finding parking spaces might be a source of verification. As one man described his own experience:

> "One way I verify my knowing so I can act on it is by what happens after I get that feeling... For example, I decide to go to a likely restaurant...and it's Friday night and it's wall-to-wall traffic... But I feel this is where I want to go, and then a parking place shows up...It's like a sign to me that I ought to just park there...And that's my way of checking it out."

If things seem to go smoothly, it may be another way to reaffirm that your knowing is on target. It's as if because you know and follow that knowing, then everything you do will fall into place easily so that you achieve that goal. One man reported having this occur when he was looking for some equipment, and suddenly felt certain that he would find it in a certain store. As he explained:

> "When everything works, when everything falls into place or is easy...it seems to happen when something is leading me there...As an example of that, a couple of years ago, I was looking for a video system, camera, and portable recorder. One day I went out to two stores and I got a sense of what was on the market, and then I remembered there was a store way across town and I felt sure it would have just what I wanted.
> So I drove there, and this was the day before Christmas, so you can imagine what the traffic was like. But as I drove up, a car pulled out right in front of the store and I pulled in. Then, when I went in, the first salesman wasn't sure the store had the item, and I said, 'Well, do you have your catalog?' and when I looked through the catalog, there it was. Just what I wanted. And I asked another salesman, and he got it for me in a few minutes, and I ended up buying it and it worked beautifully...So I feel like this feeling I had was verified, because I found this parking place right away, and they had what I wanted and I bought it, and it worked fine."

Some people find their inner knowing is verified when they ignore it, and something bad which they sensed would happen actually does. They feel they shouldn't do something, but do it anyway, and then the unfavorable outcome serves to reaffirm the value of following their intuition. One man described his experience of falling and hurting himself one time when he sensed he shouldn't take a certain route, but took it anyway. As he reported:

> "I've had certain feelings, and I'd find out they were true because I ignored them...As I found, I can verify the feeling if I don't do it. For instance, there was one time when I was walking in the railway station in London and there were two ways I could go—to the right or to the left, and it looked like the same each way. But then something like a voice said, 'Don't go

down the right; but I did anyway. So I went down this tunnel, and I ended up slipping and hurting myself...

And there have been a few other times when I've done things like that—ignored that little voice, and I've slipped up."

Still another kind of verification is when an expected outcome occurs. The outcome may not happen immediately, but you have a feeling that if you do something, something else will occur. So you do it, and that outcome occurs.

I had this kind of experience myself when I had feeling that I shouldn't trust someone. This happened when I was ghostwriting for someone who had been a client for about six months or so. At the last minute he needed something rewritten because he had given me the wrong instructions previously, so I had to do a portion of it over for him. When he came to pick it up, he was in a rush and didn't even take time to read it. When it came time to pay me, he suddenly said: "Oh, I forgot my wallet." Immediately it came to me that this was his way of not paying me by pretending he didn't have the money. He needed the project right then because he had a deadline, and assured me that if he could pick the project up now, he would bring the money that night. Perhaps I might have said something right then, but I didn't want to in case I was wrong. As events unfolded they only confirmed I was right. He didn't return that night with the money, nor the following weekend when he promised to come. Later, when I finally spoke to him about the matter, he reaffirmed that he owed me the money and thanked me for trusting him but, just as I suspected, he never paid. There was always one reason or another why he couldn't come by to pay. Yet he continued to tell me how much he appreciated my trust—as if trying to maintain face while continuing to avoid the obligation to pay.

Such an experience serves as a verification and a powerful lesson for trusting the accuracy of that inner voice. As it shows, if one senses that there will be a certain outcome as a result of a certain action, and that outcome occurs, that's a sign one's perception was correct. Accordingly, when one gets that kind of sensation, this kind of experience suggests that one should listen and avoid the action that is linked to that outcome. Otherwise you may only prove yourself correct for that unwanted outcome is apt to occur.

Deciding How to Deal With What You Know

Assuming you have decided that your feeling of knowing is accurate, the question may sometimes arise: How should you act based on what you know?

In some cases, the choice is fairly straightforward and simple. For example, your intuition tells you not to go down a certain passageway but take another route instead. It might be easy in such a case to simply follow the alternate route. Or in other cases, where your intuition is telling you to turn in a certain way, it can be easy to go with that feeling and make the turn.

In still other cases, the decision to go with your knowing may not be that simple, because you are picking up insights about someone else which you shouldn't know. For example, you may be in a situation where your voice is telling you that you shouldn't trust a person, but there is no outward reason why should shouldn't do that. As a result, if you go with your feelings, you may end up confronting or insulting someone when you have no apparent basis for doing so, just your inner feelings.

A good example of this is the situation I just described where the man claimed he had forgotten his wallet so he couldn't pay me for a project. Outwardly he seemed very sincere, and since he had been a client for over six months I had no reason not to trust him, and to accuse him would be an insulting thing to do. Yet I also had this powerfully strong feeling he was acting in bad faith.

Sometimes when you get this knowing, the issue becomes not whether to trust it or not, but how you deal with this insight after you've gotten it and you know it's correct. It can be easy to acknowledge this insight when it's favorable and tells you that you can trust someone. You can readily share your feelings if you wish and decide to enter into a relationship with that person based on trust.

But what if you are picking up terrible things about somebody? In some cases you can diplomatically withdraw. But in other cases, such as the situation I described, you are already locked into some sort of a relationship. So you have to decide. Do you acknowledge your insights? Do you tell somebody about the kinds of feelings you are picking up? Do you accuse the person based on what you are feeling, or otherwise allude to your feelings, so you have a confrontation and bring these concerns out in the open? Or do you keep these feelings hidden and continue to deal with the person based on what would normally seem true as a result of what the person is saying or doing?

The problem in knowing what to do with these sensations and insights is that sometimes they're not the kind of information you would pick up in the normal course of events, so that they can interfere with the way you normally relate to somebody or lead you to question what you would normally do. This is the case because through your knowing you are picking up something you wouldn't normally know about, for you have that inner sensitivity, that insight, which is giving you some inside information. So the question becomes, should you act on it?

For example, when the incident happened with my client, I was picking up very strongly the feeling that this person was trying to cheat me. He was trying to behave outwardly like a regular client who simply forgot his wallet and was in a rush. But inwardly, I knew that's not what was going on for him. He was trying to get away without paying. However, if I was to simply blurt out what I was feeling, that you're trying to cheat me, I would be violating a strong social norm that suggests there is an appropriate way of behaving towards people. Unless they give you some outward indication that they can't be trusted, you should behave towards others as if they are acting in good faith. It is generally not a good idea to suddenly confront a person based on your inner feelings and tell him you think he is a liar or words to that effect.

Sometimes you may be in a situation where you are picking up some powerful information through your knowing, but you may not be able to immediately act on this or reveal it, because you have to take into consideration ordinary social conventions, too. So you may have to come up with some creative or diplomatic ways to deal with the negative information you pick up about someone or something; rather than admit what you know, you might come up with some ways of acting through knowing, without making the other person aware of what you know. For instance, don't tell the person you can't trust that you feel you can't trust him—he may only deny the basis for your feelings or come up with some logical reasons why you can. Instead, perhaps find some outwardly reasonable excuses to diplomatically withdraw or prevent the event you fear from occurring.

In some cases, even though you may be picking up some inner insights, you may need to go along with ordinary social conventions because you can't openly express what you know, since you don't want to risk an unpleasant confrontation. On the other hand, you might be able to find a way to act on what you know without revealing your knowing—perhaps by some diplomatic action where you can protect yourself, while the person you don't trust can still save face.

Once you know that you know, you may still have to decide what to do with this information. Sometimes, of course, you want to act based on your knowing. But in other cases there may be other considerations to take into account so you may have to come up with other ways to deal with what you know. But at least having that knowing and the knowledge of it gives you that choice. Then you can decide the best thing to do under the circumstances.

Deciding What to Do and What You Want

Once you open up a channel to your inner knowing so you recognize it—and once you have come to trust it—you can use it to guide your life in a number of ways. This is because as you get insights about the present and the future, your confidence in that knowing will help you decide to act on it or choose not to act, whichever is more appropriate.

If something doesn't feel right, you probably shouldn't do it. If you're considering a new job and it feels wrong, perhaps it may be better not to take it. If you're thinking about a partnership with someone and you feel dubious, even though everything on the surface seems fine, maybe your knowing is trying to tell you that you shouldn't trust this person, despite his seemingly straightarrow appearance.

Likewise, your inner knowing can help you decide. If you aren't sure what to do, you can try asking yourself: "Does it feel right for me to do this right now?" If so, do it. If not, don't. Or maybe ask yourself, "Should I do this or that?", and then listen for that inner voice to give you the answer.

Your inner knowing can also help you figure out what you really want. Then, that information can help you choose. For instance, say there are three or four things you can do, and your logical side is saying: "Let's do this one." But there may be another task that your intuitive part would like to do instead. Any choice might have a favorable outcome; any option might be viable, but if you can identify the one you really want, you'll feel much more satisfied and fulfilled and will perform better in the end. The classic case, of course, is choosing a job. It's very important to get in touch with what you really want and to do it.

Knowing How to Do Something

Still another use of your inner knowing is telling you how to do something. Logically, you may feel stuck, but if you pull back, let go, and just wait for your knowing to respond, you will know what to do. That flash of insight, that little voice, that gut level feeling will give you the solution or way to go. One woman described how this experience occurred when she was changing lightbulbs. At first she couldn't seem to figure it out, but then when she stepped back, the way to do it suddenly came to her. As she explained:

> "The first time I ever encountered changing those big lightbulbs, it was like a big mystery....to make it work. I was on top of the ladder for about twenty minutes trying to work out how to do it...and I was feeling really agitated. I must have spent at least twenty minutes more getting more and more angry. And then I went down and told myself, 'Well, I'm not going to let a lightbulb defeat me,' and I decided to let go. I went off to get a glass of water and put the anger out of my mind. It's like I unlatched my brain. And then I climbed back up and all of a sudden it just seemed obvious the way to do it, and I finished changing the light. Suddenly I knew what to do."

Finding Your Way Around and Finding Objects

Often people use their knowing to find their way around or to find things. They trust their knowing to take them where they need to go.

For people finding their way around, their knowing fills in for lost directions. Or sometimes they may be in an unfamiliar town and trying to find the street where someone lives. Or they may be looking for a group of people having an event and they don't have the map. Sometimes people are able to go by their instincts. Then their knowing acts like some kind of radar to direct them.

For example, one man described how he found his way to a doctor's appointment when he wasn't sure where to go just by following his knowing. Somehow, it seemed to point him in the right direction; it told him when to turn and it even seemed to direct him right to a parking place in front of the building. As he described the experience:

"I had another example of this knowing which is very strong. I was way across town and I had an eye appointment at this hospital, but I had never been there. I knew it was out in a certain area, and I was in a rush and didn't have the exact address...

So I got in my car and I just started driving. And all of a sudden I got the feeling I should turn here, and I did—onto a street where I've never been before... So I continued driving along and then I kept getting this feeling or this voice telling me turn here, and I'd turn. And when I did, I would think to myself: 'What am I doing on this street?'

But the feeling felt so strong, I just kept going. and I ended up making a few last turns this way and there it was...So I was driving just by instinct. I never had any directions. All I knew was where I was supposed to go. I was in a part of town I had never been before, and I was going to someplace I've never been before. And by following my instincts, I got there.

I just knew when to turn, and I didn't question it. I just went with it...And in a few minutes I was there. And then, though parking in the area is usually tough, I felt like I should make a U-turn and after I did, a car pulled out and there was a parking place right in front. It really blew my mind the way all that happened, but it did."

Similarly, many people use their knowing to find objects they have mislaid or lost. Consciously they may not know where something is. But they let their logical mind go and let their knowing get a picture or feeling of where that lost object is. Or maybe a little voice tells them to look someplace and there it is.

One man described how he would take a few deep breaths to get in touch with his intuition, and after thinking: "I know where that is," he would let his knowing lead him to where the hidden article was. As he explained:

"I have had some situations where I can't find something in my house, and all I'll do is say: 'I know where it is.' And then I'll sit down, take a number of deep breaths, and I'll take two or three minutes to get relaxed and centered. And then I'll just put out, 'I really want to know where that is,' and then I find it.

There was the time after I moved, when I knew there was a certain size fastener in the house, and I hadn't seen it for five years. But I did that technique and then I got up and walked all the way downstairs and went into the garage and I went to this shelf and right to this little drawer. I reached in and there it was. I hadn't opened that thing in five years, and I felt sure it was there through just knowing. I just let go and said, 'I'm going to go and find it,' and the next thing I saw is the picture of what I want...and I felt like something was leading me right to it. So it's a wonderful arrangement. And every time this knowing happens and I find something like that, I really thank my inner self. I think: 'You really took care of me.' And that has happened again and again."

Another woman similarly reported letting her intuition lead her when she couldn't find something through using her conscious mind. She just opened up, let go of her logical thinking and followed her inner knowing.

"I've had the experience of finding things with my knowing sometimes. Like just last night, when I knew my datebook was someplace in the house. I remember looking in the car first, and then I walked through all the rooms and I couldn't find it, because I hadn't put it where I normally put it.

But I didn't get upset...I just let myself go and I tried to let my intuition lead me instead of trying to consciously say: 'Well, it should be here.'

So I just let my knowing lead me, and it led me into my workshop and the notebook was underneath some boards. I would never have thought to look there. But once I decided to trust my inner knowing, it led me right there."

Preparing for Things

You can also use your knowing to see ahead and prepare for what you see. For example, if you feel you are stepping into a potential conflict situation with someone, you can do what is necessary in advance to prepare yourself so you will do well in that situation. Or if you sense there is going to be danger ahead, you can take the necessary preparations if you decide to confront that danger anyway.

As a case in point, suppose you are planning a trip to see your mother and you know if you go on this trip there is going to be a real struggle. You can sense the coming confrontation over some problem, and as you look ahead you can see that you are going to yell and scream. Yet you may still decide: "I have to go. I have an obligation to do this." On the one hand, you are aware that your voice is telling you it's going to be tough and you're going to have this confrontation, but on the other hand you know you still need to go through with the encounter. In such a case, your voice could be a way of preparing yourself so when you meet with this person, who pushes some buttons that might set you off, you don't allow them to be pushed. You know the situation is going to be difficult. But if you're ready for it you can keep it from becoming a huge conflict. By knowing and preparing in advance, you can defuse the potential conflict and keep things under control.

Also, your knowing can sometimes urge you to do something which you don't think you need to do now, but by doing it you are prepared for something which comes later. A common example of this is when you are in a store and you suddenly get a feeling to get something, although you have no apparent use for it now. But if you get it you may find that in a short while it is exactly what you need for something you want to do.

I had this experience when I was designing games. Once when I was on a tour of someone's manufacturing plant, I saw some plastic spheres of various sizes and suddenly felt: "I've got to have that." I didn't have the slightest idea of what I wanted them for, though I experienced this strong compelling desire to have them. A few weeks later, when I was in a hardware store I saw some stove bolts of about 4″ to 6″ long in some bins and I suddenly felt this strong feeling again that I should get these. So I did, not knowing what they were for. A few days after I got them home I happened to notice them in the workshop and then saw the spheres and suddenly I saw them together as a puzzle in which the bolts were pushed through the sphere at various angles. The result was my most successful puzzle ever, which I sold to Hasbro and which sold nearly 100,000 copies. Since I trusted my knowing, that made it possible. But if I had ignored these feelings, the project would never have happened.

Similarly, a man in one of my workshops described how he sometimes got a feeling that he should buy something now, and would, even though his logic would tell him that it was ridiculous and that he didn't have any use for it. But then, a short time later he would suddenly discover it was exactly what he needed to do something. In one case, for example, by listening he ended up with just the tool he needed to do a job. As he explained:

> "My knowing helps me plan ahead lots of times. For example, many times I'll be in a store and here will be some new product on the market and I'll look at it and think, 'Hey, that's pretty keen.' And suddenly, I'll get the sense I should buy it, though my logic part says: 'Hey, you don't have any use for it'...And a lot of times, like a week later, I'll find that's the only thing I could possibly use to do something I need to get done.
>
> "Once I needed a special cutting instrument to get into a small space to cut something. And a week before, when I didn't know I would be doing this, I saw a short little hack saw and I bought it. I couldn't imagine why I would need it then, but I felt I should get it...and a week later I found it was just what I needed to get right in there and do the job...A week before I didn't know I'd be working on this thing, but I had this strong feeling and I just went with it, and I bought this thing that has fit into my life so wonderfully."

Learning to Put Aside Your Logic and Trust that Inner Voice

Sometimes it can be difficult to let go of your logic and trust your inner knowing or inner voice. At such times, you need that intuitive sense of discernment to know when to listen to your feelings rather than your logic. It's hard to define exactly what you should be looking for to be discerning but, in general, when you get that strong sense of knowing accompanied by that intense feeling you are right, that's the time to put your logic aside and go with your knowing.

For example, just recently my landlord confronted me with a new lease after I had been living where I was for over two years and had what I thought was a very good, peaceful relationship. The lease asked for an increased deposit of about $1700, a rent raise of $175—a jump of almost $1470. Plus, my landlord now wanted me to get written permission from him when I had business groups over. And there were substantial penalties if I should happen to pay late or if my bank would even mistakenly bounce a check—I could be paying over $240 for one check that bounced, even if it was the bank's fault.

My first inclination was to feel that there wasn't much I could do about this, because my landlord could more or less do what he wanted since I lived in a small non-rent controlled apartment. Also, I had been planning to remain solidly planted for at least eighteen more months while I finished current writing projects and law school. Besides, I had five rooms that were packed with furniture and was in the middle of a very busy time in my life. Logically, it seemed the thing to do was sign the lease and pay more rent, unfair as I thought it was.

But when I took some time to look within and meditate on this, the message came to me all at once: "Give notice and plan to move." This is what I did, even though logically this wasn't what I wanted to do. But I didn't have to move, though I dreamed about where I would go for a few days. Instead, after the landlord received my notice, he suddenly came to his senses, apologized for the lease and we had a long talk about how I felt about the lease and how he had written it at a time when he felt under extreme pressure. He wanted to withdraw the lease; he hadn't meant to give me what seemed like an ultimatum and really did value me as a tenant. The result was the landlord dropped his request for extra security, lowered the rent increase to only $75, not $175, dropped any demands for permissions, and dropped the high penalty clause for late payments or problems with the bank.

The result was that I saved about $5000 over the next eighteen months I planned to stay there—and it all happened by listening to my inner voice.

Thus, at times it can be fine to be guided by your logic, which is how people are commonly expected to act. But at other times, it can be beneficial to put it aside and trust your knowing. Generally, the time to do this is when you get a strong hint that your inner knowing is correct. Then, whatever your logic says, go with that inner knowing and let go of your logic that may hold you back.

This kind of going with that knowing has happened again and again in modern business when new successful entrepreneurs have trusted their feelings rather than letting logical explanations of why it won't work get in the way. Federal Express, for instance, started this way. The founder submitted his idea for the company to a professor in a Harvard Business School class, who gave him a C and said that his idea would never work. So logically, the founder of Federal Express might have put aside his dream. He went ahead and followed his feelings anyway, and of course, it worked.

Using Your Knowing to Go With the Flow

The other side of putting your logic aside to listen to and act on that inner voice is to learn to accept and trust it, so you feel comfortable acting upon it. One way to think of this process is "going with the flow." This way you let yourself be guided by that knowing you feel, and you trust that it is right and that whatever happens will all work out.

In some cases this letting go may not be easy to do since sometimes this inner push to do something can conflict with your desire to rationally know. You may want to be certain of something; you want to be sure. Sometimes this inner impulse can also conflict with your desire for security. In fact, it can sometimes be especially hard for people who are very security conscious to put their usual logic and everyday expectations aside because they feel very nervous about trusting their knowing. They don't trust that feeling it will all work out.

However, when you trust, when you let yourself go with that flow of events and listen to your knowing, I have found that somehow everything seems to work out in the end.

I had this experience when I was designing some dolls. As soon as I had the idea for something, I found the artist or doll designer I needed to execute my idea. And just as it looked like I had exhausted every possible manufacturing source, some salesperson I had spoken to from time to time about the project suddenly called to say that he and his partner wanted to set up a joint venture to bring out all of the lines. And, after some test marketing last year, the first of these are scheduled to be out soon. Along the way, there were some difficult struggles at times. At one point before these men appeared with their funding, an ersatz book publisher appeared claiming he wanted to bring out a book based on dolls. When his scheme fell apart, so did a contract I and a doll designer had with another manufacturer. But within days after that, these salesmen appeared on the scene and since we no longer had the other deal, they were interested. Likewise, there were times when it looked like they wouldn't get their money. People who made promises didn't come through. But still it felt right to wait it out and let things happen as they would. Just in time they managed to get their funding and they financed a trip I made to New York. And even though ultimately they never did get the full funding they expected, the trip to New York opened up other doors which led to the contact with a manufacturer I have now. And not only are the dolls scheduled to be out soon, but also a line of children's books.

Likewise, I have used the same type of "I know it will all work out" philosophy with freelancing, which I have been doing for over 20 years, and somehow things have always worked out. At first, going on my own seemed so uncertain and scary. I used to wonder where the next job would be coming from and would I ever work again. But after a while I developed a sense of knowing that something would come through when I needed it, and I learned to trust that feeling of knowing, so I came to feel secure. It's hard to explain, but the feeling is like knowing that when I complete one project, other projects will come into my life when I need them, and somehow, for over 20 years things have always seemed to happen that way.

In fact, I had a little incident that happened after that experience with the client who didn't pay his bill for $75 that seemed like a further confirmation that this is so. It occurred the day after I felt this knowing that this client wasn't being honest with me and wasn't going to pay. That morning the doorbell rang and some people I had not worked for in over a year were there with a new project. In fact, they had lost my phone number because it had been so long, so they came right to my address, hoping I would be there. And it turned out that the project they needed for the next day was for almost exactly the same amount as the other client who didn't pay—$72. I needed a replacement for this money I knew I wouldn't get, and almost like magic the next day there it was.

Knowing When to Act On Your Knowing

You want to look for that sensation of truth which is associated with this knowing, this sense of certainty that what you are feeling is right. When you get that powerful sense of rightness, trust what these feelings are telling you. In some cases, they may be really positive feelings that are saying to you— "Do it," but at other times they may be warnings, telling you not to do it or letting you know what may happen if you do.

When you get those feelings, you can decide whether to follow that knowing or not. Generally try to follow your strong intuitive hunches and just go with it. Your conscious mind may try to blot them out, so try to let your conscious mind go to hear that voice. Normally, if you listen to it and can discern it against all the background noise of your conscious mind and everyday life, your voice is always right.

You need to be able to put your logic aside in order to really hear this inner voice. Naturally, you need to pay attention to your logic to a certain extent to maintain a proper sense of balance, which we'll talk about more in the next chapter. But at the same time, to really pick up what this inner voice or knowing is saying, you've got to be able, when appropriate, to suspend your logic for awhile.

When you do this, it's like you are putting your logic on a shelf. You know it's there when you need it. It's as if you have a jar of supplies which give you the security you need. You can always come back to these supplies, but then you use your intuition to travel and explore away from this base.

As mentioned earlier, you need to let go of your conscious mind to hear that voice because your conscious voice tends to blot it out. It does so because your conscious talks to you in terms of logic and it keeps you in touch with the distractions of the everyday world, such as stereo sets, television sets, lights, and everyday mundane conversations. Such things help to pull you away from this intuitive part of yourself.

At times the rules and regulations of everyday life can pull you away, too. That's because they serve to tell you the way things are and how you are supposed to act. And yet, underneath these ordinary rules, you may be picking up other information that tells you, "But that's not the way it really is." So these day to day conventions of everyday action and behavior can blot out this little voice when it tries to tell you things are not quite this way, or that you really don't want to do something, although the rules tell you that you should.

Thus, you have to learn to be discerning to be aware of your knowing however it comes to you (as a voice, as a vision, as a feeling). Then you can make the decision to follow it, ignore it, or perhaps modify its message, based on what you know from the logical world. However, by tuning into that knowing at least you will have that knowledge, so you can decide and thereby have a better experience as a result of your more knowing decision.

As one man suggested in a workshop, perhaps think of this little voice or inner knowing as a very good friend who gives you some advice. Then you can decide whether to listen or not. However, be aware that if you keep saying "Hey, I'm not going to listen," pretty soon your friend is going to say, "Well, I'm not going to tell you such things anymore." After all, just like a good friend, it will lose patience with you if you're not paying attention or denying that person.

As with your friend, you have to be open and trusting in order to have your intuition continue to give you those valuable insights so you can know more. That doesn't mean you have to listen and act on everything. Rather, treat your intuition like a good friend to whom you are willing to listen and then decide. For instance, you might say: "Okay, I'm getting some valuable accurate information now, but I still have to decide what I am going to do with it." Then, you can choose. After all, when your good friend gives you advice, even though he may be right, you don't always take that advice because you still have to weigh it with the other things that may be happening in your life at the same time.

By the same token, you should respect the insights and advice you get from within. You may not always act on them. But at least you should fight against any inclination to edit, deny, or disbelieve what you receive when you get that sense of certainty and knowing. Then you can assess these inner insights in light of what you know from your conscious, logical, or everyday mind—and based on what seems most appropriate at the time, you can choose.

This way, you aren't ruled by your intuition and insights. But you can use your knowing like any other tool to help you make the best choices about what to do in everyday life.

Chapter Ten

Using Your Inner
Knowing In Everyday Life

The previous chapter dealt with recognizing your inner voice, learning to trust it when appropriate, and putting your logic aside. This chapter focuses on where that voice or knowing gets its knowing and how you can develop and apply that knowing when you need it.

Your Sources of Knowing

How does your knowing know what it knows? Where does that knowledge come from? By knowing yourself you can help to facilitate the process so your knowing can get even more information and make this available to you.

Essentially, your knowing comes from your subconscious or superconscious. These concepts of the unconscious mind are often linked together, but in effect they have a different orientation. Your subconscious looks within and contains your various feelings, impressions, and reactions about things that have happened to you. By contrast, your superconscious looks beyond and links you to the universe as a whole, so that it picks up more universal feelings, impressions, and reactions about things which exist.

Because of these facets of your unconscious you are able to pick up all sorts of information which become synthesized together into a kind of well of inner knowledge. In turn, you pick up this knowledge through your knowing, which can come to you in any of its forms as your vision, feelings, or inner voice.

It is this vast storehouse of inner information that gives you your ability to know all sorts of things, even though you may not be able to pinpoint where this information is coming from. For instance, this is why you are able to pick up an accurate insight or feeling about someone else, and in an instant you can tell exactly where someone is coming from. You may not know why you know, but you do because you experience this holistic coming together of accurate information that comes to you with this sudden rush of sensation which tells you: "Yes, this person is okay," or alternatively, "Don't trust him," or "Watch out."

Some writers, including Carl Jung, have referred to this vast storehouse of knowledge we are all connected to as the collective unconscious. It's as if we exist in a sea of unseeable thought forms and emotional waves which lap up against us constantly. But if we tune into them, we can pick up these thought forms or feelings which are flowing all around us, and then suddenly we know.

For example, when you meet somebody and get a sense of where he is coming from and whether you can trust him or not, that insight may come in an instant flash, but it involves picking up and synthesizing information from various sources in this sea of information. One source might be the immediate aura or energy field around the person, which gives off waves of energy that characterize the person, if you can see this aura. Another source might be the collective unconscious and its storehouse of general information about everything that has ever happened—and like being in a computer library, we can push a button and instantly retrieve the information we want to know. Then, too, you might be picking up information from your own subconscious feelings, impressions, and reactions.

So each time you get that knowing, such as when you meet and assess a person, you are picking up information on a number of levels, some coming directly from that person, other information from other sources. Then you merge what you know generally with what you know about that person or thing in particular, and it all synthesizes together into a sudden sensation that you know who that person really is or what that thing really means.

Increasing Your Ability to Pick Up Information

You can increase your ability to pick up information so you sharpen your sense of knowing by opening up to both your subconscious and super-conscious. Like a ship captain, you can sail on this vast sea of unconscious information and travel from the home port of your subconscious into the world of the collective unconscious to bring back the treasures of these waters.

There are various ways to speed your travels and increase the information you retrieve. For example, the Buddhists have a belief that you can send out a thread from your center and touch another person with that to make a connection and pick up information about them. In the Don Juan books, Castaneda describes how a powerful shaman travels across a waterfall by putting out cords from his body to use as a physical connection to carry him across.

We all have the ability to put out these psychic threads or connections. Then we can use them to travel psychically to pick up information about others or our environment, or we can use them as feelers or inner antennae to pick up signals which others send to us. Sometimes people do this consciously by projecting mental or physical cords out of their body. But often we may do this unconsciously too. When this happens, our feelers or inner antennae go out and pick up information which we use, without even being aware of where it comes from.

If we train ourselves to be more conscious of this process of projecting ourselves out to get information, we will gain more knowledge. There are many modalities for getting this information through projection. For example, using a projection of the cord connecting with the gut will pull in more feeling information, while a more visual projection will provide more mental information. But in either case, the information you obtain can be extremely powerful, and you can use it to supplement any information you get consciously in the course of everyday life.

Today it has become more and more important to develop these abilities, because as we grow up we tend to learn to block out these sources of unconscious information, so these conscious projections are a way of opening these channels up. Also, as a species, we have become less sensitive to the natural forces of nature, and projections can help us develop these sensitivities too. For example, researchers have shown that many animals may sense earthquakes. A few hours before the earthquake occurs the animals start behaving very anxiously, and the researchers believe that the animals are picking up some forms of energy which we normally can't sense. Yet it appears that there may be some people who have this ability too, which suggests this is a sensitivity we all might have, if only we knew how to develop it.

Similarly, children commonly have a natural ability to pick up insights which we may block out as adults, so in many ways they may be more intuitive or knowing. This is one reason that children sometimes say things that are very embarrassing to adults. They sense something about a person, such as 'This person is not very nice,' and they blurt it out. However, since such behavior is not considered socially acceptable, their parents quickly tell them not to say or think such things, so children soon learn not to be as intuitive and perceptive as they could be about these unconscious sources of information. Perhaps our parents may be only trying to teach us to control these insights or not express them, but in the process children not only learn not to talk about these inner feelings, but to shut them off as well.

A key aspect of getting more in touch with our unconscious to become more knowing is getting rid of these blocks and walls we have put up to shut it out. We need to open up these long blocked off channels and get in touch with our unconscious again so we can better pick up our sense of knowing. Then our knowing will have more information from these unconscious sources to draw from, and thereby it will have more accurate information to give us.

Picking Up What You Know

Much of this unconscious information we want to pick up is very subtle, so it can easily get submerged by our conscious thoughts or feelings, or by the sounds and sights of everyday life. For example, it is easy to lose touch with our inner voice when we have all these media images and sounds around us, or when we are in everyday contact with people who are telling us things or are otherwise bombarding us with day to day activities. Moreover, we may actively look outside ourselves to get information from all these experts, authority figures, and media people who specialize in giving information, so we may lose a sense of trust in ourselves. Also, the amplitude of many of the daily sensations we encounter is so strong that these can easily override any of the subtle feelings we feel. So our unconscious thoughts and sensations can easily get lost, and with them the knowing they bring.

Until you are able to get more in touch with this unconscious part of yourself, so you have a clear and open channel to your knowing even in the middle of everyday life, it is helpful to get away from it all so you can concentrate on getting in touch. Later you may not need to do anything special to tune into your knowing—the information will simply be there, ready for you to tap into it as you will. But in the beginning you can better make connections by finding a time or place where you can pull away from the bustle and jangle of everyday.

Finding a place of quiet, of course, helps to bring these unconscious thoughts and feelings to the surface. But if you can find a real point of stillness, you will gain an even deeper quiet than in an ordinary place.

This is one reason why it is good to work on connecting with your unconscious at night, for this is a time when the world and energies all around you are much more quiet. During the day, everything is all bright and busy. Horns are honking, many cars are on the streets, people are bustling around, and there is a much busier, wakeful energy. So you are less able to go into your unconsciousness and pull up those quieter, subtler energies. You are less likely to hear your little voice talking to you, less likely to see the fuzzy images rising up from your unconscious, less likely to feel the tugs and pulls of your inner feelings.

By contrast, at night, as the world quiets down, you are more likely to experience that inner quiet which lets you better explore, hear and see into your inner world. In fact, for some people the time period from about 2 to 4 a.m. is especially ideal, because at this time everything is very quiet. Most people have gone to bed at the end of the day and few people have gotten up to start the morning, so psychically this is a time when there is much less activity than at any other time. So some people do their meditating and focusing on what their unconscious is picking up then.

But even if the night or this 2 to 4 a.m. window isn't a good time for you, there are many things you can do to seek this quiet state of withdrawal and looking within. For example, you can select your environment so you are in a quiet place where you can get rid of all the extraneous noises and sights and sounds of the everyday world. Also, you can seek to cut out a lot of the distractions in your everyday life at certain times, so you can take a short time to look within. You can even do this in a busy office. Just find a place to be by yourself, shut the door if you can, turn off the phones or let someone else answer them. Then take about twenty or thirty minutes to get centered and look into your own unconscious to see what's going on, and then look around to pick up information from the environment and other people around you, too.

You can also use this approach in conjunction with automatic writing, which can help you record what you are picking up as well as help you focus and look more deeply into this unconscious realm. Often before going to bed, I use automatic writing to get information. Maybe once a week or every two weeks or so, I spend some time doing this. I find it a good way to get in touch with my own knowing and listen to that little voice. I can hear what it has to say about different things going on in my life and about the people I have recently met, too. You'll also find this tuning in especially helpful if you are trying to find new directions or make decisions. It can give you a sense of where you should go and it can help you feel more certain about what you are doing or the people currently in your life.

Finally, you can do things to make your environment even more conducive to getting this inside information. For example, if it's more comfortable for you, keep the room very warm, since your body temperature tends to drop when you slow down and look within. With a warm room you won't get distracted by the cold. Likewise, it helps if you have a very soft place to sit, so you feel very comfortable. Also do what you can to shut out any noise, perhaps even use ear plugs, and keep the room dark or dim. As much as possible it helps to have a very comfortable setting, where you won't have any shocks or distractions from temperature, noise, light, or the responses of your body.

In such an environment, you can best focus your mind so you can listen to that inner voice as it starts speaking and hear whatever it has to say. Or alternatively, you can see the images and visions of your inner knowing, or you can pick up information from your feelings. Whatever channel the information comes, by quieting down and tuning out the outer conscious world, you will be better able to pick up this information and know what you know.

Tuning Into Your Inner Knowing—Exercise #15

The following exercise is designed to help you tune into your knowing or inner voice to obtain this information. You will ask for information about something that will happen in the next few days, so you can check out the accuracy of the information you receive. Find a quiet place to get relaxed, and preferably turn the lights down low or turn them off.

To begin, just become very relaxed. Lie down if you wish. Focus on your breathing for a few minutes as you calm down.

While you're focusing on your breathing, pay attention to the point of consciousness in the center of your head. Imagine it any way you want to—as a point of light, as the inner part of you that you feel is your center, or as a little voice that speaks to you. Recognize that this is the center of your sense of knowing, the center of your understanding of the information that comes in from your unconscious.

Now imagine yourself having a conversation with this inner part of yourself. You can ask it a question, and maybe it will acquire a certain form, like a screen, or maybe it will be like a wise person. Or perhaps it may be like a powerful beam.

Whatever form this inner part of you takes, try to see yourself in dialogue with it, and know that when you want to you can always ask this inner voice some questions, and this inner voice will tell you the answers.

To get the answer, you just have to listen and put aside your judging and your criticizing, and your tendency to analyze whether something is right or wrong. For when you listen, this little voice will tell you the truth.

If there is something you have been concerned about, some decision you need to make, you can now start asking questions and talking to this part of you, this point of knowing, and you will find it knows all sorts of things.

For instance, some of your questions may have to do with what you are going to do tomorrow. The day after. Over the week. You may have some questions about who you are, what you want to do. Maybe you want to know some information about somebody in your life, such as a friend, a person you're very close to, a relative. Again, just ask any question you want.

Sometimes you may notice that the information you get is very different from what you would normally say or think logically, but at other times it may be exactly what you might think when you are not in an altered state of consciousness.

If you do get similar information to what you already know, just see it as a reconfirmation of what you know. Often your little inner voice may tell you when you already know something, and that's fine. Or it may tell you new information or even conflicting information, and that's fine, too. Such information is telling you to take another closer look, for now you may be seeing the real truth that underlies what only appears to be on the surface.

If you wish, you might ask some test questions just to verify the information that you're getting. This will help you see how accurate your little voice really can be.

For this test, maybe ask a question about something which you don't know about consciously, but maybe your voice will know. For instance, maybe ask if when you get home, will something be in a certain place in your apartment or house. Or maybe ask whether a letter is going to arrive or whether somebody is going to call. Ask something you can verify within a day or two. You may be surprised at how accurate your little voice is.

Now, on your own, just ask some more questions, whatever you want. And know that this little voice will always be there for you. At times you can tune into it when it's very quiet, and this can be a very good time, a very relaxed time to get in touch with your inner voice.

But also know that your inner voice is there too at times when you're very busy, and sometimes you can ask a question and get a quick answer, like a yes or a no. For instance, you can get a sense of 'Should I do this?' or 'Should I do that?'

Sometimes you may even feel your inner knowing pushing you like a pendulum. A certain direction might be a yes; another direction might be a no.

Recognize that you can communicate with your inner knowing in a lot of different ways, and as you become more sensitive, you'll find that these communication channels increasingly open up. And you can use whichever channels you prefer.

For your inner knowing can communicate with you verbally as this little voice. It can communicate through your feelings, or it can appear to you through your vision. You can tune into it on any channel, or on more than one. And the more you tune in, the more you'll be in tune with this inner knowing or little voice.

In some cases, you may get the feeling that you need to withdraw for a little bit to communicate with this little voice. If so, fine. Just take that time to get away and ask what you need to ask. So sometimes before you make a decision, know that your little voice is there for you, and maybe delay making your decision right away. Instead, pull away for a little bit and ask your question so you really know.

Now, if there are any other questions you have, go ahead and ask your little voice. Then, when you feel ready, say goodbye to that voice or to your inner knowing, in whatever form it takes. Know that you will be able to come back at any time and talk to that voice. You will be able to tune into your knowing and get the information you need. And you will be able to know that you know.

But for now, just let go of that knowing and when you are ready, open your eyes and come back into the room.

Working With Your Inner Voice or Knowing

When you go within, using an exercise such as the previous one, you may find your inner knowing responds to you in a number of ways. It may take the form of a pinpoint of white light, especially if you have been using this image in previous exercises. It may come to you like a disembodied voice of wisdom. Or it might take animal or human form. Or perhaps it might appear like a radiant spiritual being. Just speak to it or greet it in whatever form it comes.

Even if your inner knowing appears in the guise of a comic character or otherwise seems a little ridiculous, that's perfectly fine. You can still get valid information, and these personal traits help to personalize your knowing so you can better communicate with it. One woman, who had a rabbit and the nickname "Bunny," reported that her inner voice appeared to her as Bugs Bunny telling her to do this or that. She found the advice helpful, even if she thought the appearance of the rabbit was strange. A doctor working with the inner voice as a source of healing reported that one man created the persona of "Freddie the Frog," and found he could have long talks with this creature who gave him wise and useful advice.

To some extent, you can relax when you go within and let your inner knowing come to you in whatever form it takes. Then, you can communicate with whatever form your knowing assumes. Also, you can take a more active role to develop a clearer image or a character for your knowing, so you can communicate with it more closely and thereby obtain even deeper and more accurate information, just as you would when you develop a close relationship with a long-term friend.

One good approach, if you find your knowing communicates with you in a certain way, is to develop it further in that direction. For example, if your knowing comes to you as a voice, perhaps give it form or add a personality, and then try to learn more about who this being is. This way you can really get to know your inner voice because it becomes like a real person or animal. If your inner knowing comes to you as a feeling, maybe get more into that feeling and perhaps feel it more intensely. Alternatively, if your knowing comes to you as a voice and you would prefer not to see this assume a particular form, perhaps pay more attention to the qualities of this voice, or just continue to talk to that voice as a voice. Or perhaps imagine this is the voice of a very wise person you can't see, such as the Wizard of Oz behind a screen. You don't have to feel you have to make this voice visual, and many people prefer not to visualize a particular person or being associated with it. For them the inner knowing is just a powerful, often all-knowing voice. So whatever way your inner knowing comes to you, just develop that a little more.

In a sense you might consider this development as a process of personality construction. It's like you are creating another personality within your inner self. If you want, you can create and communicate with more than one inner personality to gain insights in different areas. For instance, one persona may be especially knowing about other people, one about your work and career, and another about your problems with love and relationships. The process may sound a little bit like the way in which the ancients called on different gods to advise them about different areas of their life. But here you are in active charge of the process—you are knowingly creating these personas within yourself. It's like you are the director who's doing the casting and writing the script.

This personality creation process is possible because we all have different sides within ourselves, and it's possible to take on different qualities at different times. For example, when you call on that wise person for information, you are tapping into your inner wisdom, so you may suddenly feel very wise and knowing. In fact, this feeling of wisdom you experience when guided by this other inner personality may express itself in your physical being as well, such as in the way you hold yourself, talk, and move.

There may be times that you want a very serious wise being to guide you, but there may be other times when you want to have a more free-spirited type of person to help you make decisions. In the first case, the wise being may be the type of person to call on for advice about your work or money, but you may feel the more free-spirited being is more appropriate when you are making a decision about a trip.

As long as there is a certain part of you that remains in control of all this, you can call on these personas as you want, and then you can decide whether to use their advice or not. In some cases, people involved in magic will call on the assistance of ancient gods and other spiritual beings with a long tradition. Or they may even go into trances and assume these personas. The process is much the same in creating a persona for your inner voice, except that the people working with ancient gods and known spiritual beings are drawing on a whole range of personality characteristics associated with these deities and beings, due to historical associations. You can, of course, call on these beings if you wish, but you don't have to. You can build up the persona of your inner knowing from any sources.

However you do it, the key to success is staying in control as you make this inner part of you more and more real. Some people involved with working with magic and other realities become too deeply involved and lose control. They start thinking they really are that inner voice, and they throw themselves so totally into that created reality that they lose touch with their rational conscious part. So you need to keep that sense of balance which we'll talk about more in the next chapter.

Basically, you want to let this inner part of you go. You want to learn to work with it closely and trust it. But at the same time, you still need to keep your rational part there to guide things and determine how far to let your inner voice go. This way you can obtain and use the insights you gain in a very balanced way.

Summing Up

In summary, you can learn to develop a close relationship with your inner knowing once you learn to recognize it, trust it, and develop ways of relating to it to get the information and advice you need. In some cases, you can simply ask questions and get a yes or a no advising you what to do, but many people have an ongoing dialogue with their inner knowing or voice. They might talk to it directly, or they might use a process like automatic writing or journal keeping to aid them in their communication.

You may also find this knowing communicates with you in different ways. For some people it's more of a sense of feeling; others may meditate and will hear a little voice, still others may see images and forms. Or perhaps you may have a communication going on through a number of channels at once. Whatever form this communication takes, you can still develop it further by creating a persona for your inner guide or perhaps a series of personas representing different parts of yourself. If you want to draw on the personalities of known beings with a history, this is fine, or you can create any animal, human, or symbolic forms you want. You can even have a wise armchair talk to you, if this helps you tap your inner part.

This process will help you connect with your subconscious or super-conscious that is the source of your knowing or inner wisdom. This is not a part of yourself which you are normally in touch with. But as you start working with this part of you more and more, you will gain more access to it and you can direct it to get more insights for you. For example, through this channel you can tap into the collective unconscious, pick up insights about other people and discover things about yourself.

These insights and answers come from the unconscious level and they result from a kind of synthesis of knowledge from many different sources—from within yourself, from other people, from your immediate environment, and from the collective historical unconscious, which draws on the thought forms created throughout history and throughout the world. So your inner knowing is like a radar screen picking all of this up. But you also need to keep a balance between all the information you are getting from your inner voice and what is happening in the everyday world around you. This means you've got to synthesize the knowledge you pick up from this inner world with the inputs you get from the outer world as well. This way you create a harmony of inner and outer, intuition and logic, thinking and feeling, knowing and doing. And then you can best use the information you get from your knowing to help you in everyday life.

Chapter Eleven

Taking A Solo To Contact The Forces Of Nature And Your Inner Self

Once you have a firm foundation in seeing and working with dreaming, projection, and your inner knowing, you are ready to take the solo. This is a time when you go out by yourself into a natural setting and seek to get in touch with the forces of nature which exist outside of you and within yourself. Then you can learn to work with these forces to increase your abilities to do all of the other things.

In a sense, the solo acts as a kind of a bridge between the abilities and awareness you have developed now and the more powerful abilities and awareness you can develop in the future as you work with these skills more and more. As such, the solo really has two purposes. On the one hand it is designed to help you assess where you are now and ask any questions you have now so you get immediate guidance. On the other hand it is designed to make you more aware of the powerful energies of nature inside and outside of yourself, so you can call on them in the future to be even more powerful in whatever you want to do.

When and Where to Go on a Solo

When you go on the solo you will spend about a half-hour to an hour alone in a quiet natural setting at night. You can go to a nearby park, to the beach, or even find a comfortable spot in your own backyard. And if you have a chance to do this in a pristine wilderness setting, this is even better because the experience will be that much more concentrated and intense.

The reason for working in darkness is because then you are better able to see the subtle forms and energies of nature. Otherwise, they are too easily overlooked in the hustle and bustle of the everyday world. Also, at night the active energies of the day settle down and it is easier to get calm and relaxed, become quiet and look inside. It is easier to be open and receptive in this calm and quiet state.

How to Prepare for a Solo

To prepare for a solo you should dress warmly, since you will be outdoors for some time at night. If you are doing this on your own, take a watch or clock to let you know when the time you have set for the solo (about 30 minutes to an hour) is over or if you prefer, use your own internal clock to inform you when the solo feels over. Another possibility is to go to the site with a friend or take the solo in a group with each of you widely separated from one another. Then, one person can monitor the time and come to get you when the solo is over. It is also helpful to take a flashlight (or go with someone who has one), so you can easily see where you are going until you get to the place where you will do your solo.

You should pick a place to do this where you feel comfortable and where you won't encounter curious people. Public park or beach areas can be fine, but be sure the setting you have chosen is likely to be safe. If you have a power object you are working with, such as a long walking stick or staff, it helps to take it with you. One reason is that it can help you feel safe, both on a psychic and a physical level from both the forces of nature and from actual intruders, respectively.

As you approach whatever site you have chosen, be quiet and stop any talking on the way in. This will help you settle down and get in the mood to be alone for awhile and look within.

When you get to the general area of the site, choose a place within it that feels right for you. If you are with a group of people taking the solo at the same time, make sure there are at least 40 or 50 yards between you.

Some typical spots might be by a tree, on an overlook, in a grove, or by a large log. Just go by your feelings and choose a place which feels comfortable, safe, and perhaps even powerful.

Then, sit down and get comfortable. An ordinary sitting position is fine, or perhaps assume a cross-legged position and sit up straight with your hands outstretched to be more receptive to the energies and forces around you.

Once you feel settled, get relaxed and let yourself be open to the energies of nature. It's as if you are putting yourself out there in nature to get in touch and you are saying: "Here I am." In doing so, you want to be in a receptive state, so that you see whatever you see, or hear whatever you hear, or let your inner voice tell you whatever it wants to tell you. Then quietly listen and notice what you experience.

If you wish, you can also imagine a protective circle around yourself. Some people find this makes them feel more comfortable, since they feel that it will keep out the energies of nature and other influences they don't want to intrude. If you do decide you want such a circle, you can simply visualize it around you, or if you prefer, project out a ring of strong protective energy around yourself. Another possibility is to create a protective dome all around you, either through visualizing or projecting your feelings. You can also use a power object to draw this circle or dome if you feel more comfortable with that.

In any event, whether you have a protective circle around you or not, open yourself up when you are ready and experience whatever happens now.

What to Expect on a Solo

On a solo you may have a wide range of experiences, but normally it's a very calm and peaceful kind of experience for most people.

Frequently, you may see forms emerge in nature. Sometimes these may appear as concentrations of energy that seem to take on solid form, and often these will appear in the shadows or near natural objects, like trees and bushes. Or you may notice sparkles or pulsations of energy travel through the air. Sometimes you may see these energies take on human or animal forms, and if you wish you can talk to these forms or listen to them if they have anything to say. You can variously think of these forms as projections or constructions from your mind, as interpretations you are placing on the energy forms you see, or as real energies you are perceiving in nature. However you think of them, such experiences are common, and you can later work with these forms and energies you see to help you get information and make decisions about subsequent actions.

You may also find that you are looking within yourself and tuning out the environment around you. This may often occur when you have questions you want to ask yourself about something or have upcoming decisions or choices to make. Then the solo becomes an especially helpful way to have an intimate dialogue with your inner self and find your answers through your knowing.

In many ways you will also find the solo is like an extension of your own personality. So if you feel very calm and peaceful, you'll generally have a calm and peaceful experience. On the other hand, if you are going through a very tense and emotional time in your life and can't get relaxed before the solo, you may have a more intense and emotionally heightened solo experience, too.

You may find that the solo can be a time to additionally review current concerns you are thinking about. But now, in this deep receptive state, you may often get new information and insights so you can respond to these concerns in more creative, productive ways. For example, if you have been stuck about something, such as what to do about a person you're having a conflict with, your inner knowing may offer you some good suggestions on what to do.

Some Examples of Representative Solos

The following examples of solos illustrate these general principles of what a solo is like. For example, my own experience was the typically calm, insightful solo. I went with a group to a large forested area along the coast of Northern California, and after we hiked along a wooded trail for about 45 minutes we came to a meadow. I found a spot under a tree that felt very calm and restful and I sat down there, feeling like I was almost in the center of this large open meadow. To prepare, I visualized a protective ring around myself and I found I felt very calm and comfortable. Then I asked questions about various things, some of them quite mundane, and my inner voice came up with some answers that really worked. At the time I had been concerned with losing weight, which I wasn't doing very successfully. So my voice suggested an alternate approach I hadn't tried before—'Take a vitamin pill of any kind before each meal to remind yourself you are on a diet.'—and when I did so over the next 10 days, my weight dropped to the lowest it had been in several years. The subject might seem mundane, but the insights were certainly valid, and you can, of course, seek information about much larger, more significant issues for you.

Another person who was very dramatic and emotional in his nature had a much more dramatic, eventful solo. While he was meditating he heard loud crashes all around him, and he saw the images of beings careening through the air. At one point he saw a large fox flying around and it was seemingly calling to him to follow, but he resisted. Then he saw a large hole open up which led to an underground passage. After this he heard a child crying for help and he felt this was still another test to get him to step outside of his protective circle. But again he resisted, and he felt as if the evil presence that was sending these temptations was going away.

This kind of solo is definitely quite different from that which is experienced by most people. But this man had a background of studying magic before and he normally tended to make everything he experienced into something very grandiose and elaborate. In fact, he had been meditating for a few days about a week earlier because he had been going through some rough times in his everyday life, and he felt his experiences in this solo were a continuation of this. It was as if he was already going through a personal crisis and psychic battle in his life, and everything was already very emotional and traumatic for him. So he had a lot of deep questions to ask in his solo. Then, after he asked them his ongoing personal battle was played out here.

By contrast, a woman who was a very stable career-oriented person had a very calm and peaceful experience like mine. She thought about her warm feelings for a friend she had known for years and then she gained a feeling of recommitment to her career.

Another man who tended to be very alone and suspicious had a solo experience that tended to intensify these feelings. He felt extremely isolated for the 45 minutes he was alone and he felt like the forces of nature were consciously ignoring him because he had almost no experience of anything.

Rather, he went blank for most of the time he spent on his solo and he felt intensely alone and bored.

As these examples show, you will often find that the solo helps to highlight who you are and it plays up what you are especially interested in.

Some Instructions to Keep in Mind When You Do Your Solo

Once you are ready to go out on your solo, you can use the following instructions as a reminder about what to do and what to pay attention to.

When you begin your solo, you can start by making a circle or protective space around yourself. Or if you prefer, just sit down and get comfortable.

Once you are comfortable, be receptive and open. It's like you are saying: "Here I am universe," or "Here I am nature, and I'm ready to be receptive. Just tell me whatever you want to tell me."

Then, be aware and notice any sights or sounds. Notice if there are any forms of nature around you. You may experience this as a sense of presence that something is there. Or perhaps you may see visual forms or hear unusual noises. The way in which the forces of nature communicate with you depends on the way in which you perceive things.

But however you choose to communicate with nature or perceive, be open to answers—about yourself, about others, or about events generally.

As you'll find, this solo is a way of getting in touch with your inner voice or knowing, and you are very open to nature as well. So be open to any advice and suggestions, and this experience may help you to make decisions.

Don't try to consciously ask questions. Just let them come into your mind, and try to let go of your conscious thinking. Or if you do consciously ask a question, then listen to the answer. Don't try to call forth that answer yourself. Just let it come to you. Let your inner knowing respond and control the experience. Don't try to direct and control it yourself.

Taking Some Time to Assess and Evaluate the Experience

After your solo is over you should take some time to briefly assess what you learned and consider what you might do now, if anything, as a result. If you have done the solo on your own, you can do this on your own too. Perhaps use a notebook if you wish to record the highlights of your experience and note your reactions to what happened in the field. Or if you have gone on a solo with a group, take about a half hour or so to discuss this.

This group sharing can be a good time to learn what others have done on their own solos, and perhaps their insights about what happened may give you some additional insights about your own experience.

The following comments from a small workshop illustrate the kinds of experiences and observations that can come out of a solo and show how the review process can produce some suggestions for working with the information gained from the solo.

One woman reported she had some fears at first when she started her solo, but later, in the discussion, she realized that these fears were not so much about the solo but about confronting her inner self. She recognized that she should look more closely at how she really felt so she could act accordingly. As she stated:

"I was scared at first, and I started thinking about my fears. But then I started asking some questions and I got answers to different things. So I began looking at the different sides of my life.

And then as I felt more comfortable confronting these things, I began to look around me and I talked to the trees. Then I saw some movement and I listened to the sounds.

So I guess what happened is I realized that these fears were coming from inside me, not from the environment. Once I realized this, I found this a safe place to communicate. So I began to learn some new things about myself and then I felt ready to look outside.

But at first, when confronted by these fears, I didn't want to believe my inner self. So when I asked questions like, 'Can you do this or that?' I heard all these voices telling me I can't. Then, as I saw these fears were coming from within, these voices went away. I think I may have pushed them away myself. But in any case, that's when I started feeling comfortable and safe and felt able to look outside."

This review or discussion of what happened can also help you think of things you should do in the future to make your next solo an even more productive experience. For example, one woman who doubted the wisdom of her inner voice came to realize that it would be helpful if she had a dialogue with it next time. Then she could express her doubts to this voice and get some response from it explaining why it gave her the answers it did or where it got its information. As I told her during the workshop discussion:

"If you're doubting your inner voice, maybe have a dialogue with it. You believe you can't do something but your voice says you can, so maybe ask it 'Why do you think I can do it?'

Also, since you're telling yourself 'I can't,' you might ask yourself 'Why do you think I can't?'

In other words, try to get underneath your outward feelings and fears to see what's really going on. And this dialogue with your voice can help you probe more deeply so you start getting answers to your questions and more insight into yourself."

In another case, a woman who reported feeling some fear about being alone in the dark realized that next time she could put up a protective circle or dome of white light so she could feel more comfortable and safe. In our discussion I suggested:

> "If you feel unsafe in the environment but it really is a safe place, you might perhaps set up a protective circle around yourself. Just imagine yourself in a dome of white light so that you feel comfortable and very protected.
>
> Sometimes it can be good to look at your fears and understand what they are telling you. But at other times, your particular fears might not be rational, and it's at those times you can help protect yourself against them by doing something like visualizing this protective circle or shield."

This review period can additionally help you process the insights you have gained and learn how to apply them in specific situations. I had this experience in my second solo. I had a powerful feeling of being very free, and one of the insights that came to me was that it was time to go in new directions. As a result, I felt I should see a particular incident that happened as a break between the past and the future and as a possible subject for a new book. In the solo, the exact direction to go in wasn't clear, but then I used the review process as a means of thinking about possible alternatives.

You can likewise use this post-solo review to both prepare for a better, more productive solo next time, and to consider in a more rational frame of mind how to begin putting the information and insights from your solo to practical use.

Repeating the Solo

Consider your first solo just a beginning. Later on, when you feel like it, this is something you can repeat again and again. A good time to do it is when you have questions about something which you haven't been able to answer through other means and you need some time alone to do some deep thinking. You can use it to help you make difficult decisions, too.

Thus, whenever you want, find a quiet place out in nature and let yourself tune into the elements or forces of nature. Then, once again experience whatever you experience.

Chapter Twelve

Developing Balance
And Personal Control

The Need for Balance

As you develop your intuitive abilities—your abilities of seeing, dreaming, projection, and the like—it's important to use these with balance. This way you can incorporate them into your life in a harmonious way, and you can feel balanced and integrated. Your goal should be to 1) balance out the use of these intuitive abilities with your everyday rational approach to the world and 2) use these abilities to achieve balance in what you do in life. You want to have balance in both your goals and the methods you use to achieve them.

Balancing Your Intuitive and Rational Abilities

The first key to a balanced approach to life is being aware that there are two sides of yourself—the intellectual, rational side, which corresponds to the more mundane everyday world of outward appearances and experiences, and the more intuitive, creative side, which has the ability to see into other realities. To achieve balance, you need to keep these two sides in perspective, so they work together and complement each other.

As you learn how to become more intuitive you don't want to spend too much time getting involved in seeing and projection, so that you lose touch with everyday reality. On the other hand, if you're not enough in touch with your intuitive abilities, you can get so caught up in everyday reality that you lose your perspective and sense of balance, too.

So the ideal is to have both. The way to do this is by using your insights into the intuitive world to gain information and guidance. Then, you can take that knowledge and apply it to everyday life to make your own life better and adapt to everyday experiences and changes. This way you can feel a sense of assurance and calm, whatever happens. You won't get overly upset when difficulties occur. And you can be flexible in response to events. Whatever occurs, you can look on your experiences and say, 'Okay, I've gained what I need to learn from this particular thing and now I'm ready to move on to something else.'

By having this balance you can feel a sense of power and control over all aspects of your life. As appropriate, you can respond and adapt to events, or when you wish, you can act to take charge and shape those events yourself. It's like stepping into the control room of your life. By being balanced you give yourself that power as the coordinator and director to keep things in control, so you can react and adapt to everyday life in the best possible way.

Keeping Your Life in Balance

The ideal is to achieve balance in all aspects of your life—physical, emotional, and intellectual, and in your relationship with your self, others, and the world as a whole. Your intuitive powers can help you do this by sensing how you should respond in a particular situation.

In the physical sphere you want to take care of your body and your well-being. Again there's that ideal of balance. For instance, on the one hand you want to eat and enjoy, but you don't want to over-indulge. On the other hand, you don't want to diet to get too thin, because then you don't have enough strength.

Likewise, in the emotional sphere you can use your intuitive powers to help you stay on an even keel. And you can use them to help direct the use of your intellect, too, so you seek and obtain the appropriate knowledge. They can also help balance out how you feel about and perceive yourself, relate to others, and see yourself in the larger universal picture.

The following chapter describes the various ways you can use your intuitive abilities to help achieve this feeling of balance and control in your life.

Using Your Powers For Positive Ends

One of the most important keys for staying in balance is using the abilities you develop in a positive way to help yourself and help others. Otherwise, if you start using these powers for negative ends, you will find this negativity will come back at you, because the universe is like a big balance scale. In effect, when you put out a certain amount of negative energy, some other negative energy will appear to balance that out, although these types of energies may be expressed in different forms. For example, you may put out a negative thought and receive back negative actions, or you may act in a negative way and that may produce negative feelings. But the two forms of negativity will appear—the original negativity and the reaction, because the second arises in response to the first as a way to keep the scale in balance.

You might also look at the process of keeping yourself in balance as playing a kind of game with rules. It's like the universe is a game board with millions of players, and the basic rule is that there is a certain justice in the universe, which some call karma. It's a rule of fairness and balance, and according to this rule the universe responds back to the things you do in kind. So if you are doing good things, you'll get the support of the universe. But if you do bad things, you'll get bad things back. The process may not happen immediately; it may take some time before the action of the rule of justice takes effect. Just as in playing any game, the referee may not immediately see your foul and give you a penalty, or at times the scoregiver may not observe and reward your score. But in the long run, what you do will be noticed, so that generally what you put out will come back to you. It's like hitting a ball against a backboard. Hit a good hit, and you'll get a good return. But hit one too hard or at a wrong angle, and you'll probably have difficulty dealing with the ball when it comes back to you.

Discovering and Acting from your Center

Another way to stay in balance is to use your intuitive powers to discover your true will and act from it. In fact, one of the reasons for training to use these techniques is to look within to discover this true will and develop the knowing so you know how and when to act. Working with the forces of nature in the field and doing intuitive exercises can help to give you these insights. But then you have to ask yourself, what do you really want from life for yourself, so you have this central purpose and recognize your true will. Once you are in touch with this, you will have more focus and therefore more power and control in everyday life.

As long as you continue to act from this sense of commitment and direction, you can feel very much in balance and in control over what you do. Yet, since there are times when you can be thrown off of this center, you need to be on guard against situations that can cause you to lose this direction. One way is to prepare yourself in advance for such situations and perhaps avoid them. Or if you notice that a situation is occurring which is pulling you off balance, pull yourself away from it.

For example, if you get into an argument with someone you know, it can be easy to get upset and you can forget to stay centered. You may lose your sense of calm balance and feel out of control. Therefore, if you experience this happening, you might work on calming down, focusing on what you really want from that relationship, or perhaps pull yourself away from the situation, so that the angry emotion goes away and you get back to being centered again. Then you can move from that center back into that relationship again, if you feel it is beneficial for you overall, and try to work things out as smoothly as possible. If not, then perhaps see this experience as an indication it is time to break the connection and move on to other things.

Developing Balanced Relationships With Others

These intuitive abilities can also help you in developing more harmonious, balanced relationships with others. One reason this occurs is because the insights you gain will help you to be more sensitive to others, so you have a better sense of where they are coming from. You can use this knowledge to have more acceptance and compassion for others, which contributes to having a good relationship. Acceptance means accepting people where they are at, while compassion means being more sympathetic and understanding of others. With acceptance and compassion you can not only have a smoother relationship in the here and now, but you can help others move on and simultaneously develop yourself.

This process works, for when you seek to help others you are gaining something for yourself too—sometimes in the immediate satisfaction you get from helping, sometimes in the return help the person may give to you, and often both. It's part of the balance in the universe. You may do something altruistic to benefit others, and later that benefit you have given out comes back in some way to benefit you. So altruism is balanced out with your own self-interest, whereby you gain when you help others gain as well.

A good example of this is the teacher. A teacher may give something to other people in the form of knowledge. But she also gets something back when she experiences satisfaction in seeing others learn and grow. And even a person whose whole purpose is helping others gets something back. There's a certain satisfaction that comes from seeing the realization of one's goals.

Likewise, when you're helping other people, you're doing things for yourself at the same time. So there's a balance in doing both. And that's fine. You want that balance in a relationship, so everybody wins. There's a balance of self-interest with what you are giving to others which is the basis of a good relationship, whether that relationship is a personal or business one.

And you do need that balance. For if the relationship is primarily based on your own self-interest, eventually it will fall apart because the other person will feel exploited. Or if there's too much altruism, and you don't feel you are getting enough out of the arrangement, you will eventually start feeling resentful, and the relationship will fall apart for that reason, too.

It doesn't matter whether the relationship is primarily personal or business. The same principles hold. For example, the people who are the most successful business people in the long run are those who are providing good products and services to others, so there is a real benefit they are giving. And that comes back to them in the form of their own profit from the benefit given.

It's the same with your own personal development. If you can provide services or benefits to others that they find useful, they will respond in ways that benefit you. People will like you, want to be with you, do things for you. Or if you have a service, they will pay you for it.

Thus, there's a kind of social balance in the world which helps to link and unite us to each other. And as long as there is that reciprocal relationship based on the cord of altruism that pulls us toward others and the cord of self-interest that pulls others towards us, the relationship stays in balance. It's as if the ties of altruism and self-interest are equal, so we are in equilibrium with others. Their pull on us and our pull on them is about the same, so we are both in balance with each other.

To achieve this state of balance you will find it very productive to both work on satisfying your self-interest and on helping others, because in the long run you will get back from them what you put out, and that will satisfy your self-interest, too.

Working with People of Good and Bad Will

The formula of balancing altruism with self-interest works when you are dealing with people who are coming from a place of good will. In this case, when you do something for other people and they feel good, they will want to do something for you in return. As a result, with such people you want to be altruistic and helpful, because the benefits you offer will come back to you in kind.

By contrast, if you realize that people are not acting from a good will place, this approach doesn't work, because when you try to do good things for them, they may try to take advantage of you. So you have to be aware of this possibility and protect yourself accordingly. In turn, you can learn this through your sense of knowing which gives you information on whether to trust someone or not.

For example, Tony tried to be very understanding and help a client in rewriting a project for him and meeting his deadlines. But later, as Tony realized, this client was not coming from a place of good will. Instead, he was overly demanding and self centered, so that the more Tony tried to be helpful and see things from the client's point of view, the more the client tried to take advantage of Tony. He did so by making Tony appear to be in the wrong when he wasn't. The client kept telling Tony he had followed the instructions incorrectly, when in fact it was the client himself who repeatedly gave Tony the wrong instructions in the first place. In a case like this, when you recognize that someone is coming from a place of ill will and wants to take advantage of your good will, you have to close up and conceal your vulnerability. You may need to respond by being equally tough or perhaps cutting off the relationship entirely, since it may be more profitable to deal with only those people who are coming from good will and seeking win-win solutions. It may not be worth it to get caught up in a win-lose encounter with a person coming from an ill will orientation.

It's important to make this good will/bad will distinction in dealing with people, so you can be ready to put up your guard if need be. Normally you can expect people to come from a good will place, though motivated by self-interest. A businessman may seek to gain a good profit, but he will also recognize that if he doesn't provide a good service he will lose in the long run by losing clients. By contrast, the con artist who doesn't think of the future may make a short-term gain, but he will lose in the end. He may get what seems like an excellent bargain now because he has been a hard-nosed and crafty negotiator. But then he may find the person who feels cheated will never work with him again, and may warn his friends as well. So in the long run the con artist will fail.

The best approach is to start off by coming from a good will place yourself, which means being open and trying to help other people, so they feel good. But if you feel that people are taking advantage of your goodness, then cut this approach off. This way of responding is part of the balancing process. You start by putting out a little bit of yourself, and if other people respond in kind so they appear to be coming from a good will place, too, then you can keep going. You can open up and offer to help them even more. Likewise, if they respond positively, so can you. For as long as this good will/good will arrangement prevails, you can relate to the other person in a spirit of openness and trust, which is ideal. After all, when we're working with good will people, that's the optimal state. It permits us to work together in peace and harmony because there's trust; everyone involved is seeking a win-win relationship.

However, not everybody is coming from this place and some people are waiting for others to open up and show their vulnerability. You do have to be ready to watch for such people if necessary, and then you can either put up your protective barriers or get out of the situation.

As an example of how this works, I was at a meeting of a community conflict resolutions group and an extremely angry woman was there describing how many other people in her apartment building had been treating her badly. They had been making noise and blaming her for making noise herself, and now she was upset because her landlord had given her an eviction notice and she thought he wanted to get rid of her. However, what had really led to the situation was a breakdown in communication, so that the woman thought her neighbors were trying to make noise to disturb her and they thought the same of her. So everyone was thinking and acting as if the others were coming from a place of bad will. And if that was true, there could have been no resolution.

But as soon as the woman vented her own complaints and was willing to listen to the others, she became aware that her landlord didn't really want to get rid of her. He just wanted some peace and quiet and thought the eviction was the only way to get this. When she heard this, she was willing to make some concessions to cut down on some of her own noise and another neighbor said she would be willing to do the same. After this, almost miraculously, the battle of the neighbors calmed down, and this woman who had come to the meeting like an angry shrew turned into a little lamb who was so thankful that the conflict resolution group had somehow helped her cut through this thicket of hostilty. Yet, what really made this good outcome possible was the neighbors themselves, since they all wanted to come from a good will place. So once they saw that in each other, they were able to begin to trust and work together once again.

Whenever possible open yourself up to come from a place of good will if others are willing to do the same. But if not, be ready to close down again to protect yourself. Use your knowing to sense where people are coming from, so you can decide. The result will be more balance in your relationships.

Sharing Your Power with Others

Another key way to stay balanced in your relations with others is to be aware of the power relationship you are in with them, and to feel comfortable with the amount of power you each have. For example, if you are the dominant partner or usually take the initiative in a relationship, that means the other person has given some power over to you. Or if you usually follow the other person's lead, that means you have given that person power. If you feel comfortable with that balance, fine, but if you feel the person has too much power over you, take some of that power back; or if you feel you want less control in that relationship, give up some of your power.

Probably the most common out-of-balance situation is when you feel overpowered or manipulated by someone else. A common reason this happens is that we give people power over us, but aren't aware that we have given them this power. One man at a workshop reported this power problem with a long-term friend who was extremely influential over him—too influential. Yet, he felt he couldn't break away. "I really feel cramped around him," he said. "My whole body even cringes when I do something he doesn't like. I can feel his disapproval sweep all over me."

However, as the man came to realize, he only felt his friend's disapproval because he had given him that power. Originally, when they had first become friends, they had a more equalitarian relationship. But the friend started becoming increasingly authoritative and demanding, while the man became more submissive. As a result, he felt overly controlled. After awhile he recognized that the man had only gained this power over him because he had given it up. So he could take that power back from his friend and get that control again; and this is what he did. One day he stood up to his friend. "I took back the power," he explained. "I told him: 'Okay, you've done enough. Now I want to make my own decisions. I want myself back.' And so he gave me back the power and went on to take control of someone else. It was hard to make that break. But at least I now feel free."

Keeping a Balance of Power and Good Will

Perhaps one way to think of balancing out your relationship with others is to think of yourself as a captain over your own personal growth. In this role, and you can direct your power and control to achieve your desired goals. Also, you work with and help others along the way and you share some of your power with them in the process.

In effect, as a ship captain, you are steering through this waterway that is like life. Accordingly, when the sea is calm and things are working, you can go full speed ahead. But when the sea is rough and things are not working, you need to slow down or pull back and you must seek to protect yourself from the possible dangers around you.

In other words, as long as everything is peaceful and harmonious, that's a sign all is safe, so you can keep going ahead. But as soon as you see the waves starting to swell or feel the winds blowing or changing direction, you know it's time to maneuver appropriately to move your ship in another direction and change course or at least proceed more slowly and cautiously. When the storm calms down, you can move on ahead as before.

By being aware and ready to respond, you've got that control over the ship of yourself. At the same time, realize that all the other people that you deal with are like the passengers on your ship or part of the crew. And most of them will work and cooperate with you. For instance, they'll help you put up the sails or they'll go where you ask them to go on the ship. For they have an understanding of the power relationship you have worked out between you, and they are coming from a place of good will.

However, if you see someone on your ship who is trying to take over as captain, you know you have a power problem to deal with. Or if you notice someone who is trying to sabotage the voyage and keep the ship from going where you want, you know you have a person acting from a place of ill will. So though you may expect and hope that things will sail along smoothly, you still have to stand guard and be ready to act should problems arise. You shouldn't become paranoid, but at the same time you can't trust completely. You need that balance to keep your ship on its proper course.

Dealing with Challenges and Keeping Your Balance

Commonly, when you sail that smooth course, keep things in balance, and do good, positive things, life will proceed along smoothly and you'll feel the sense of peace and harmony that comes with that. But occasionally you may encounter some obstacles and challenges along the way. It's like someone is throwing you a curve or giving you a test to see if you can handle what happens, so you don't get lulled into thinking everything is easy and become blase.

However, when you do get through these tests, you will find you have come out a stronger, better person because of them. You know more because of the experience and you discover you have new powers and strengths you may not have thought you had. Or you will develop these powers and strengths then as a result of encountering and mastering the experience. For example, you may find yourself in a difficult situation, such as giving your first speech or taking on a new and more responsible job, and you're not sure you can handle it. Then when you find you can, you will feel this great sense of power and mastery that you have done it.

These kinds of problems can occur in a number of ways. In some cases you might encounter a situation where you feel you couldn't have gotten through it unless you had developed special powers or had special protections, such as happened once to Michael. He was out in the desert and his car was ready to break down, yet he drove along feeling a sense of inner strength and protection. When he drove into the gas station, getting extraordinary gas mileage, the attendant expressed his amazement: "I don't understand how you did it. You were driving without any shocks, and by all rights you should have run out of gas. I've never seen this kind of car go so far on one tank before."

In other cases, you might find yourself repeatedly exposed to a series of difficulties and come out better for the experience. You have learned from them, rather than letting their cumulative effect destroy you. In this type of situation, the individual effect of one obstacle might not seem particularly great, but then as problems occur, the impact mounts up until the problem can seem overwhelming. It's like the universe has suddenly turned it's disfavor on you. But when you can look at that series of difficulties, figure out how to deal from them, learn from the experience to do better in the future, and in essence, turn the whole situation around, you suddenly get a huge charge of power. It's like you've turned a negative into a positive and have achieved a synthesis or a balance in that way.

Gaining Strength Through Overcoming Your Difficulties in Achieving Goals and in Relationships

Two of the major areas where you may encounter challenges and difficulties are in achieving your goals for success and in personal relationships. But in either case, as you overcome your fears or find that you can do something you didn't think you could do, you will gain an inner strength and become more centered and balanced.

I had this experience after I received my doctorate in sociology. I had managed to get it by just writing papers and not taking any tests so, although I had the credential, I wasn't sure I really deserved it and I had avoided these tests because I was afraid of them. I thought maybe if I was tested, I would find I couldn't do well and for me that was very disturbing. However, after getting the degree I felt the need to show myself that I really could do it. So for three years I sat in on anthropology classes and seminars and actually took some tests—not because the grades were recorded anywhere, but because I wanted them for me. In fact, one of the classes I confronted and mastered was a statistics class, which was something that had always terrified me. But once I finished that and learned that if I had gotten a grade it would have been an A, I felt like I could do anything. For I had met this challenge that had frightened me and I had overcome it.

I also used to be terrified of public speaking. But I met the challenge head on by joining Toastmasters. Likewise with with my other early fears, one by one, I encountered and overcame them, and each time I felt a surge of confidence that there was more and more that I could do.

I think that's true for anyone. You can find that power in yourself, if only you confront the obstacles that stand in your way. And with each obstacle overcome, you will feel more power and control, for the more you do this the more you discover you have all the capabilities that you never thought you had.

Likewise, you can come through problems in relationships to gain more inner strength. One woman reported some devastating experiences she had when a few of her relationships ended. "I felt like I wanted to die," she said. "I felt like I would never live through it. I had become so dependent on these people that when they left it was like the end of the world for me." But after a few such incidents, she came to feel stronger and she learned to be less dependent on people in the future. As she reported, "I got this inner strength and I discovered parts of myself that I didn't even know were there. And so I learned. And I feel like I'm a better person now as a result."

This inner strength helped her in making an ethical choice and breaking out of a bad relationship, and when she made the choice which she felt was right, she felt even stronger as a result. Another woman named Sarah gained a feeling of such strength, when she had to make a choice when her mother broke her leg and needed her help. But her boyfriend wanted her to join him for the weekend, as she usually did. But Sarah felt her obligation to her mother had to come first, so she chose that, although it resulted in losing her boyfriend. Initially, the loss felt devastating, but as Sarah thought about it she felt she had done the right thing, and she felt a surge of spiritual strength as a result. As she described the experience.

"I had to choose between being with my lover or helping my mother. I was torn, but I picked my mother. I told my lover that I was going to be with her, and as a result my lover dropped me. He told me, 'You picked her, you know.' So he wrote me a Dear John letter and I went through this experience like death and dying...

Yet all of a sudden I thought, Well, I did the right thing. I thought if this person is going to drop me over my helping a relative, my mother of all people,then I don't want to be with that person....

I can't explain it, but when he left I went through this terrible-death like experience. I felt almost suicidal. Like if I was near a tall building or in the wrong spot at the wrong time, I would have done myself in. I was really in the depths of despair. But a few days later what came to me was that I made the right decision. So even though I lost my friend, I gained spiritually because I did what was best..

And as soon as I realized that, I got this inner strength that I never felt before. Like I found out that I don't really need people that much—that I have this inner strength to help me...I had been relying on this person so much and I realized I that I didn't need to do this anymore. I realized this person wasn't everything I needed. But you never really know that kind of thing until the person's gone. You think you need someone when you don't, simply because he's there. I found this a real growing experience, and I came out of it a much stronger independent person."

Also, anyone in an overly dependent relationship can find new strengths in themselves when they break away, for they suddenly realize they can do many things they thought they couldn't. There have been many examples of this in situations where a dependent woman's husband or lover goes off to war. Suddenly he's gone and she feels a great loss. She may feel very scared at being alone and having to now fend for herself. But then she discovers she can do all these things and gains a new personal independence for herself. This may sometimes break up the relationship when he comes back if he can't accept this, because she has taken some of the power back that she had given him. But whether the relationship endures or not, she has grown as a person by discovering more of her inner strength.

You can become similarly stronger by facing the various obstacles and challenges that present themselves along the way and calling on your inner powers to help you do this. Then you will commonly feel an increased sense of balance and harmony that accompanies this feeling of inner strength.

The Risks of Things Being Too Easy

You have seen some of the benefits of overcoming difficulties. By contrast, if things are too easy for you, you risk not developing this inner power. This is the case because if you initially obtain victory after victory, or if things at first come very easily to you, you may become weak or lose that inner spark.

An example would be the spoiled child who is given most everything while he or she is young. He or she therefore usually develops very little ambition to achieve. This occurs because such children develop the attitude: Why work for it when it's freely given? It's easier to do nothing, so these people have very little desire to achieve as they grow, despite prevailing opportunities.

In contrast, many people who become truly successful are those who have had real struggles. A prime example of this difference in development is shown by what happens in high school. Here often the most popular kids are the least successful afterwards, because they are part of the "in" crowd that values a superficial attractiveness. On the other hand, many of the least popular high school students who really work hard and struggle are the ones that bloom afterward. They have honed their skills in the fire of hard work.

And that's true for many people who suffer a lot of hard times and struggles. If they overcome the challenge, they come out much better for it. Some studies have shown that the entrepreneurs who have really made it big in business have failed an average of seven times, and then they make it through.

The process of personal development and growth is thus a little bit like what happens when a piece of soft metal is put through a flame. The flame strengthens it; it hardens the metal into something solid and strong. Likewise you can strengthen yourself by going through the flames or challenges in your life. For if things are too easy, you can lose perspective. You can start taking things for granted and think everything is so easy. But the world isn't like that. It's full of uncertainty, challenges, and obstacles along the way. But you can overcome most if you persevere.

Dealing with Bigger and Bigger Challenges

As you move forward along the path, you may find that the challenges become bigger and bigger. You have overcome one obstacle, but then another appears. However, now you are even stronger, so as the bigger challenges appear you are better able to deal with them. When you do, your accomplishment is that much greater.

A common example of this is the student in school. As he or she advances, the courses become harder and harder, the information more and more specialized and difficult to master. But at the same time, the student knows more, so he or she can understand the more difficult subject. And the degree received at the end for achievement reflects this. It is more valuable the higher the student goes.

The same sort of process occurs in sports. The good player moves on to greater and greater challenges, and as he does there are both more risks and more rewards. Think of the person who enters a motorcycle contest. When he first gets started and travels slowly, there isn't a great deal of risk involved. But as he learns more and goes faster, the potential for danger rises. But he also has more skill, so he can take on more danger and then usually come through successfully. To be sure, at times he may go too far and then will fall back. But that is all part of the process of growing and getting better. At each stage of growth there will come a breakthrough, and the person will move on to a much higher level of achievement and skill.

Likewise, the same kind of process occurs on the psychic or spiritual level, although here the challenges often come in the forms of unknowns as you explore other levels of reality. In a sense, you are exploring new frontiers or realms of consciousness as you delve into yourself and your personal powers. But just like the student or the athlete, the further you go, the more challenges you take on, the more able and skilled you will become. There may be risks in the process because you may gain self-knowledge or other knowledge that may be difficult to deal with at first. But just like the student or athlete who perseveres and overcomes a challenge, you will be better able to deal with whatever comes next. So the further you look into the unknown, the more you will know about this normally unconscious other world and the more you will be able to tap these powers and apply them in your everyday life. This occurs because you know more, so you can do more, and your challenges, achievements and rewards will be that much greater as a result.

Recognizing Your Own Limits

While part of growth is taking on and overcoming these challenges, it is also important to approach these challenges in a balanced way. And that means knowing how far to go. You have to take into consideration your own limitations and the limitations of others, so that you move ahead, but not too far.

Knowing how far to go is part of the whole process of knowing and recognizing what you know. At certain times, you may realize you can surpass past limitations and then it's time to move on. But at other times you may not be ready, and then it is best to wait. In other words, be ready to take that calculated and knowing risk at times, when it seems appropriate for you to confront a challenge and move on to another level. But at other times, be ready to wait when the challenge is too big for now.

Thus, part of balance is being aware of your own limitations. You want to move on but you also have to balance that by knowing when to hold back. You have to balance doing by not doing too much, and the key to this balance lies in your paying attention to what you can do and what you know.

Recognizing Yourself When You Overcome Challenges

When you do overcome some challenge, it's good to recognize yourself in some way. It's a way of reminding yourself that you have accomplished something, that you have gone through the challenge. It's a kind of self-appreciation which will help you feel good and motivate you to continue on to deal with still more challenges.

Some ways to recognize yourself might be to give yourself a pat on the back to acknowledge yourself; give yourself a little certificate of recognition; or say to yourself: "I've accomplished this." To keep things in balance you can use a small symbol or small act of recognition to recognize when you have overcome a small or fairly ordinary type of challenge. But if you have overcome something big, you might have a celebration. Take yourself out to dinner; go out with someone and do something special; maybe even make up a certificate of graduation or a pin that indicates that you have moved on to another level. Many organizations use such recognition ceremonies or graduation symbols when their members achieve something or pass some test. You can do the same to recognize yourself.

Accepting and Responding to the Flow of Things

Another way to gain balance in your life is to accept and go with the flow of events in your life. By moving with the current you let yourself flow with the waves, rather than fight against them, and you'll find that everything seems to happen much more smoothly.

With this approach things will seem to flow into your life when you need them, and you'll find yourself worrying less because there's no need to worry about something before it's ready to happen. You'll feel that when things are ready to happen, they will, and you will feel confident that you will be ready to do whatever needs to be done at the appropriate time.

One woman at a workshop who approached life this way reported that it seemed to work for her. She would think about something she wanted, feel confident this would happen, and then find it did. As she commented:

> "I've sometimes had the experience where I know I needed the money by a certain time. For example, I once moved into a place when I was out of work and I needed $300 by a certain date to pay the rent. I didn't know exactly where it was going to come from, but I had the feeling that I would get the money. And I did.
>
> Well, I've found that has happened again and again. I know I need something, and I send out this message to the universe that I'm going to get that. And somehow I'll find a way. I'll get the money or whatever. And it's really amazing, the way it seems to work. I ask and what I need seems to come into my life. I don't just sit there and wait for it. I go and do whatever I normally do. But I put it out; I ask for it, and the universe seems to respond."

I have had the same sort of experience myself over and over again. I have felt a need for something and then, almost as if the universe is listening, an event soon occurs and exactly what I need appears in my life. For instance, about twenty years ago I started working as a freelance writer. At first it was very scary because at times I would feel like I was never going to get another project in. But then, as soon as I finished one thing and had some space in my life, someone would call and I would get in another project. So after a time, I began to feel that somehow there is this natural flow, and I've learned to accept the process. It's like the tides going in and out. When the tide goes out, you know it's going to come back in again, so you don't have to worry that that will happen. I've come to see the ebb and flow of work in much the same way. I've come to feel there will always be another project coming in to fill up a space in my life whenever I need it. And for twenty years, that's the way things seem to have worked.

If you have that kind of approach to whatever happens in life, you can keep the hard times in perspective because you know they will flow back out again and the good times will flow back in again, much like the tide.

Being Flexible in Dealing with Stress

When you adopt this 'go with the flow' approach, it will also help you to be flexible so you can better deal with stress. Stress is an ordinary part of everyday life and people commonly feel this whenever they face a new situation they have to deal with.

The difference between people that are successful in dealing with the situation and the stresses they feel and those that aren't is that the successful people are centered, balanced, and flexible. They don't let the stress they feel overcome them or deflect them from overcoming a challenge if this is something they want to do. They don't feel upset by the difficulties they face. Rather, they just look on the situation as another challenge to overcome, and they go with whatever challenges the situation presents. They feel confident they can handle whatever comes up.

The process is a little like being a reed in the water. By bending with the waves when the tide washes in, the reed can snap back up again when the tide washes out. But if the reed tried to stand straight and firm, it would probably break apart under the stress. So be like the reed yourself and bend in response to stress. Then the stress will flow back out without breaking you, much like what happens to the reed in the water.

Being Prepared to Deal with the Unknown

Besides being flexible in dealing with stress, you should also be prepared to deal with the unknown generally, by recognizing that everything in life is uncertain and subject to change. If you are responsive to the unfolding of events as they happen, you can go with the flow and achieve a better outcome.

For example, if something happens that seems to be a negative event, you may be able to avoid any bad consequences by being prepared. Then you can simply get out of the way. Or perhaps you can gain some important knowledge from the experience or act on it to turn it around.

You need to be prepared to deal with the unexpected consequences of what seem to be good things too, because sometimes you can end up with bad results if you don't deal with a good event properly—and this outcome can throw you off from where you are going.

A prime example of this is someone who wins the lottery. Normally, you would think this would be a wonderful event and the big winner can feel he has achieved that pinnacle of success —money, fame—he can feel like he suddenly has it all. However, I have read of a number of cases where these winners have run into difficulties because they haven't been able to deal with their good fortune. They may have arguments with friends and relatives who come to them seeking help or who are jealous. They may get persuaded to make bad investments and lose much of their money that way. Or they may become so grasping now that they have money that they fail to act ethically or fairly. In one case, a big jackpot winner claimed his friend, who gave him some money to gamble, had nothing to do with the jackpot—because the winner wanted it all. So the two formerly good friends ended up in court and not talking to each other instead of sharing the good fortune which was really due to their joint efforts.

People who have other kinds of good things happen can similarly encounter problems if they aren't prepared to deal with their good fortune in a reasonable and balanced way. For then things can go wrong and they can end up losing their success.

Still others may lose what they have gained because they take it for granted. They don't continue to work for the future —such as the person who takes an exam, does really well, and then doesn't prepare for the next one, with bad results.

So you have to realize that even success and good fortune can be very changeable. They can be very fleeting or suddenly disappear because life is full of unexpected events, and you generally have to keep working to keep them in your life.

Sometimes people feel that there is an abundance in life, and all they have to do is think it is there and it will be theirs. But it's not that easy. You have to work for that abundance. Certainly a positive attitude can help you bring good things into your life. But at the same time, you have to recognize that there are all sorts of difficulties you may encounter out there, and you have to be prepared for them when they occur.

It's all part of the process of keeping a balance. On the one hand, you want to do all you can to achieve success and good fortune. But at the same time, you have to recognize that there are a number of difficulties in the world. So it's important to be prepared to deal with all of these things—the good, the bad, the unexpected, and change. In the process, you need to have a positive outlook and try to make the best of what happens, because that will help you in achieving success. At the same time recognize that there are some real problems in the world and we have to face them. Then you can best balance out the positive and negative as you chart out your own course and steer through the ups and downs and through the unknowns that are continually popping up in life.

Chapter Thirteen

Overcoming Any Blocks To Personal Power And Charting Your Own Course

Becoming Aware of the Barriers

As you do move ahead to gain more power you may, from time to time, feel stuck or feel you aren't moving ahead as fast as you like. When such problems arise, this is the time to ask yourself: Is something holding me back? And then ask: What can I do to get through it as efficiently as possible?

The reason for asking these questions is so you can look at what might be the barrier holding you back, for you may need to deal with the barrier first before you can move on. There are a variety of ways to do this.

Share What's Bothering You

One way to deal with a difficult situation that's making you feel stuck is to share the problem. Talk about the situation with a neutral third party to get some feedback. Or if you are in a conflict situation with someone, it can often help to open up and share what's bothering you with that person, though in a calm, non-confrontive way. By dealing with the problem directly and finding a solution, instead of keeping it buried and letting it fester, you can move on with a minimum of conflict to something else.

Make the Problem Smaller

Another way to overcome a conflict situation is to cut it down to size. Imagine the problem is smaller, and if you are dealing with a person who is difficult, see that person as smaller, too.

You can do this mentally by seeing this situation or person as very small or growing smaller. And you can add even more impact to your decision to cut a problem down to size by literally cutting out a very small picture of that problem situation or person.

One woman at a workshop used to do this effectively at the suggestion of one of her aunts. As she described it:

> "Sometimes it may be difficult to understand or overcome a problem because you are so wound up in it. Even your analytical mind analyzing it won't help. But I had an aunt who suggested that whenever something really bothers you, cut out a picture and use animals or symbols or whatever to make a collage. Then, when you cut out a picture of the person who's bugging you, you make them very small. But you make all these birds, or animals, or other things in the collage very big.
>
> And I found this really worked, because you really see what's bothering you in a new perspective. Usually that person who's bothering you seems overwhelming, but then you cut them down to size and the problem seems to fade away."

The reason this type of approach works is because you take something that is bothering you and then symbolically you make it smaller in some way or you get rid of it. You bring it down to your own level so you can deal with it and overcome it. And the result is you feel an emotional letting go or release.

Distance Yourself from the Problem

Another approach to overcoming conflicts is to distance yourself from a problem situation if you find you are thinking about it too much and this thinking is not helping you solve the problem. In this case, it may be best to tell yourself that this is what you are doing and to let the problem go. Also, you might look at this situation and ask, 'What can I learn from this?' or think 'How can I use this beneficially?' You can then try to either accept the situation as it is now, or try to turn it around in some other way or do both. The value of letting go or learning from a situation and moving on is then you don't dwell on the situation too much or get stuck in it, which can hold you back.

Letting go or distancing yourself from a situation may not always be that easy. Sometimes it can be very hard to let go of the situation, even though intellectually you know that it's silly to think about it. Yet there's an emotional hook that keeps you tied.

For example, one woman in a workshop had an ongoing argument with her neighbor over a tree on her property. The neighbor complained that the tree blocked his view, but the woman had the right to let her tree grow as it did. One weekend, after she returned from a short trip, she discovered that the top of her tree had been hacked off. She was furious at her neighbor, because she was sure he had done it. For weeks she continued to simmer in anger until finally it came to her in a meditation that she needed to tell her neighbor what she thought, so she could release her anger and put the incident behind her.

Similarly, if you find yourself caught in thinking about some situation that has bothered you, to achieve balance you need to release and let go. It's fine to think about how you can handle a bad situation in the future so you can learn from it. But if you find yourself reviewing a situation over and over again in your mind to look for alternatives, at a certain point your thinking is no longer productive. You're just going over the same ground again and again. That's the time to put a stop to your thinking and chase those thoughts away.

To do so, however, you've got to break the habit pattern or groove of thinking you have built up, as well as the emotional tie. You've got to disconnect. One way, is to pull out some benefits from the situation so you can feel there's a good pay-off after all. Then your thoughts of this negative situation will likely fade of their own accord.

But an alternative might be to simply do some act to symbolically indicate you are letting go. That action will create the break. For example, you might do some kind of banishing ritual, such as writing down the incident on a piece of paper and then tearing it up or burning it to show that the situation is finished. Or perhaps set up some time to think about how you can learn from the situation, and after you have come up with all the things you can learn, tell yourself the incident itself is over. You have gained all you can from it and are ready to move on.

Using Your Knowing to Find a Solution

Your knowing can be a particularly valuable tool in both perceiving barriers and deciding on the best way of overcoming them. It can help you assess the situation so you know how far you can go and so you can choose among the possible alternatives. Also, it can help you know when to pull back when it is appropriate.

Michael, for instance, used this knowing in a number of tense situations to resolve a problem. In one case, a woman was taking a solo to get in touch with her own powers. She she was on a cliff and soon she began having some strange experiences in which she imagined that some spiritual beings were coming towards her and were enticing her to walk off the cliff to go towards them. Michael sensed that something potentially dangerous was happening to her and he got there in time to draw her back.

In another case, Michael was working on an ambulance run when he encountered a situation where one man was threatening another person with a gun. But he was able to calm the situation down by just getting a sense of what he should do. He spoke to the man with the gun in a way that convinced him to put it down and move on. And another time Michael saw two friends arguing at a campsite, and again he sensed exactly what to do to act quickly to calm them.

Essentially, this knowing can occur in a difficult or crisis situation to let you know what to do to solve it. The way it works is you just sit back or let your mind go and you imagine or think to yourself: 'What can I do now to deal with this situation?' And almost instantly, some insight will suddenly appear.

For example, this is what I did in the incident with my landlord, described earlier. I looked to my inner knowing to tell me what to do, and it gave me some excellent advice, which saved me about $5000.

Thus, when you listen to and trust your knowing, you can sense what is needed to resolve a problem and come up with that. By tuning in and developing this ability, you can use this sense of knowing when it comes to you to know the appropriate time to say something or act to achieve a balance or a resolution to a problem.

Tuning Into Your Knowing To Overcome Any Blocks or Turn a Difficult Situation Around—Exercise #16

The following exercise is designed to help you tune into any blocks or barriers you are experiencing in your own life and find a way to turn the problem around. You can use the suggested images in this exercise or create your own series of images to help you tune in and make changes.

Start by getting very relaxed maybe concentrate on your breathing for a few moments to calm down. You can notice your breathing going in and out, in and out.

What I'll be doing is giving you a series of images to think about, and each time you will have a chance to imagine how you can deal with and overcome one of the problems facing you.

To begin I'd like you to think of any difficult situation or problem that is facing you in your life. I'd like you to imagine that you are seeing this problem as separate from yourself, as a little mound of dirt which you are looking at. Now see yourself walking around it, looking at it, and realizing that this problem is apart from you.

As you look at it, think of how you might move it, or make it smaller by pulling some dirt away from it. Or maybe you can find some material to cover it up. Or perhaps bring somebody over to help you figure out what to do to get rid of this pile of dirt and solve your problem.

You might think about how you might turn this pile of dirt around to change it or do something different. And know that as you change this pile of dirt, you are also changing your problem.

Now take a few minutes to ask yourself about the situation you see in that pile of dirt. You want to deal with it as efficiently as you can to get rid of or solve the problem. So ask yourself things like: 'What can I do to solve it? Change it? Who might be able to give me some help?' Then let your mind go and see what suggestions and solutions come up.

When you feel ready, you can walk away from that situation and see the pile disappear or disintegrate. Or take your shovel, and shovel the pile away. It is gone now for you have found a way to resolve that problem. You just have to put that situation into practice now and make it work.

When you're finished with that problem, you can go on to look at another one and resolve this too. And this time, imagine that you are watching a performance in front of you. It may be on a stage or screen, or maybe you're watching it on TV. Or perhaps listen to the story unfolding on the radio if you prefer.

Whatever you are viewing or listening to, just focus on it for a few moments. You'll see a problem that concerns you revealed there as you listen or watch.

Now see yourself as the director. You are in charge of that performance and you can guide it however you want. So now imagine various ways in which you can make this performance different. Ask yourself: 'Can I change the people? Can I make the situation different? Can I change myself? Or maybe can I make some changes in parts of the scenery?' Then think of all the changes you might make.

At the same time you make these changes, see yourself growing stronger and stronger. Recognize that you are in charge of the performance, and you can direct it as you wish. Also, realize that you have the power to stop it at any time, because maybe the performance isn't as important as you think.

Finally, choose a third problem. Or if you wish, take one of the preceding problems if you want to look at it in another way.

Now imagine that you've got a group of experts around you. These are people that you can turn to for advice about what to do to resolve a problem. You can ask them for information, and you'll find they have lots of ideas.

Now start asking them some questions if you want. You can ask them what you can do now to turn things around. Ask them: "What can I do differently to overcome my problem." Listen to what they say. Ask more questions if you have them to get specific guidelines on what to do.

Then when you feel finished and complete, when you're ready, come back into the room and open your eyes. You should be feeling good because you've come up with some good ideas and solutions to deal with your problems.

You can use the above exercise to deal with all sorts of problems in all areas of your life. And you may find that different images evoke different types of problems. For example, one woman found when she looked at the screen she saw a noted radio doctor who gave her tips on what to do about her health. Then, when she spoke with her team of advisors, they told her what to do about a person she was having difficulties with. With their help, she made him smaller by symbolically taking a shovel and pushing him down into the pile of dirt. As she described it:

"When you said to make the dirt pile smaller or move it around, I just saw the problem dissolving. I thought it doesn't matter anymore what the problem is because we're greater than the problem.

And then I realized that this man may not be happy with what I'm doing, but I'm ruining my life trying to please him... I've been ruining my life because I realized that I'm making him this big monster... But he's just a person, and I don't have to be afraid of him anymore. So I started shoveling him into the ground.

And then he became this little tiny man. He was like a paper doll looking up at me. But I was way up here—this big giant woman. And then he simply dissolved and became a spirit and flew away like a bird.

So in the end, I felt free."

Learning to Be Flexible In Response to Challenges -Exercise #17

Your ability to be flexible and adapt can also help you deal with the problems and challenges you encounter on the path to greater personal or spiritual development. You have to expect to have various challenges and stresses along the way, because part of personal development is seeking new challenges so you grow. As a result, these challenges in the form of obstacles and barriers to overcome will continually be popping up.

Therefore, you should be flexible and willing to adapt and bounce back, so that whenever a problem comes up you will try to work it out as quickly as you can and then move on. That way you don't get stuck in it or worry about it.

It doesn't matter if the problem you encounter is serious or minor. If you have this basic attitude of being flexible and moving on, you will generally come up with a good solution, so this approach will work. For example, say you are in a dangerous situation such as a mugger confronting you. If you can think of something very quickly, you can probably talk yourself out of the situation. Or suppose it's a more mundane situation, such as lost keys. If you're responding with flexibility you might simply ground yourself and relax, and in this state of calm you might suddenly remember where the keys are. But if you suddenly start panicking by thinking of what may happen, you may not only not find your keys, but you will likely get extremely upset.

Your ideal should be to have the ability to adapt and stay in control of the situation. And at the same time, you want to move on and grow as a result of the situation, too.

The following exercise is designed to help you become more flexible and adaptible by thinking of new ways to respond to a variety of situations. There are a series of images suggested. You can use them all to work with different situations, or if you prefer, select those images that work best for you—and feel free to develop your own.

Once again, close your eyes, calm down, and get relaxed. Get centered and focus within. Perhaps pay attention to your breathing going in and out, in and out.

In a few moments, we'll be thinking about how you can be flexible in situations so you can decide when it's best to move on and how to do that. I'll be giving you a series of images, and again you can work with all of these images, or choose those that feel most comfortable.

First, I'd like you to take any situation where you feel you have been stuck, and imagine that this situation is holding onto you like quicksand. So you really feel trapped and stuck.

Take a moment to feel that feeling and see yourself in some quicksand on a beach. The situation is holding you down like that. But you notice a rope along the side and you can use that to pull yourself up and out.

The situation you are in is like that. You can get out of it too. So imagine yourself doing something like pulling on a rope to get yourself out. And then see yourself walking away, just like you're walking away from that pit of quicksand on the beach.

Now choose another situation—or even the same one if you want to work on it some more, and see yourself in a campsite, and imagine that this situation is in a tent that is plugged into the ground. It's like this problem is stuck in the ground inside the tent, too.

However, know that whatever the situation is, it is something you can walk away from. You can leave it there in that tent. Or if you want, there might be some things from the situation you might want to take with you. A few good experiences, a few memories, some insights you have learned. If you want, you can stop at the tent, open the flaps, look inside and pull out whatever you want from that situation and take it with you. And then you can leave it all there and move on.

Also, if you wish to completely eliminate something from your past, you can destroy it too. You can imagine it in the tent, and then you can light a match, and destroy that particular thing that's holding you back. Then, as you see the flames rise up you feel very free, and you know you have that ability to move and go on to other things, and you know that nothing is holding you back anymore. You feel completely free and ready to move on.

Now take another situation or the same one and imagine the situation you want to change or leave behind is in one town. But you are packing up and moving on. You can travel anyway you want.

If you want to take the train, see yourself at a train station. And perhaps imagine the situation you are leaving in a warehouse. But you are getting on the train and traveling away.

Or if you prefer, you can go to a nearby airport and take the plane. And when you do, you are leaving the situation behind. It doesn't have to come with you. It's in the past. It's gone. And again you feel that sense of release. You are free of one more piece of baggage from your past.

If you want to take another situation or the same one, here's one more image of transformation and change you can work with. This time, see yourself writing down a brief description of the situation. Perhaps you are in your bedroom or in your office writing it down. And you have a piece of paper or book before you.

Notice that there is a small stove near you. After you have written down your description, you turn on the stove and put the piece of paper with your write-up of the situation into the stove to burn it up. If you wish, you can tear up that piece of paper into little bits and then burn it up in the stove. Do this now.

Now that you have gotten rid of these situations that have been bothering you, realize that you can always get rid of any problems and difficulties that are bothering you in the future. You can do this because you always have control of yourself. You can step aside from whatever the problem is and walk away from it. You can look at it from a distance. You can tear it up and destroy it or burn it. And then you can go on to other things.

However you want to do it, you can always move on. Now, what I'd like you to do is take any situation and use any approach you feel comfortable with to destroy this problem and then move on. Realize you can destroy it, change it, put it behind you and go on to new and better things.

Wherever you are, see yourself traveling away from the problem situation you want to leave behind. If you're in quicksand, pull the rope and walk away. If you're in a campsite, you can leave the tent behind and walk across a nearby meadow. If you're taking a train or plane, you can travel away and arrive in a new setting. Or if you have just burned up your problem, turn off the stove and walk out of the room.

Whatever you do, the situation from the past is now behind you. You're ready to step into a new situation, a new setting. Go there and see it. Just look around and experience what this new situation is and feel very free.

Know that you can always bring this new situation into your life. You merely have to see it is there. For once you see it, once you visualize it, you can act on it to actually make it happen. See yourself doing this now. You're going towards this new situation, this new goal, doing whatever is necessary to make it happen. And it is happening now. Then when you feel ready, come back into the room.

Being Ready to Take Action

Once you know what the barriers are, once you are aware of challenges you want to overcome and the direction you want to go, you can take action. You can use these shamanic techniques for practical purposes to help you accomplish your goals. By working on becoming integrated in all your aspects, you are more ready to take action and deal more profitably and efficiently with any situations as they arise in life. And as discussed, this integration comes from being balanced.

The approach to shamanism described in this book is designed to provide a very pragmatic approach to your own personal development—one you can use to gain the information you need so you can know how to act in everyday life.

The approach is a little like spiritual capitalism, since you are developing yourself spiritually and intuitively. But at the same time, you are using these techniques to make your life work more efficiently, smoothly, and productively. You are trying to do what works. So much like the capitalist, you are investing in yourself and your own personal development in order to get a payoff in the everyday world in the form of results which will help both others and yourself.

So unlike some of the more meditative, withdrawal-oriented approaches to personal or spiritual growth, this approach is designed to be practical and action-oriented. You want to use those techniques that work; you want to be practical and apply what you learn. When you work with the various techniques like seeing, dreaming, ritual, and mental projection, you don't merely want to use them to learn more about yourself or better understand how to work with nature and the spritiual world. Rather, you want to take the information you gain about yourself, the forces of nature, and the spiritual powers to apply them to your own life. Then you can better deal with everyday situations as they arise, and when you are ready, move on.

Getting Unstuck and Moving On

To take this action and move on, you have to be unstuck from the past and meet ongoing challenges and problems as they come up. So if you feel stuck in anything, you need to pull away and let go to move on.

One common way of being stuck is repeating old patterns by doing something over and over again. For instance, you can be stuck in a relationship with someone that is going nowhere, stuck in a holding pattern of arguing with neighbors, stuck in a job which has become boring or is no longer a challenge. In such cases, it may be time to put whatever is making you feel stuck in the past so you can go onto something else where you can continue to grow. Whether it's a personal relationship that's holding you back, a work relationship that's gone sour, anything that makes you feel like you are repeating something over and over, or a particular situation which you feel is destructive or hurtful to you, let it go and move on. Also, if you are around a negative kind of person, such as a neighbor, friend, or work associate, and you feel their energy is pulling you down, or if you find yourself thinking too much about a negative situation, it's time to let go, too.

In short, there can be many different reasons for feeling stuck, but whatever the situation, when you feel this sense of being trapped it's time to put the situation in the past and move on.

Moving to a new place or travel can sometimes be a good way of cutting loose. I found this freeing myself. About ten years ago I was really feeling stuck in the San Francisco Bay Area, because I had been here for about ten years and I felt a need to get away for a little while. I needed a new environment, a new culture for a breath of fresh air. As a result I found a teaching job in Georgia for about six months, and I came back feeling very refreshed. I was ready to fit right back in and consider the Bay Area home again, and I felt committed that this is where I wanted to be. But to feel that way, I had to first get away so I could experience that feeling of freedom. I had both roots and a base, but I knew I could get away and be free too.

A brief vacation can give you the space you need to become unstuck. Often people can feel trapped by whatever work they are doing because of the regularity and repetition of it. But if you take off for awhile, you can come back invigorated and renewed, and perhaps with many ideas for new projects. When I went to the Soviet Union last summer, I had been feeling stuck because I had been doing the same thing for so long, though I basically liked what I was doing. When I returned, I had new ideas for books, games, new travel programs, all sorts of things. But I had to first get away to get renewed.

Using Key Markers In Your Life to Help You Move On

One way to help you get unstuck or move on is to use key markers in your life to mark a break with the past or a shift to something new. Our society already has a number of these which many people use, such as the dates marking the beginning of new seasons, the end of the school year, and New Years, when people make new resolutions. So we have a lot of designated endings and beginnings in our society which are institutionalized ways of moving on.

However, you can create your own markers which signify your own ending or graduation from something. In fact, you might think of these personal endings and beginnings as part of a series of cycles of different lengths of time. Some may be fairly long — say five, seven, or ten years—for long-term projects. But others may be much shorter, even a matter of months, weeks, or days, for different kinds of activities. So you can complete different things and mark this with graduations at different times.

Perhaps one way to think of the process is to imagine that your life is like a stage, and there are different parts of you, like characters in a play who are acting and moving on and off the stage at different times. While some of these characters have much larger, more important roles in the play, others have only a brief time to do their act.

In turn, you can develop different levels of graduation recognitions depending on the amount of time you have spent on something and its importance in your life. For example, if it's just a small sort of accomplishment or a fairly short cycle, then give yourself a similarly brief recognition, like a pat on the back or the acknowledgment: "I've done it." But for something of larger importance in your life, perhaps have a celebration or create a little certificate of graduation, as mentioned earlier. Rituals and ceremonies provide self-recognition and they are a way of letting your community of friends and associates know you have moved on, too.

Besides giving yourself achievement recognitions, you might also give yourself permission after an accomplishment to do something you want to do. This is a way of telling yourself that you've earned the ability to do more because you've tested yourself and have come through successfully. You can use this permission as a form of a reward for what you have done in the past. But at the same time, this permission looks ahead to the future and opens a door for you by telling you that you have gained more power and skill by what you have accomplished, so you have the ability to go on and do more. In other words, your permission is both a reward and a way of allowing yourself to do something else that maybe you thought you couldn't do before. But now you are telling yourself you think or know you can do it, and you are allowing yourself the space to let yourself do it. This way your permission can help you move on, too.

Chapter Fourteen

Recognizing Your Inner
Source Of Personal Power

Finally, as you move along the path, you will find that you gain more strength in whatever you do, if you recognize the bond between yourself and the cosmic and realize that this is a key source of your strength and power. Moreover, this link will help you feel a greater sense of commitment to yourself and to your path because it will give you a feeling of your larger purpose as part of the total world order, where all things are, on some level, interconnected and empowered through their relationship to everything else. By recognizing this link you will feel more power because you will realize that everything you do in your feelings, actions, or thoughts has some impact on everything else, because all are part of this universal link.

The Importance of Belief in a Positive Outcome

Given this interconnection of all things, it is important that you approach whatever you do to move ahead and gain personal power with this belief: the belief that things will all work out well as long as you are committed to your own positive growth and continue moving ahead on this path of personal development. The reason your belief is so important is because in this interconnected universe our beliefs translate into the thoughts, feelings, and actions which help to create the very thing in which we believe.

Whether the universe is basically good or whether it is a neutral place where things can be either good or bad, if you have the belief or knowing that the universe is basically good, then the universe will generally manifest itself as being good to you. Though you may encounter some difficulties along the way, in the long run you can believe that things will work out and they will.

Thus, you want to have this sense of trust that somehow in the long run things will have a positive outcome. If you believe that there's some force out there that cares for you, is concerned about you, and is looking out for you in some way, then that belief will give you a feeling of security and confidence that can help you in achieving what you want. This belief could be a projection from yourself about your belief in a positive, benevolent universe, or you could be really getting in touch with this force out there. But in either case, this positive belief will give you the feeling of assurance that you can accomplish what you want to do, and that power arising from your belief will help you achieve your goals. By the same token, this belief will help you in calling upon the forces of nature which are inside you and outside you and manifested in different forms (i.e., the forces of fire, air, earth and water), to help you in achieving these goals.

Trusting Your Own Powers

Your trust in your own powers to gain these goals will also help you achieve them. It all comes back to making a commitment to your own growth and then having the faith that you can do it. Then you move ahead with that faith, trusting that whatever happens, you can meet that challenge and do whatever needs to be done, and by doing so all will work out in the end.

Even with this trust, at times you may question the possibilities of your own power, because you are uncertain about how much power you have, or you might be afraid of losing the powers you possess. And so you may worry: "It's not going to work." Or you may fear "I don't have these special psychic abilities." Or if you have used these powers once or twice and have seen them work, you may wonder: "Can I do it again?" Or you may even be scared that you can because you aren't sure you can handle all this power. However, when such doubts arise you have to be able to put them aside and trust.

I had such concerns myself when I was first taking self-development classes in which I learned some psychic awareness techniques. While these psychic classes were going on I was taking another class on mind-body relationships, and I thought I would try out these techniques on another woman in my class. When I did I suddenly saw all of these things about her I never would have known through my normal senses. I used the technique of visualizing an image of a rose in front of the energy centers of her body and interpreting what was going on in her life based on what happened with the rose. When I did this I picked up a lot of disappointment and despair and hurt, and what really scared me when I got some feedback from her later is that what I saw was true.

I found it scary to know all this on two levels. On the one hand, I felt a little afraid that this was real power I was working with, for it was allowing me to see what I normally couldn't see. And I felt a strong sense of responsibility that went along with this because I was picking up very private information, not generally available to others. Yet at the same time I felt concerned because I was afraid I had just been able to see this way once and I couldn't do it again.

So for awhile I pulled back from using these powers, which many people sometimes do. They are afraid of their own abilities and powers, because using them brings both risks and responsibilities as well as the rewards. But eventually I got back into exploring these powers again. I realized that there's this little part of us that might doubt or have fears; but that this skeptical part of us is what can hold us back.

Thus, at some point I realized we all need to put this skeptical part of ourselves aside and trust. You can try this yourself, and once you do you'll find, as I have, that things generally seem to work out in the end, even though there may be some initial difficulties or no logical explanation as to why things should work as they do.

Sometimes, even though something doesn't make sense, if you believe in or trust your knowing or feelings enough, you should just go with the insights you receive. It's hard to explain, but once you have made this commitment to yourself and the development of your own personal powers, you should have faith in yourself and the universe. For once you do, you will feel a power that's out there which is concerned about you and cares about you. And if you should encounter any problems, this power will push you through and you will continue to grow, for we all grow by overcoming these challenges and obstacles.

Now it may be that this power outside is really there or it may be a projection from inside of you. But in either case, this trust will help you go on because it will help to remove any fears of failure that can be a major obstacle in your way. This is because if you have these fears you can get stuck in a situation and make the failure happen by doing things to bring the failure on. But if you approach the world with a feeling of trust that everything is all going to work out, this belief can help you grow stronger so you can make what you believe in happen. I don't know if this force is out there or within yourself or both. But whatever its source, if you move ahead with faith or trust, you'll find that somehow things will generally work out.

Feeling A Sense of Power and Trust—Exercise #18

The following exercise is designed to help you feel the sense of your own power and to feel this trust in yourself and the universe.

Begin by doing whatever you need to feel comfortable and relaxed. Concentrate on your own breathing if this helps.

Now just imagine that you are surrounded by a warm, flowing feeling. You're feeling very comfortable, very cozy. Perhaps you're sitting by a flame or fire, which is causing this warm feeling around you. And if you wish, just watch this flame or fire and feel very comfortable, very warm.

Notice that this feeling around you is like a very protective envelope, and you feel this envelope of energy surrounding you. You can feel it vibrating, pulsating, and you feel it infused with all kinds of good feelings and warmth.

Perhaps you also feel or see the sun glowing, and you feel its warm rays coming down on you, making you feel all warm and glowing.

Also, you may see somebody near you who you feel very protected by. Or perhaps this feeling of protection comes from a force or an energy. But whatever it's source, you feel very protected, very safe.

And you continue to feel very warm and very strong, because of all this powerful energy. You know you can always call on this energy or force, and whether you see this force outside yourself or coming from within, you know that force is always there. It's a very loving, warm force and it has lots of power, and you can always call on that power.

In fact, this power is like an aura or envelope of energy that surrounds you, and that same energy is there in the fire in front of you or in the sun.

And you can draw on this energy whenever you want. And it can sustain you if you encounter any difficulties.

You may experience that energy coming from a very helpful person or advisor who is near by.

Just feel that energy, that force, which is all around you, in front of you, above you, and in others. And know that you can always turn to that force or that energy or that person for the help and sustenance and protection you need.

Also know that you have this knowing inside you that things will always work out. You have this sense of trust in yourself and the universe. It's a little bit like having a guardian angel or spirit or being around you to protect you. Such beings may come from your inner self or they may exist separate and apart from you. But wherever they come from, know that their power is there.

You can call on this power as you wish. Should you do any ritual, you can always call on this power or force; and you can ask your guardians or helpers for help.

Or should you ever feel alone sometime, know that this power is always within you or without you. And it can help center you, so if you ever feel unbalanced or uncertain about things, you can call on this power for stability or strength.

Likewise, if you're ever confronting somebody who you feel unsure of, who you're not sure you trust, or who you feel some hostility towards, you can always look towards this power around you or within you. And you can call on it to come around you to strengthen you and help you deal with the situation, whatever you have to do.

Also, if you feel hassled or distressed by everyday life, you know this force is around you and within you to help you in that situation, so it's there for you then, too.

Or if you have a project to do, you know you can call on this energy to help you get it done. Or if you have some concerns about money, you know this force will always help you come through.

The force is always there, so trust it. It's a power that's within you, without you. A power that's always there.

So just repeat this to yourself over and over. And at times when you are feeling doubts, bring up these images of power and trust or tap into this feeling of strength and power that wells up all around you and within you. Thus, you constantly feel this loving, glowing warmth. So the image, the feeling, is constantly with you. Or perhaps it is there in the form of a voice that calls to you and says: "I am here. I am here with you."

For this power, this energy is there in many forms, and you can call on it, see it, feel it, trust it, and bring it with you wherever you go.

And perhaps when you wake up in the morning or before you go to bed at night, you can take a few minutes to see this image of power, or feel how it feels, or hear a voice of power calling to you.

And during the day or night, you can call on it too, to get its strength. For wherever you are, you can always call on this force or power. Just know that, and feel this strong feeling of power and know that you can trust it and it will help you trust.

So now, take a minute or two just to feel this energy around you, and continue to see this energy, feel it, or hear it. Just quietly focus on this feeling or vision.

Then, when you are ready, you can come back to the room. But always keep this image or vision or voice with you. And know you can call on it anytime. Whenever you need it, it's always there and you can always trust it. For it's around you; it's part of you; it is you. Now, just come back into the room and open your eyes.

Staying in Practice

The approach to life and the exercises described in this book will help you in achieving personal power. However, to make this approach work effectively for you, it's important to work at this regularly and make a commitment to doing this.

Developing personal power is like developing any skill. You have to keep at it. You have to practice. So if you want to be able to use your seeing, dreaming, projection and other skills easily, you have to stay in touch with them and use them on a regular basis.

This is true for any form of meditating or working with altered realities. If you just meditate or use these techniques once a month or even every two weeks, it's not going to be as effective as if you use these techniques regularly. Thus, if you are making a commitment to your own personal growth, part of that commitment should be a commitment to practice. It doesn't have to be much—even 20 to 30 minutes a day can be enough.

But the point is that you've got to practice to make these techniques a regular part of your life. Once they are, the formal practice may no longer be necessary, for now you are using these techniques automatically. They have become a part of you.

ABOUT THE AUTHOR

Gini Graham Scott, Ph.D. is a nationally-known author of over 15 books, as well as a speaker and seminar/workshop leader, specializing in shamanism, creativity, personal development, and conflict resolution techniques. The holder of a Ph.D. in Sociology from the University of California at Berkeley, Dr. Scott has written two previous books on shamanism and working with altered states of consciousness: *Shaman Warrior* and *Mind Power,* and two other books on shamanic techniques will be out in 1989. Other recent books by Dr. Scott include *The Creative Traveler* and *A Citizen Diplomat in the U.S.S.R.*

As a recognized expert on shamanism and mental imaging, Dr. Scott has written numerous articles on these topics. She is also a popular guest on national talk shows, having appeared on the Phil Donahue Show, the Sally Jessy Raphael Show, and other talk shows in New York, Los Angeles, Chicago, and San Francisco.

A third year law student, Dr. Scott is also a game and toy designer, and she has recently received national recognition for her game *Glasnost: The Game of Soviet-American Peace and Diplomacy.*